THE PHILOSOPHY OF KNOWLEDGE

THE PHILOSOPHY OF KNOWLEDGE

KENNETH T. GALLAGHER

FORDHAM UNIVERSITY PRESS
New York

© Copyright 1982 by FORDHAM UNIVERSITY PRESS
© Sheed and Ward, Inc., 1964
All rights reserved
LC 64–19903
ISBN 0–8232–1095–2

Second Printing 1984
Third Printing 1986
Fourth Printing 1990
Fifth Printing 1994

Gallagher, Kenneth T.
    The philosophy of knowledge / Kenneth T. Gallagher.
    Originally published: Sheed and Ward, Inc., 1964.
    Includes bibliographical references and index.
    ISBN 0-8232-1095-2.
    1. Knowledge, Theory of. I. Gallagher, Kenneth T.
BD161 .G35   64–19903

To
KATHLEEN AND TERENCE
Lucida spei sidera

Printed in the United States of America

CONTENTS

PREFACE		ix
PREFACE TO THE NEW EDITION		xi
1.	THE STATUS OF KNOWING	3
	Wonder	
	The Situation of Common Sense	
	Scepticism	
	The Existential Aspect	
	Analogy of Knowledge	
	Method in Epistemology	
2.	THE CRITICAL DOUBT	24
	The Paradox of Error	
	The Discovery of the Cogito	
	Subjectivism	
	The Escape Route	
	Dream and Reality	
3.	THE POINT OF DEPARTURE	44
	"Inside" and "Outside"	
	The Bi-polarity of Consciousness	
	Being-in-a-World	
	The Epistemological Circle	
	The Question as Irreducible Beginning	
4.	THE PROBLEM OF PERCEPTION: I	68
	"Naive Realism"	
	Locke and Representationalism	

      Berkeley
      Contemporary Views
        a) *Scientism*
        b) *Sense-Datum Approach: A Way Out?*
          1) *Moore, Russell, Broad*
          2) *Ayer and Phenomenalism*
        c) *Linguistic Analysis*
          1) *Stebbing's Paradigm Argument*
          2) *Ostensive Signification*
          3) *Wittgenstein, Ryle, and "Ordinary Language"*

5. THE PROBLEM OF PERCEPTION: II   103
    Scholastic Solutions: Preliminary
    Virtual Realism
    Evaluation of Virtual Realism
    Summing Up
    Puzzles About "Objectivity"

6. THE SEARCH FOR THE UNCONDITIONAL   128
    The Primitive Assertion
    First Principles
    The Priority of the First Principles
    Causality and Determinism
    The Critique of Hume and Kant
    Evidence, Certitude and Doubt

7. CONCEPTUAL KNOWLEDGE   153
    Universals
    Nominalism
    Conceptualism
    Meanings and Instances
    Judgment
    Concepts as Creative Apprehensions

8. THOUGHT AND EXPERIENCE: I   179
    On "Knowing Essences"
    Dewey, Pragmatism and Truth
    Social and Historical Dimensions

Contents

9. **THOUGHT AND EXPERIENCE: II** — 207
   Induction
   Hume's Objection
   Ayer's Tautology View
   Von Hildebrand and Philosophical Insight

10. **EXISTENTIAL TRUTH** — 226
    On the Nature of Evidence
    Kierkegaard and Subjectivity
    Marcel: Problem and Mystery
    Transcendence and "Proof"
    Free Certitude

11. **INTERSUBJECTIVE KNOWLEDGE** — 251
    "Other Minds"
    Direct Knowledge of the Other
    I and Thou

12. **REMAINDERS** — 276
    The Philosophy of Science
    Moral and Aesthetic Experience

13. **REPRISE** — 290

    RELATED READING — 297

    INDEX — 303

PREFACE

In preparing this volume, the following intentions have been principally in mind: to provide a text which covers the standard topics treated in a course in epistemology and at the same time to present these as living questions; to provide a generous amount of historical information on what representative thinkers have held on these questions; to provide extensive reference to those aspects of the problem of knowledge which have emerged in contemporary philosophy; to provide a book which actually deals in a directly reflective philosophical manner with both classical and contemporary problems.

The aim, then, is both informational and philosophical, and a central philosophical point, conveyed both directly and obliquely, is that reflection in the philosophy of knowledge is still *going on*. Therefore, an attempt has been made to give a more open and unfinished air to the discussions than is customary with a textbook. Footnotes are deliberately more frequent than is usual, with the aim of convincing the student of the current and continuingly dialectical character of the issues, and also with the sheer informational intention of acquainting him with the literature; they are meant as an integral pedagogical part of the course.

Although the book has been written from a definite philosophical standpoint, every effort has been made to render it easily utilizable by those who do not share this standpoint. As indicated, all standard topics in the customary epistemological course are treated in a relatively straightforward manner, and it is hoped that an instructor who prefers to confine himself to these topics, without bothering about less familiar matters, will be able to do so simply by selecting the proper sections. Conversely, one who wants to roam farther afield should find ample material from which to choose. It is unlikely that every topic in the book could be covered in a course of normal length.

My primary debt of gratitude in connection with this book is to Mr. Philip Scharper, an outstanding editor, whose suggestion originally inspired it and whose encouragement and generously cooperative attitude made its writing a pleasant task. My thanks also go to Dr. Bernard B. Gilligan of Fordham University, for many illuminating and extremely helpful conversations on the philosophy of von Hildebrand. Finally, I should like to seize what seems to be a good opportunity to signalize the ancient debt which I owe to Rev. David C. Cronin, S. J., of Fordham University, in whose classes my preoccupation with epistemological problems was long ago awakened; generations of Fordham students will join me in their esteem for this philosopher, an irrepressible mind and a classroom teacher *sui generis*.

Grateful acknowledgment is made to Fordham University Press for their permission to reprint material in Chapter X which first appeared in my *The Philosophy of Gabriel Marcel,* 1962; and to *International Philosophical Quarterly,* for permission to use the paragraph on Proust, in Chapter V, which first appeared in an article, "Recent Anglo-American Views on Perception," IV, 122–141.

KENNETH T. GALLAGHER

Fordham University
   February 1964

PREFACE TO THE NEW EDITION

In the central and continuing debate of philosophy, that between the Sophists and Socrates, this text attempted what might be called a "socratic realism," defending the objective and even absolute value of our knowledge, while grounding it in the dialectic of human existence. It is hoped that this approach, and the ensuing encounter with the broad epistemological tradition to which it leads, will continue to be serviceable for those seeking a text in the undergraduate course in theory of knowledge.

The opportunity has been taken to correct a few errors in the text, and a section has been added to the bibliography (see *ADDENDA*, pp. 300–302) calling attention to some of the significant works appearing in the interim since original publication; as is the case with the main bibliography, this aims to be selective rather than complete, in the belief that this is more useful.

This much might be added: of all the sections departing from familiar or standard issues, the author would regard Chapter 10, "Existential Truth," as of most philosophical importance.

KENNETH T. GALLAGHER

Fordham University
June 1982

THE PHILOSOPHY OF KNOWLEDGE

1 *THE STATUS OF KNOWING*

WONDER

"All men by nature desire to know." Aristotle begins his metaphysics with this thought and he seems to believe that this urge to know not only can be realized but actually is realized in his own work. Not without reason has he been called the "master of those who know."

But two generations earlier Socrates had built his own philosophical career on a somewhat different foundation, the conviction that no man had knowledge. His interpretation of the Delphic oracle's pronouncement that "No man alive is wiser than Socrates," came down to just this: no man had knowledge, but other men thought they knew while Socrates alone knew that he did not know.[1] This was his sole claim to pre-eminence, and it may strike us as a rather meager one.

At first sight we would seem to have here two rather sharply opposed views of the human condition: on the one hand an affirmation of a universal and realizable desire to know, on the other a seeming affirmation of universal ignorance as the natural predicament of man. But there is still another aphorism which will help to reconcile these two approaches.

Philosophy, says Plato, begins in *wonder*.[2] It *is* primarily wonder (*to thaumazein*), and no man who lacks this capacity can ever attain to philosophical insight. Since this sentiment is derived from

---
[1] Plato, *Apology*, 21–23.
[2] Plato, *Theaetetus*, 155.

Socrates and shared by Aristotle, it may well repay a closer examination.

The "wonder" which is spoken of here should not be thought of as equivalent to any sort of "curiosity" or need to collect information; nor is it like the bewilderment one might feel in the face of an elaborate mechanism, whether the mechanism of an IBM 705 or the clockwork of a carbon molecule. Philosophical wonder is not primarily before the complicated and abstruse, but before the simple, the obvious, the close at hand. It is the obvious which is most unfathomable, and it is in the region of the near at hand that the great philosophical questions have emerged and in which they continue to dwell.

What is change, being, motion, time, space, mind, matter? Of such questions has the career of philosophy been made. Among them all, perhaps the paramount one is that which Socrates singled out for primacy at the beginning through his adoption of the maxim "Know thyself": Who am I? What does it mean to be a self, and to be just this self which I uniquely am? Here we have a perfect coincidence of the obvious and the mysterious: the maxim "Know thyself" turns us to that which is at the same time nearest at hand, and yet most distant.

And with this we meet at once the ambiguous compenetration of the near and the far which characterizes every genuine experience of philosophical wonder. Wonder begins with the obvious, but it is as if it begins with a "distancing" of the obvious, an endeavor to retain the immediacy of the questioned datum while bathing it in an aura of absolute strangeness. In one sense, nothing could seem odder than to question a thing which is already present to us: for if it *is* present, then we know it as present, and it would even seem that we have already to *know* what it is in order to ask what it is. This is the peculiarity of which Plato speaks in the *Meno*.[3] To find something we are looking for, we must already *know* what we are looking for; therefore, to find the answer to our question about "what" things are, we must be able to recognize it

---

[3] *Meno*, 80; *Theaetetus*, 196–200; cf. *Phaedo*, 73.

The Status of Knowing

as the right answer, and so must already know it. A paradox, no doubt, and probably a crucial one, for it directs our attention to different meanings for "knowing."

St. Augustine provides a famous example in *Confessions XI*, when he says, "What is time? If no one asks me, I know; if I wish to explain it to someone who asks, I do not know." Philosophy consists largely in asking these questions about what I already "know." Of course I know what I mean by "I," "self," "being," "real," "mind," "matter," "change," "time," "thing," and so on. That is, if no one asks me, I know; I simply inhabit their obviousness, their commonplace-ness. This kind of obviousness, however, is really a very derivative realm; it is a realm in which assumptions, conceptual and linguistic schemes, objectified systems of thought, social and cultural custom, have interposed themselves between reflection and original experience. What I know is what "everybody knows," and hence what nobody really knows.

When, therefore, the philosopher withdraws from the "obvious" of the commonplace, he does so in order to restore himself to the freshness of existence as it actually wells up in its perpetually renewed origin. It is this obvious towards which he moves in wonder. He is trying to think existence primordially. It is always there to be thought, always powerfully and overwhelmingly there, always giving itself to thought, but always not yet thought. And thus, the philosopher feels man to be, as Heidegger has said, the "strangest" of beings, nearest and farthest from the secret of things.[4]

Now this condition of the philosopher should not be taken as a misfortune. Rather it is a privilege. Socrates' position is not really as contrary to Aristotle's as it might seem. Granted that all men by nature desire to know, perhaps the first step towards the kind of knowledge that Aristotle had in mind is the Socratic realization that we do not yet know—that the world of the everyday is a realm of *seeming* knowledge.

Perhaps every advance into philosophical knowledge remains

[4] Martin Heidegger, *An Introduction to Metaphysics*, trans. by Ralph Manheim (New Haven: Yale Univ. Press, 1959), pp. 146–151.

tributary to man's experience of himself as the strangest of beings. This experience may even be, as we shall see, itself a kind of knowledge, perhaps the highest kind. What is clear, at any rate, is that the desire for philosophical knowledge of which Aristotle spoke cannot be pursued in the attitude of the commonplace within which everyday thought operates. The element of wonder before the mystery of existence is a constituent of the philosophical question and no philosophical knowledge is possible except in function of that wonder.

Philosophy does not consist so much in a set of formulated answers as it does in the entering into a certain kind of question. Philosophy is the *awakening* out of acceptance, just as Plato emphasized for his own purposes in the myth of the cave.[5] It is the turning away from what "everybody knows" towards the real as it is delivered to my lived consciousness. Wonder, then, has this strange double-aspect of placing me before my experience, yet placing me before it as something altogether strange.

From this point of view, it might be said that the philosophy of knowledge is co-extensive with philosophy. The search to explore and express the richness of reality is always concomitantly an effort to decide what I *know* in any given area. Philosophy is essentially reflection. And reflection is essentially critical. I cannot, therefore, have a metaphysics which is not at the same time an epistemology of metaphysics; nor a psychology which is not an epistemology of psychology; nor even, for that matter, a science which is not an epistemology of science. That is, every philosophical science (and indeed, every science of any kind) when fully constituted and ideally achieved would contain a built-in epistemology in the sense of a critical reflection upon the status of its own assumptions, procedures, and conclusions.

In another sense, however, there is a real point in treating epistemology as itself a special manifestation of the philosophical quest. In this sense, the enterprise of Descartes, of which we shall speak in the next chapter, introduces a radically new epoch in the

[5] *Republic,* Bk. VII.

The Status of Knowing

history of thought. For it represents the stage at which philosophical wonder makes itself its own object. Now instead of simply wondering at the reality of change or time or self, philosophy wonders at *knowing* itself. Man's question turns back upon itself. A new era begins in which he makes *his own search to know* the object of a further search: how do I know that I can know? By what right do I question? Perhaps my wonder has no right to exist —perhaps it is useless, and I am forever shut off from the reality I seek to know. With this question, philosophy may be considered to come into possession of its own essence, for it would seem that there is nowhere further to go.

With the Greeks and the Medievals, thought stretches beyond the taken-for-granted in the object towards the really real. With Descartes and the moderns, thought seeks to surpass the taken-for-granted which might be part and parcel of thought itself, to allow its own pellucid light to appear to itself. At this stage the general problem of knowledge emerges as a separate pre-occupation: knowledge becomes problematic to itself.

THE SITUATION OF COMMON SENSE

The historical movement of reflective thought which culminates in the emergence of the separate problem of knowledge can be analytically retraced. At the initial phase of both historical and analytical processes is the situation in which common sense finds itself. The posture of common sense is a confident one mainly because it is an uncritical one. The "man in the street" (which is not the name for a special plebeian brand of human, but simply means everyone when he is not deliberately philosophizing) finds himself in possession of a large stockpile of items of knowledge, about which he is securely certain and which he would think it frivolous to question. Maritain is no doubt right when he points out[6] that this store of common-sense beliefs is a mixed one, comprising on one level such primary insights as the principle of non-

---

[6] Jacques Maritain, *The Degrees of Knowledge*, trans. by Gerald B. Phelan (New York: Scribner), 1959, pp. 82–84.

contradiction, but reaching down through many more dubious social convictions to a grab bag of intellectual remnants. What all the various levels have in common is that they contain items of knowledge which the possessor regards as a terminus and in which his thought comes to rest.

Common sense thinks it knows lots of things: I exist; I have a body; I have a past, with which I am in contact through my memory; my five senses put me in touch with an external world which is outside me and independent of me, but which I can understand as it is in itself; other men exist—there is experience beyond my experience; there is a past of humanity, history; I am certain of various moral and political principles by which I live and conduct myself in respect to the rest of humanity; and so forth. The last item, however, suggests what is too easily overlooked, that "common sense" has an historical and cultural coefficient: much of what was perfectly plain to the Greek mind in the age of Hesiod is so much nonsense to the modern democratic man. Once this is realized, we walk more warily in describing the mental condition of common sense as "certitude."

Common sense is well aware that it is often deceived, that mistakes are possible. Optical illusions, errors in judging distance or color, and such total vagaries as hallucinations are common enough. Yet common sense does not use the existence of these erroneous beliefs to question the status of its true beliefs. A man may be very frequently deceived, but until he utilizes his deceptive experience to call the nature of his veridical experience into question, he is still comfortable within the confines of common sense.

For that reason, the modern man is not completely at home in the posture of common sense. For the discoveries of science do not allow him to let them merely coexist with his beliefs about the reality of his familiar world. Once he has "learned" from science that the world as it is out there by itself is a swirl of atoms, he cannot help being puzzled as to how this world fits with his own perceptual picture. He sees colors, hears sounds, feels warmth and cold. But apparently in the universe that science investigates these don't "really exist." Then he inevitably is driven to wonder about the status of the things he does perceive. Are they inside his head, a mere private universe, quite different from nature as it really is?

Once this distinction between appearance and reality has wedged its way into consciousness, it need not stop at factual difficulties. For in grasping this distinction, consciousness grasps itself as a subject distinct from the objects of its knowing, and then is tumbled into the whole radical difficulty of how it can ever be sure that it has reached the real object and not simply an apparent object. If knowledge aspires to see things as they really are, how do we know we have reached things as they really are? In fact, how do I know that I am not totally confined to appearances, and that there is anything at all beyond appearances?

Just here is where epistemology is not only possible but necessary. A thought which has reached this stage of reflection cannot be satisfied by a return to the unreflecting assurances of common sense, but must press forward to a new plane. The certainty which epistemology now seeks is made possible by a doubt—it is a cure for a doubt; which is to say, it is essentially reflective. Every one of the assertions of common sense can be summoned before the reflective question. When epistemology settles or allays these doubts, we may get a reflexive certitude which is more entitled to the name than the incurious acceptance of the pre-philosophical man.

SCEPTICISM

The objection is naturally raised at this point that in acting thus epistemology is proposing a chimerical goal for itself. For, if we are to demonstrate the validity of our knowledge, we will already be making use of our knowledge and therefore already presuming its validity. Some, like Etienne Gilson, have therefore argued that there *is* no problem of knowledge, since the critical question cannot be consistently raised:[7] realism, for them, is an absolute presumption of thought, and any attempt to justify realism already

---

[7] Etienne Gilson, *Réalisme thomiste et critique de la connaissance*, (Paris: J. Vrin), 1947.

represents a concession, if not a surrender. For this position, knowing puts us in touch with the real, and that is the end of it.

There is more than one way of responding to this objection. To begin with, we may start by acknowledging the positive insight contained in it. What it stresses is the unconditional attachment of thought to reality, and this surely requires stressing. The existence of knowledge, and the partial transparence of knowledge to itself is an ultimate and irreducible given. Thought exists, and the existence of thought testifies to its own openness to being. No denial or doubt of this openness can be successfully carried through. That is why the position of the absolute sceptic is the most vulnerable in the whole domain of philosophy. What the absolute sceptic contends is that man's mind is incapable of attaining truth—that we can know nothing for an objective certainty but are confined to the free play of our own subjective opinions. Unfortunately for him, however, the very attempt to express his position involves him in a denial of it. For he holds at least one judgment to be objectively true—his own. He holds it as objectively true (and not a mere subjective opinion) that man cannot know objective truth; he is certain that he cannot be certain. The traditional accusation that the sceptical position is self-nullifying and literally absurd seems fully justified.

No matter how he twists and turns, the sceptic cannot help implicitly denying what he is explicitly affirming. Suppose he contents himself with merely *doubting* whether our thought puts us in touch with reality. Even so, he does not escape inconsistency, for this doubt of his is not a frame of mind in which he merely happens to find himself; it is, he maintains, the *correct* position, and he argues with me that I ought to give up my dogmatism and espouse his conscientious refraining from judgment. Yet to hold his position as "correct" or "right" is to believe that in this one case he has reached the objective state of affairs and seen what the proper response to it is. Even if he goes to the heroic length of remaining silent, of taking no position at all, still he does not escape inconsistency. For he has not lost the power of speech—

his silence is not a misfortune but a decision, and a response. This is the way things are, he says in effect, and the proper response is silence. But what he is contending is that we cannot know the way things are, and so his silence is a testimony against his own view.

Although the refutation of scepticism tends to sound negative (to tell us what we cannot do) it really has a positive consequence. For what it actually reveals is what Gilson insists on: at some level thought is unconditionally attached to being, attached in such a way that it cannot successfully deny its attachment. We thus reach the unconditional value of affirmation, when we realize that it is impossible to affirm our inability to affirm. That is why an inspection of scepticism is very useful, even though there does not seem to have been anybody in the history of philosophy who could literally be called an absolute sceptic as that role is cast by epistemology. Not even Pyrrho or Sextus Empiricus quite measure up.[8] The relativism of Protagoras probably comes closest.[9] His *homo mensura* doctrine ("man is the measure of all things") is an attempt to limit the value of *all* affirmation to the one who makes it; just as what tastes good to one is not necessarily tasty to another, so, he says, what is true for one is not necessarily true for another. Regardless of the dearth of historical examples, it is instructive to state the extreme form of scepticism as one of the antecedently possible answers to the epistemological question as to the truth-value of my knowledge. Once we have seen the im-

---

[8] Pyrrho (c. 360-c. 270 B.C.) gave the name Pyrrhonism to scepticism. On Sextus Empiricus (c. 250 A.D.), the foremost of the ancient sceptics, whose *Outlines of Pyrrhonism* is the fullest presentation of the views of this school, see esp. Venant Cauchy, "The Nature and Genesis of the Sceptical Attitude," *The Modern Schoolman*, XXVII, pp. 203-221, pp. 297-310.

[9] For the relativism of Protagoras (c. 481-c. 411 B.C.), see Plato's *Theaetetus*, 160-162; and for his ethical doctrine, see Plato's presentation and rebuttal in *Protagoras*. Another sophist, Gorgias (c. 483-c. 375 B.C.) is also the subject of a dialog by Plato, one of the most powerful statements of the ethical position of Socrates and Plato. Gorgias' threefold sceptical formula was: a) Nothing is b) If it is, it cannot be known c) If it is known, it cannot be communicated to others.

possibility of adopting this answer, we have also seen that thought is irrevocably open to being.

THE EXISTENTIAL ASPECT

Allowing proper weight to Gilson's position does not entail accepting it wholly, however, for there is much to be said in rebuttal. We may hold with Maritain, for instance, that the aim of epistemology is not so much to answer the question of *whether* I can know, but *to discover the conditions under which I can know, the extent and limits of my knowing.*[10] This seems a proper definition of the aims and scope of the philosophy of knowledge, and it does not involve us in any inconsistency. On this program, epistemology does not vindicate my right to affirm, but it maps out and circumscribes the range of that right.

Nevertheless it will not entirely do to stop here. While there is much justice in the insistence that realism is a presupposition of thought and that it cannot consistently be questioned, there is also something highly significant in the fact that men have thought it possible to question this "un-questionable." Maybe they have not been justified, maybe the question has not been a *real* question but only a psychological morass in which a confused mind found itself. But it is nevertheless a fact significant for epistemology that the kind of knowledge available to man will allow him to get into this psychological morass. Perhaps not every sort of knower would be subject to the extremes of sceptical doubt: the possibility of scepticism is therefore the revelation of something important about man's mode of knowing.

Man can get himself into the plight which some epistemologists assure us is epistemologically anomalous, the plight of worrying whether he is not totally estranged from the truth, whether his mind's acts of "knowing" are not empty. This is not merely an academic issue, for man's desire to know is not just a matter of

---

[10] Maritain, *op. cit.*, p. 73.

disinterested curiosity, or a drive for formal correctness. It is a matter of existential *concern*. "What can I know?" is just another side of the metaphysical question, "What is?" or "What is real?" Here we ask "How far can I be attached to what is real? How can I assure myself of my contact with being?" Man's knowledge is an attempt to *express* to himself his attachment to being. The fact that it is the prey to doubt is, then, an ontological revelation of the nature of man and inevitably relevant to epistemology.

Ontologically, the ground of doubt is in man's finitude. Unless man were the kind of being he is, he would have no epistemological problem. But because he is limited in the way he is, this limitation extends to his entire being, *even,* apparently to the knowledge which he can really be said to possess. Man is not a being with limitations; he is limited being. That is, there are not two factors in man, one entirely being and the other a kind of limiting boundary—but even in the respect that he *is,* he is not. Man's whole being is shot through with nothingness; his knowledge arises out of that being, so that even where that knowledge is, one might say, quite "indisputable," the little worm of nothingness can begin to gnaw on it. Let us say that we *know* that the world exists: but wait, and before long there flowers within that affirmation the blossom of nothingness and doubts: perhaps I am wrong, perhaps I am deceived, perhaps I am only dreaming.

Without elaborating too far, it may be pointed out that the role of nothingness in knowledge is only one manifestation of a spectre which threatens man's being in various guises. Think of the role of death, time, separation from others, loneliness, failure, opposition to my will, sin, despair—all experiences in which the presence of nothingness is searingly felt. In keeping with more than one contemporary philosopher, we may single out the modality of *time* as especially crucial. For time, as the mode of human existence, cannot be regarded as negligible to the understanding of human knowing.

Man's knowing is a function of his mode of existing, and his mode of existing is essentially temporal. Man's existence is always not-yet-accomplished: he is the unfinished being, who is in the process of making himself. Man is not man in the way a stone is a stone or a table a table. These things are simply identical with themselves, complete, realized, solid, without a fissure in their existence. They are what they are. But as both Kierkegaard and Sartre agree in emphasizing, man is not what he is: he must become what he is.[11] To be a man is not to be a simple self-identity, in the manner of a stone, a table, an atom. Man's existence is open to the future because it is open in the present; man is not at any single moment identical with himself, in possession of his own being. That man exists temporally is not only a statement about an extent of time, but a statement about human existence at any moment of time. Man is a becoming which never at any moment coincides with itself: man is not what he is. Time is possible because man is not a simple self-identity but a being forever non-coincident with himself.

If this is so, if man never simply "coincides" with himself, but is always other than himself, beyond himself, then man's knowledge, too, can never be a matter of simple "possession." Just as man does not inertly coincide with his being, so he does not coincide with his knowledge. Just as man's being is a perpetual becoming, an achievement, so his knowledge is a perpetual achievement, a prize ceaselessly rewon. Once we grasp in all naivety the truth that time is a real component of human existence, we will never be inclined to approach epistemology without reference to it. And once we cease to think of knowledge as something we either "have" or "do not have," as a static acquisition, many difficulties will appear in a new light. If knowledge is a modality of human existence, then it is subject to the same limitations as that existence; just as man is not what he is, so he does not know what he knows.

---

[11] This is a continuing theme with Kierkegaard. It is the central subject of his *The Sickness unto Death*; see esp. the opening lines of this essay. See also Jean Paul Sartre, *Being and Nothingness,* trans. by Hazel Barnes (New York: Philosophical Library), 1956, p. lxvii.

The pathos of human existence consists in man's struggle to surpass the nothingness in himself and to found himself in steadfast being. So, too, the pathos of human knowledge is in its struggle to found itself unreservedly in the steadfastness of certitude. I want unreservedly to be, and I want unreservedly to know. My effort to be *certain* is one side of my effort to *be*. I want to anchor myself beyond the nothingness of doubt. But every struggle to be and every struggle to know takes place under conditions which plunge it again into becoming. This does not mean that the whole process is futile, that the cynic's view of life or the sceptic's view of knowledge is justified. What it means is that epistemology must begin with a double recognition: *human knowledge exists, but it exists subject to the conditions of human existence*. One who begins by erecting a false ideal of knowledge as a set of objectified formulas atemporally straddling the minds which think them, will tend inevitably either to a sterile and abstract dogmatism or to the abject frustration of the sceptic. That human knowledge is subject to the conditions of human existence cannot destroy its cognitional value. It is only because of our integral human existence that we know at all, and our mode of existence, which makes knowledge possible, cannot be regarded as a threat to it.

ANALOGY OF KNOWLEDGE

For what, after all, does it mean to "know?" This is a question which many will feel should have been asked at the beginning, but there are certain advantages in postponing it until now. What is immediately clear is that there can be no question of a "definition" of knowledge, since to define something is to render it in terms of something else which is more simply intelligible; that is impossible in the case of what is itself simple and ultimate. Since knowing is an ultimate and irreducible event, it cannot be conveyed in terms more fundamental than itself. Synonyms like "awareness" or "consciousness of" serve some explicative purpose but cannot take us very far. What is, however, desirable, is to indicate the possible range of applicability which this word has, for this will prevent us from identifying knowledge with some particular brand of knowledge.

We speak of "knowing how" to do things (drive a car, type); "knowing that" certain facts are true (Columbus discovered America, two and two are four); and also of simple "knowing" by acquaintance (the location of our house, or the identity of a friend). These common uses only *begin* to indicate the diversity of possible significations in the word, since each contains a further diversity in itself and reveals various ambiguities to our inspection. We may be undecided, for example, whether the word *knowledge* deserves to be applied more to the one who "knows how" to find his way in a certain neighborhood because of a lifelong acquaintance with it or to one who knows how to read and follow a streetmap of it; who "really" *knows* the route? Or we wonder whether the child's knowledge of the fact that his mother loves him is knowledge of fact or knowledge by acquaintance, and if we have difficulty in classifying this and myriad other sorts of "knowing," we may eventually wonder whether they should even be called "knowing."

Many a man will decide in the end that only a certain variety of knowing is "really" deserving of the term knowledge. This is what Bertrand Russell does when he reserves the term for the brand of knowledge available to the scientist and allots it to others only to the degree that they approximate scientific status.[12] A milder form of this restriction might be the precept of Vere Childe that to deserve the designation, knowledge must be communicable in a symbolic manner. Thus, by definition, I could not be said to *know* something except insofar as it was capable of being embodied in an objectified form.[13] This is in some ways close to the familiar contention that the only real knowledge is that which is available to all and "publicly verifiable"—so that the face which

[12] Bertrand Russell, *Human Knowledge* (New York: Simon and Schuster), 1948, pp. XI, 52.
[13] Vere Childe, *Society and Knowledge* (New York: Harper and Bros.), 1956, pp. 4, 19.

The Status of Knowing

the world presents to the artist or the poet has no cognitional value, since it is not there for a neutral observer.

In spite of the superficial plausibility of these contentions, it is against just such an unwarranted initial restriction of knowledge that the epistemologist must resolutely set himself. Paradoxical as it may sound, we cannot begin the philosophy of knowledge by deciding what knowing is and then discover what measures up to this definition. On the contrary, what is required is an initial openness to the multifaceted meaning of "knowledge" as that is discerned by critical review. We must hold open the door to the possibility that the ways of knowing may be multiple and that each of these ways may be thoroughly entitled to be denominated by the term "knowledge."

This point can be put more strongly. Not only *may* the ways of knowing be multiple, it seems that we ought to expect that they be multiple. To expect that knowing would have one "univocal" or identical meaning is actually what is incongruous. The Thomistic philosopher especially ought to be prepared to see this. It is his doctrine of the analogy of being which prepares the ontological ground for this expectation. It is a fundamental premise of Thomism that "being" is not a univocal term, but rather an analogous one, that is, it means somewhat the same thing and somewhat a different thing in its various uses. The similarity which binds beings together and allows them all to be designated by the same term ("being") is not the possession of some univocally or identically shared "property," but rather a community of resemblance. All things are alike in that they are being, but they differ also in virtue of their being. Therefore, their mode of being makes them like every other thing, but also makes them different from every other thing.

Now if there is an analogy of being, we also ought to expect that there is an analogy of knowledge.[14] Whatever knowledge is,

---

[14] L. M. Regis, O.P., *Epistemology*, trans. by Imelda Byrne (New York: Macmillan), 1959, p. 67. For a notable attempt on the part of a thinker in the Thomistic tradition to explore the analogical range of knowledge, see Barry Miller, *The Range of Intellect* (London: Geoffrey Chapman),

and however impossible it may be to define it, what is clear is that it is oriented to being. *If knowledge is to mold itself on the contours of being, it too must be analogous.* If the being of person, stone, beauty, justice, thought, color, number is only analogously similar, then the knowledge which is the orienting of consciousness towards person, stone, beauty, justice, thought, color, number, must be analogously knowledge. To regard it as a shortcoming of our knowledge of another person that it cannot be expressed in terms satisfying to the scientist is equivalent to treating a person and a scientific object as univocally being; to ask that beauty provide credentials acceptable to the neutral observer is to ask it to be what it is not.

Man's knowing, as Heidegger rightly says, is *a-letheia*:[15] It is the unveiling of being. In as many ways as there is the unveiling of being, there are that many ways of knowing. Traditionally, epistemology has tended to confine itself to sense perception and intellectual cognition, the latter being somewhat narrowly conceived. But this does not appear sufficient. Knowledge is the event by which human consciousness emerges into the light of being. We cannot prescribe in advance how being is to be revealed. The proper initial attitude for the philosopher of knowledge is a kind of humility before experience, which is simply equivalent to a total openness. It is an attitude not unlike that which William James called "radical empiricism," and which he so nobly cultivated himself;[16] or that which José Ortega y Gasset has referred to as "absolute positivism," which is not to be confused with the shallow positivism of those who arrogate to themselves this title.[17]

1961; the growing interest of modern Thomists in the questions of affective and poetic knowledge, and in the cognitional import of value experience, is indicated in the interesting first chapter of this book.

[15] Martin Heidegger, *Being and Time*, trans. by John Macqarrie and Edward Robinson (New York: Harper), 1962, p. 256.

[16] William James, *Essays in Radical Empiricism* (New York: Longmans, Green & Co.), 1912.

[17] José Ortega y Gasset, *What is Philosophy?*, trans. by Mildred Adams (New York: W. W. Norton & Co.), 1960, p. 125.

The Status of Knowing

Philosophy, the effort of reflective thought to let experience recognize itself, must not commit the mistake of trying to stuff experience into cubby-holes prepared in advanced. The proper task of the philosopher is not to begin by denying cognitive value to any dimension of experience, but to seek to discern what modulation occurs in the term *knowledge* as it is applied in various realms. Knowledge may mean one thing in science, and another in history, metaphysics, moral experience, art, interpersonal knowledge. Epistemology must reckon with this spectrum of signification, and not approach its subject too narrowly.

METHOD IN EPISTEMOLOGY

Accordingly, even the tendency, common among Scholastic philosophers, to see the critique of knowledge exclusively in terms of an assessment of *judgments* may be misdirected. Its obvious plausibility lies in the fact that the claim of "knowledge" is closely tied to the fact of *assertion* (or denial). I may feel that I only really know what I can assert, and that the question of truth only arises in respect to the judgment in which I assert that such and such a state of affairs holds good in reality. Such, in fact, is the basis for the familiar conception of truth as "the adequation of thought with reality." If what my judgment asserts actually holds good, then my judgment is said to be conformed to the real and ergo true. Until some judgment is made, the question of truth is not clearly raised. Experience, it is felt, is neither true nor false, but simply is; concepts (green, grass) as separate apprehensions are neither true nor false but simply grasps of realizable meanings. But judgments *assert* something ("The grass is green.") and are either true or false in their assertion.

Now, while there is not the slightest doubt that judgment plays an extremely crucial role in human cognition, it still remains true that the problem of knowledge should not be equated with the problem of the truth-value of judgments. Knowledge is no doubt intimately linked to *expression,* and expression normally finds its utterance in judgment, but epistemology is really concerned with the question of the *ground* of judgment. The truth-value of judgments is really decided in terms of evidence, and the real preoccupation of epistemology is with the question of evidence. This question is wider than the question of judgment. It is even possible that there may be a real sense to saying that I *know* more than I can express in judgment.

Thomistic philosophers are, in effect, conceding this in their discussion of "connatural knowledge."[18] Connatural knowledge is knowledge which arises because of an affinity of the knower for the realm about which he judges. For example, the artist knows what is right in a picture even though he has not studied aesthetics; or the good man knows virtue in a manner distinct from that of the ethical theorist. But this means that there is an evidence available to the artist and the good man which is lacking to the theoretical knower, and therefore the epistemological question of the value of judgment is really a question of the admissibility of evidence. We can go further: the wife's knowledge of her husband's love is expressed in her whole life and not merely in the occasional explicit judgments in which it might crystallize. Could there even be kinds of knowledge which we could not even express in judgments at all? Such might be the poet's knowledge of nature, the political hero's knowledge of his own calling, or the lived knowledge of the body in perception.

As soon as attention is turned from the judgment to the evidence upon which it is reared, any overly narrow preoccupation with the form of thought is left behind. The question of evidence is not simply a question of predicating concepts of sense-particulars. It is a question of the emergence-to-view of dimensions of the real. And this emergence may easily overflow the bounds we have habitually set for cognition. There is a constant tendency to treat ideas, judgments, and reasoning as cognitive and other facets of experience as cognitionally irrelevant. But as Gabriel Marcel,

[18] On connaturality, see Miller, *op. cit.*, chapt. 7; and Jacques Maritain, *The Range of Reason* (New York: Scribner), 1961, pp. 22–29.

The Status of Knowing

among others, has brought home to us, we need only think of the revelatory role of love or of hope to see the artificiality of these divisions.[19] Love can be a principle of knowledge, an instrument of vision. Far from being irrelevant to the question of knowledge, love can be the *means* by which a certain kind of knowing can occur. One who *loves* another person, *knows* him better than one who does not. Perhaps the reality of another is only fully there for one who loves him. And conversely, my love for another person can open the possibility of a kind of self-knowledge which would otherwise be inaccessible to me. One who does not love another may not *know* himself.

None of what is said here can be taken as anything more than tentative and propaedeutic, for clearly these truths, if they are truths, need considerable buttressing. They are only advanced by way of anticipation at this point, and in order to set the tone for the most appropriate mood to undertake the critique of our knowing. There is every reason to think that the judgment occupies a special place in human knowledge, and to a large extent it is true that epistemology must pay special attention to it. But it must be seen as included within the question of evidence. And further, the judgment itself must not be conceived after the fashion of a pure logician or grammarian. The judgment is the expression of the self's assimilation of reality. It cannot really be appreciated apart from the total dynamism of the subject by which reality is revealed to me. A conviction of this will prevent any premature impoverishment of experience on the part of the epistemologist, and it will also prescribe the method he will follow in his critical review.

This question of method is the last introductory point and should not need laboring. The philosophy of knowledge, as the attempt to assess the cognitive worth of experience, ought not to be overburdened with the paraphernalia of technical terminology, nor with the elaborate presuppositions of any philosophical

---

[19] Gabriel Marcel, *Homo Viator,* trans. by Emma Crauford (Chicago: Henry Regnery Co.), 1951.

system. It should look as directly as possible to experience and it should use ordinary language. This is not to say that it can ever succeed in being without presuppositions, since even ordinary language embodies theoretical categories. But it will avoid approaching its task with a thought-schema already consciously prepared; to do this would be to insert that schema between reflection and the reality it is seeking to reach.

Russell's acceptance of the normative character of scientific knowledge commits this fallacy, for not only does it tend to exempt this knowledge from critical review but it casts the shadow of the "taken-for-granted" across the whole of human experience and hides it from our reflective gaze. The same charge may be levelled at the admirable work of Louis Regis, who carries on his epistemological review within a fully constituted framework of Thomistic categories.[20] In order to survey knowledge, we must comprehend it, Regis holds, against the prior comprehension of the meaning of immanent action, the distinction of act and potency, matter and form, substance and accident, and so forth. This will not do. It immediately turns us away from experience towards interpretation. Likewise, Frederick Wilhelmsen's propensity for approaching the subject in a strenuously psychological manner and mingling the explanation of the what of knowledge with the how (couched in the Thomistic language of species, intentions, immaterial forms, and so forth) blunts his epistemological point.[21] Right, here, seems to lie on the side of those like Fernand van Steenberghen who stress the need of epistemology to build all analyses on a *descriptive* method and to confine itself to non-technical terminology.[22] If Georges van Riet is correct, it is useless to search the pages of St. Thomas for a solution to the epistemological problem, for this problem did not exist for St. Thomas.[23]

[20] Regis, *op. cit.*, pp. 151ss.
[21] Frederick D. Wilhelmsen, *Man's Knowledge of Reality* (Englewood Cliffs, N.J.: Prentice-Hall), 1956.
[22] Fernand van Steenberghen, *Epistemology*, trans. by Rev. Martin Flynn (New York: Jos. Wagner), 1949, pp. 22–25.
[23] Georges van Riet, *L'épistemologie thomiste* (Louvain: Editions de l'Institut Supérieur de Philosophie), 1946, p. 636.

The Status of Knowing

On the same general terms, it is not too fruitful to answer the epistemological problem in language and categories borrowed exclusively from St. Thomas, for these categories were discovered in answer to quite different purposes, either metaphysical or psychological. It is unlikely that St. Thomas would continue to address himself to the question with an excessive reliance on these terms if he were alive today. If we are to justify the existence of epistemology as a separate and independent inquiry, we ought to cultivate a deliberate independence of a terminology which may be illuminating in other directions, but is apt to be blinding here. By the time we get through mastering typical technical notions, we have left the freshness of experience far behind; at length, instead of dealing with existence as it gushes pristinely forth, we find ourselves closeted with brochures describing it at third hand. Whatever price may be paid in foregoing the precision which technical language can provide, it seems to be compensated by our avoidance of the airless atmosphere to which it confines us.

2 THE CRITICAL DOUBT

THE PARADOX OF ERROR

With the refutation of absolute scepticism, epistemology only stands at the threshold of its philosophical undertaking. For to say that we cannot doubt the capacity of the human mind to attain truth (its openness to reality) is not the same as saying that we cannot doubt anything that common sense is "sure" of. A mitigated scepticism, far from being absurd, is rather the first counsel for fruitful reflection. Error exists. This means that one datum with respect to human knowledge is that it is capable of co-existing with error. Not all of our knowledge is on equally firm footing. Therefore, the critical enterprise in which epistemology undertakes to review the value of our habitual knowledge can be construed as an attempt to discriminate between what is solid and what is fragile in our common-sense convictions. The difficulty is, however, to find a criterion in terms of which this discrimination can be made. What is the hallmark of well-grounded knowledge which will serve to distinguish it from spurious "knowledge?"

One of the most radical and ingenious attempts to answer this question was that made by René Descartes.[1] Descartes conceived the plan of using doubt to overcome doubt. One way of deciding what is unconditionally certain and indubitable is to see how much can be doubted. If we systematically attempt to call into doubt as much of our knowledge as we possibly can, we will eventually

[1] 1596–1650.

The Critical Doubt

reach a point that is impervious to doubt, and then our knowledge can be built on the bedrock of absolute certitude. Doubt pushed far enough will eventually uncover what is indubitable, if such exists. His suggested procedure, which has the attraction of an uncompromising rigor, has been referred to as the "universal methodic doubt." It is universal because it will be extended without limit, or until it becomes self-limiting; it is methodic, because it is a means which reflective philosophical thought utilizes as a method of attaining truth; it is a doubt, not in the sense of a lived quandary, but as a calling-into-question performed by thought.

Sometimes Descartes' starting-point is mistakenly regarded as a version of absolute scepticism but actually he is at the precisely opposite pole to scepticism. What the sceptic wonders about is whether we can attain any truth; what Descartes wonders about is why we should ever fail to attain truth. For him the problem of the philosophy of knowledge is not how we can know but why we should ever fall into error. Error is a scandal for thought. There is no question for Descartes that the mind is capable of attaining truth; he had probably as much confidence in the capacity of thought as any man who ever lived, and his procedure could with more accuracy be regarded as that of a rationalist than that of a sceptic. He is so convinced that the mind ought to be reaching truth that error becomes a complete anomaly for him. And it would not be too hard to see error as Descartes saw it. For we must remember that error is quite a different thing from ignorance, which is merely not-knowing. It is easy to see that a limited thought might be ignorant of many things; it might not see them. That presents no pressing problem. But error does not consist in failing to see something; it consists in thinking I know what I do not know, or in thinking I do not know what I know.

Once this incongruity dawns on us, we will be arrested by the paradoxical character of error. As a comparison: If I were asked, "Do you see the book on the table from where you are sitting?" I would answer either "Yes, quite easily," or "No, I can't see it from here." In the first case I would be seeing, in the second not seeing; the first case would be analogous to knowledge, the second to ignorance—but neither would entail error. But surely a man who is seeing something knows that he is seeing it, and one who is not seeing something knows that he is not seeing it. Therefore, how is error even possible? The same situation is repeated whatever kind of "seeing" is involved. If I really "see" the answer to an algebraic problem, I have solved it and know the answer; if I can't figure it out, I do not know the answer. In the first case I have knowledge, in the second ignorance—in neither case do I have error. If I really see the correctness of philosophical reasoning, I assent to its conclusions; if I do not see it, I do not assent. In the first case, knowledge, in the second, ignorance (not-knowing)—but again no error. But obviously people do make mistakes in mathematical problems and obviously philosophers do disagree (which should not be, since disagreement implies error and not only ignorance).

There is a spontaneous tendency to dismiss this dilemma with the expostulation that it is a pseudo-quandary; it is simply that we become inattentive or careless, and that we are not alert to the full conditions of the problem. Thus, a man who looks quickly may mistake a shadow on the table for a dark-covered book or one working out a problem may mistake a 3 for an 8. Error, the suggestion is made, intrudes because we go about our thinking rather carelessly. Now although from one standpoint this just pushes the whole problem back one step further (how can inattentiveness infect knowledge?), it is rather close to what Descartes himself was disposed to believe. Error is essentially inattention. But then knowledge is essentially attention. And one who wishes to avoid error and to attain unconditional knowledge, has only to rouse himself to an unflagging effort of attention. This is really what Descartes himself attempted to do. If I ask in respect to every one of the assents which I give to the purported "truths" which I "know," whether this assent is really justified, I am asking "Do I really see what this assent implies that I see?" If I have the hardihood to withhold assent in every case in which I cannot affirm upon attentive inspection that the evidence to warrant this

The Critical Doubt

assent is really present to me, then I will avoid all the error which is caused by inattentiveness.

All the other sources to which error is frequently ascribed are only effective insofar as they generate inattentiveness. Thus, prejudice, pride, self-will, fatigue, combativeness, haste, emotion, etc., are only influential in giving rise to error inasmuch as they are the several ways in which the gaze of my thought is rendered inattentive. Therefore, if I demand attentiveness of myself, I have eliminated the real source of error. This demand is implemented by turning myself resolutely to the evidence upon which any given assent is supposedly based. Just so, the man who mistook the shadow for the book could correct his error simply by asking himself "Now am I really sure that I see what I have asserted that I see? Let me look carefully and make sure." He would then turn reflectively to the visual evidence and banish his doubts. So it ought to be with all errors, in Descartes' estimation. If we are inflexible in our demand that our assent be withheld except in those cases in which we can be sure that the evidence is present, we will never go wrong.

To be sure of this presence of the evidence, Descartes suggests that we need only to ask, "Is there any possible basis for doubt that things might be otherwise than I assert?" Let me make the active effort to doubt that the evidence is really there, and I will be able to underwrite my assent unconditionally, if it deserves it. Thus, "How much can I really know?" is a question which can only be answered after I determine "How much can I succeed in doubting?" It is in the rigor with which Descartes prosecuted this second question that his fulcral contribution to philosophy consists. For he carried his doubt farther than most men would have been prepared to carry it. Let us follow him through the successive stages of this doubt.

THE DISCOVERY OF THE COGITO

We can begin with the deliverances of the philosophers of the past, for they are quite easy to doubt. They are, in fact, what started Descartes on the path of dubiety. As a student at the Jesuit college of La Flêche, he had received the usual training in Scholastic philosophy common to the curriculum of the day (a day now widely stigmatized as the decadence of scholasticism). To put it mildly, he was not impressed. The widespread conflict among the philosophers of the past caused him the same dismay that it has caused many a mind before and since. That there should be such a cacophony of voices on issues that mattered so much to man was distressing indeed.

As to whether the conclusions of the philosophers could be doubted, the answer was clear: it is the easiest thing in the world to doubt what has been endlessly doubted by philosophers themselves. Philosophical disagreement is a kind of mutual disparagement of philosophical evidence on the part of philosophers themselves. The reason for the possibility of such doubt was not far to seek. The philosophy of the past had been too ready to admit probable or merely plausible reasoning into a domain that should have been reserved purely for *necessary insight*. What philosophy seeks is certitude and certitude is only possible on the basis of coercive evidence; only *necessary* reasoning should have a part in the philosophical venture. Once anything else is allowed to participate, we get the hodge-podge of plausibilities and implausibilities which philosophy had become.

Nor was it one whit more difficult for Descartes to treat as less than certain the "knowledge" of the science of his day, since it was largely built on the shifting sands of philosophy itself. This, we must remember, would have been easier in a day when science was so largely dependent on inherited Aristotelian notions of physics. Let anyone ask himself how hard it would be for him to treat as less than indubitable the fact that there are four fundamental elements, water, earth, air, and fire, that each of these has its "natural place" (that of fire being "up," and that of earth being "down") and he will at once perceive that the conclusions of science could not offer much resistance to the critical doubt.

But surely, one may feel, there remains a whole set of ordinary beliefs that still stands after these speculative constructions have

The Critical Doubt

been swept away. Perhaps we might treat the rough laws which common sense makes for itself about the predictable and reliable behavior of bodies as only highly probable (as Hume was to do later), and perhaps we might fairly easily succeed in impugning the reliability of our senses which so frequently subject us to illusions, but still, that the bodies about which the senses and the roughly approximate laws speak exist and have their being independent of us, is not this evident? That other persons exist, whose life and consciousness are not mine, is not this undeniable? Or that my own past exists, my past which my memory retains and assures me of, how can this be disputed? But let us listen to Descartes himself on this score.

He will admit that it seems unreasonable to doubt many things, "For example, there is the fact that I am here, seated by the fire, attired in a dressing gown, having this paper in my hands and other similar matters." But he goes on:

> At the same time I must remember that I am a man, and that consequently I am in the habit of sleeping, and in my dreams representing to myself the same things or sometimes even less probable things, than do those who are insane in their waking moments. How often has it happened to me that in the night I dreamt that I found myself in this particular place, that I was dressed and seated near the fire, whilst in reality I was lying undressed in bed! At this moment it does indeed seem to me that it is with eyes awake that I am looking at this paper; that this head which I move is not asleep, that it is deliberately and of set purpose that I extend my hand and perceive it; what happens in sleep does not appear so clear nor so distinct as does all this. But in thinking over this I remind myself that on many occasions I have in sleep been deceived by similar illusions, and in dwelling carefully on this reflection I see so manifestly that there are no certain indications by which we may clearly distinguish wakefulness from sleep that I am lost in astonishment. And my astonishment is such that it is almost capable of persuading me that I now dream.[2]

---

[2] *Descartes Selections,* edit. Ralph M. Eaton (New York: Scribner's), 1927, pp. 90–91. All page references to Descartes are from this volume, and are from the *Meditations.*

This is the famous "dream doubt" of Descartes. His point is easy to grasp. When I dream I seem to find myself among objects which are real, independent of me, and out of my control. And yet they are not real and independent of me. How do I know that I am not always dreaming, that the world which I believe to have its being outside me is not really a figment of my imagination? As for my body, which seems so irresistibly real, the body which I inhabit in a dream seems equally real and is but the insubstantial wisp of fantasy. This is Prospero philosophising: "We are such stuff as dreams are made on"; or the mood of Schopenhauer, "The world is my idea." This is philosophy at play with a vengeance. But it is more than that. For it carries a melancholy note, though a muted one. For what expires in the collapse of the world into dream is not only the cloud-capped towers and the gorgeous palaces, but also the people in them: my friends, my beloved ones, the persons in whose reality I had counted myself blessed, are now figures met in a dream, not other than me at all but hollow projections of myself.

Yet thought still clamors for its rights. Even if I am dreaming, still there are truths which withstand the general catastrophe, truths which I can still affirm as unconditional. Two and two are four, whether I am awake or asleep; a square has four sides in both the dream world and the world of common sense. Is there any way in which the methodic doubt can break the defenses of such seemingly impregnable truths? Well,

> As I sometimes imagine that others deceive themselves in the things which they think they know best, how do I know that I am not deceived every time that I add two and three, or count the sides of a square, or judge of things still simpler, if anything simpler can be imagined?[3]

If I sometimes make errors in mathematics without realizing it, what assurance do I have that I do not always make errors? This

---

[3] *Ibid.*, p. 93.

consideration is somewhat weak, and Descartes, in seeking to reinforce it, now reaches the extremity of his methodic doubt. This is the hypothesis of the evil genius, by which he manages at one stroke to shake the foundations of every ostensible item of knowledge he has, including mathematical truths. Why should there not be some higher power who is toying with me for his own purposes and who causes me to be filled with all manner of baseless convictions? Perhaps I am even the only person in existence and my entire experience is phantasmagorical, a film of illusion projected by some power malignantly bent on perpetually deceiving me, and to which no object whatever corresponds outside of myself:

I shall then suppose . . . some evil genius not less powerful than deceitful, has employed his whole energies in deceiving me . . . I suppose, then, that all the things that I see are false; I persuade myself that nothing has ever existed of all that my fallacious memory represents to me. I consider that I possess no senses; I imagine that body, figure, extension, movement and place are but the fictions of my mind. What, then, can be esteemed as true? Perhaps nothing at all, unless that there is nothing in the world that is certain.[4]

But what then? Is this equivalent to a state of paralysis? Is there anything that can escape this universal collapse? Strange as it seems, there is:

But how do I know that there is not something different from those things that I have just considered, of which one cannot have the slightest doubt? . . . I myself, am I not at least something? But I have already denied that I had senses and body. Yet I hesitate, for what follows from that? Am I so dependent on body and senses that I cannot exist without these? But I was persuaded that there was nothing in all the world, that there was no heaven, no earth, that there were no minds, nor any bodies: was I not then likewise persuaded that I did not exist? Not at all; of a surety I myself did exist since I persuaded

[4] *Ibid.*, p. 95.

myself of something . . . But there is some deceiver or other, very powerful and very cunning, who ever employs his ingenuity in deceiving me. Then without doubt I exist also if he deceives me, and let him deceive me as much as he will, he can never cause me to be nothing so long as I think that I am something. So that after having reflected well and carefully examined all things, we must come to the definite conclusion that this proposition: I am, I exist, is necessarily true each time that I pronounce it, or that I mentally conceive it.[5]

This then, is the rock upon which Descartes' doubt finally comes to rest: *cogito, ergo sum.* I think therefore I exist. *No matter how far the acid of doubt eats, it cannot consume that which is the condition for its own existence: the existence of the doubter.* My existence as a self, then, is the ultimate indubitable which no doubt can eradicate. Even if I am universally deceived, the act of being deceived is an act of thinking, and it delivers up the existence of the one who thinks and is deceived.

Some clarification of Descartes' point is required. First of all, it must be noted that in respect to the content of the cogito, what is delivered to him is simply his thinking self. The implied complete formula is: *cogito, ergo sum cogitans.* I think, therefore I am a thinking being. What the cogito renders indubitable is just that which is necessary to constitute it as cogito—and this means the existence of a *mind,* a conscious substance. It does not guarantee the existence of a body. Quite otherwise. When he reached the cogito, Descartes was not at that point assured of the real existence of his body, which might still fall on the deceptive side of his experience. It may be a body which only seems to be real, a dream body. Much more reasoning will be necessary before he can infer any other status for his body.

[5] *Ibid.*, pp. 96–97. A remarkably similar point had been made by St. Augustine twelve centuries earlier in his dialog against the sceptics (*Contra Academicos*). Let us accept your belief, says Augustine, that I am universally deceived, and yet there remains one ineluctable truth: "fallor, ergo sum,"—"I am deceived, therefore I exist." Augustine did not go on, however, to extract the methodological cornerstone of his thought from this truth, as did Descartes.

The Critical Doubt

But what is there from the beginning, given absolutely, given as the condition for doubt itself, is that I, as a thinking being, *am*. More briefly it may be observed that when Descartes speaks of "thinking," he is not referring exclusively to reasoning proper; seeing, hearing, feeling, pleasure or pain, willing, considered as conscious operations, are all included within this term. Even though the status of their objects may be in doubt, the conscious operations are not in doubt. Thus, the mirage of which I am (deceptively) aware may be unreal, but my act of being (deceptively) aware of it is real.

The objection is sometimes raised against Descartes that the cogito does not actually represent his only original indubitable, that it is actually the product of an inference, and therefore presupposes that the premise upon which the inference is made is antecedently known. What this objection supposes is that the "therefore" in Descartes' aphorism indicates that we are dealing with an enthymeme, a suppressed syllogistic inference, which, expanded into full form, would read like this: "All beings which think, exist; I think; therefore I exist." Here both the premise and the rules for the syllogism are prior to the syllogism and the cogito itself would require the previous justification of both of them.

This objection, however, is not well taken. The cogito is not reached as the result of an inference, and the ergo is not the ergo of the syllogism. What Descartes means is that my full personal existence is delivered to me in the act of doubting. I do not find doubt and then infer that there must be an "I" who doubts; rather, this "I" is delivered in the act of doubting. It is not inferred, but co-immediately present; thinking is the ego in its manifestation. The awareness of doubt is the awareness of myself doubting. The ego's existence is therefore known intuitively, and not inferentially.

SUBJECTIVISM

It is apparent that the plight in which Descartes finds himself with the discovery of the cogito is not an entirely comfortable one.

While it gives him an irrefrangible certitude, it does so at the expense of minimizing to a degree the scope of this certitude. For the subject which Descartes has uncovered in the cogito is a purely private, isolated subject. At this stage, he is certain of the existence of absolutely nothing but himself as a thinking being. Evidently this is unsatisfactory, and he is faced with the task of making his way out to the world which is other than himself starting from a purely private ego. The task will prove to be an imposing one, not only for Descartes but for many a modern philosopher.

The difficulty must be stated in all sharpness in order for its magnitude to be appreciated. What is presumed in Descartes' conception of mental life, as this is developed in his mature thought, is that the data of consciousness are purely subjective states. This is implied in his ability to conceive all the data of experience to be without self-certifying objective reference. Even if nothing whatever existed besides myself, I could still have exactly the same experiences that I am now having; therefore the fact that I am now having these experiences does not prove that they exist as anything other than my own states of consciousness; therefore finally, since consciousness as conceived by Descartes does not have an immediate objective reference to anything other than myself, if such reference is to be established, it must be as the result of some kind of reasoning.

What we have met here in a stark form is the problem of subjectivism. This problem is a formidable one indeed, since it amounts to this question: if all of my consciousness initially has the exclusive value of a subjective state of my own individual psyche, how do I ever learn the nature of anything other than myself or even rise to the awareness that there is anything other than myself? This question cannot be taken lightly, for in one form or another it is the question with which modern philosophy has been wrestling since Descartes. It is a question which arises in all its acuteness when we conceive of consciousness in a certain manner, the manner in which Descartes conceived it. But the

The Critical Doubt

problem is not only Descartes', since his way of conceiving consciousness is a way which will appeal to every human mind at a certain stage of reflection. It is the outlook of those who are called "idealists," and it is therefore convenient to introduce at this point the familiar distinction between *epistemological realists and epistemological idealists*. The formulations of the position of each is deliberately broad, for reasons that will become apparent later.

a) Epistemological realism holds that my consciousness puts me in touch with what is other than myself.

b) Epistemological idealism holds that every act of knowing terminates in an idea, which is a purely subjective event.

It is to be noted that the word "idea," from which epistemological idealism derives its name, does not refer exclusively or primarily to "universal ideas" or concepts in the strict sense. Any conscious undergoing of an experience is an idea, so that, seeing red, tasting something sweet, feeling a twinge of pain, being joyful, hoping, choosing, etc., are all ideas. They are data present for a conscious subject, in the opinion of idealists, "mental events." As mental events, they are modifications of an individual mind, and hence subjective. Epistemological idealism as defined above is hence equivalent to subjectivism. And the problem for a conscientious subjectivism is unmistakable: if *every* act of knowing terminates in a purely subjective event, then how can I ever utilize my knowing to arrive at the existence of anything other than myself? And if I cannot, then how do I know that anything other than myself really exists?

Now one answer to this question that is possible is that I *cannot* know. This is the reply of the position known as solipsism, according to which my self alone (*solus ipse*) exists—or at least I can only be sure that I exist, while the existence of things other than myself remains problematic. Obviously, solipsism, even more than absolute scepticism, remains more an hypothetical extreme for speculation than a genuine alternative. That is why nobody can point to any philosophers who have been solipsists. If really convinced solipsists have existed, they have, for evident reasons, never earned themselves a place in the textbooks of the history of philosophy.

The awkwardness of solipsism is amusingly illustrated by an episode recounted by Bertrand Russell.[6] Russell tells us of a letter he once received from the logician, Mrs. Christine Ladd Franklin, assuring him that she was a solipsist and expressing surprise that lots of other people were not also solipsists! Nothing could better illustrate the academic character of this position—and yet it is not only useful but essential to take notice of it. For, granted that nobody psychologically and existentially could sustain a stance of solipsism, the problem for the epistemological idealist or subjectivist is how, given his conception of consciousness, he can logically avoid it. If *all* consciousness is subjective, how can I *ever* be conscious of anything other than myself? It really seems that a single-minded idealist would find great difficulty in avoiding, speculatively, the solipsistic conclusion. What actually happens, as will be seen, is that those who begin by adopting an ostensibly subjectivist starting-point, eventually believe themselves to have discovered some feature of consciousness which is exempt from a purely subjective status and which *also* has objective reference. Unless they were to do so, they would be perpetually confined to their own individual psyches.

THE ESCAPE ROUTE

To call Descartes' conception of consciousness a subjective one is to oversimplify and to do scant justice to his thought, and in an attempt to present a rounded picture of Descartes, we would have to give a far better balanced exposition than the present one. We may offer the excuse that the present examination is interested in only certain aspects of his thought. That there really is a subjectivist peril in his approach, is indicated clearly enough by the

---

[6] Bertrand Russell, *op. cit.*, p. 180.

urgency with which he himself sought to escape it. If he had stopped with the cogito, he would have had merely the certitude of the solipsist, but no thinker is content to stop there. What is needed is an escape route from the cul-de-sac of subjectivism, and it is interesting to observe the route which Descartes took.

He reasons that by a careful reflection on the first truth (the cogito) he will be able to discern what in it guarantees its truth and thus to use this feature as a criterion for further certitude. Why does he find it impossible to reject the truth of his own existence? Because, he tells us, he perceives it so "clearly and distinctly" that doubt is rendered impotent. But if it were thinkable that a reality which was thus given clearly and distinctly might nevertheless be falsely given, his certitude would be baseless. Then in the very recognition of the indubitability of this clear and distinct given is also contained the recognition that nothing which is given clearly and distinctly can be false. Accordingly, we "can establish as a general rule that all things which I perceive very clearly and very distinctly are true."[7]

Needless to say, a great deal of criticism has been levelled at this procedure of Descartes, some of it misguided. It has often been supposed that this passion for clarity is simply a transposition into philosophy of Descartes' own fabulous skill in and admiration for mathematics. Whatever psychological justice there may be to this, it is not quite correct to equate Descartes' emphasis on clear and distinct ideas with a predilection for definition and exactitude. The somewhat unfortunate phrase refers principally to the evidential character of a datum, rather than to its exactitude; Descartes is concerned with what he elsewhere called the "simple," which others have thought of as the self-evident, the self-given, the luminous, the intelligible.[8] What he is continually emphasizing

---

[7] Descartes, *op. cit.*, p. 108.

[8] On this, see Norman Kemp Smith, *Studies in the Cartesian Philosophy* (New York: Russell and Russell), 1962, pp. 35–37. It is a fact, however, that his own examples tend to be rather abstract: "extension, shape, motion, and the like."

is the intuitive character of knowing: what I see, I see. The clear and distinct is that which shines in its own light.[9] His stand is this: however much positive, non-derivative reality is contained in a clear and distinct idea, that content is *real*; the distinction between subjective and objective is suppressed, and thought reaches what has unqualified cognitional value.[10]

The question is, do I possess any other un-derivative, positive, and self-luminous notions besides that of my own existence? Descartes finds another such idea in my idea of the infinite being, God. The meaning of this idea is perfectly luminous (clear and distinct). If so, it has, in respect to whatever positive content it contains, unqualified reality. This idea exists. There must be that in reality which sufficiently accounts for whatever positive reality this idea contains. But I am a limited being; therefore, I cannot be the adequate cause of my idea of the infinite. Nor can I regard this as an idea which I put together by combining other ideas of which I might be the adequate cause. No combination of finite aspects will ever give rise to a notion of the infinite. Rather just the opposite, for Descartes. The notion of the infinite is not really negative—it is positive. I could not even recognize something as *limited* unless I had a prior standard against which to measure its limitation.[11] This is more easily seen in his conception of God as Perfect Being; perfection is the primordial notion and the recognition of the beings of experience as im-perfect is only possible if I possess the more fully positive notion of the Perfect. Then the only adequate cause for the existence of the idea of the infinite, perfect being *is* the infinite, perfect being.

[9] It is true that he conceived of a universal science in which all these "simples" or luminous insights could be linked by a necessary chain of intuitive inferences, in which all human knowledge could be welded together, but that is not essential to the present context.

[10] Descartes, *op. cit.*, p. 115.

[11] *Ibid.*, pp. 118, 139–142. Descartes' argument is a version of the ontological argument of St. Anselm, which has been accepted in various forms by philosophers like Leibniz, Spinoza, and Hegel, but which is rejected by St. Thomas and the Scholastic tradition in general.

The Critical Doubt

There still remains the question of the "external world." How do I overcome the doubt as to the real existence of material things outside of me and independent of me? To do this Descartes has recourse to two things: the nature of the perfect being and the nature of my sense experience. My sense experience is not a conscious creation of myself. On the contrary, the data which present themselves to me in perception are often imposed upon me against my will and desire. As a senser, I am a receptive consciousness and therefore not an active cause. The data which I sense must therefore owe their existence to some cause other than myself. But why could not this cause be God Himself rather than bodies? As far as Descartes can see, such a possibility is incompatible with the nature of God as a perfect being. As perfect, He is perfectly veracious and cannot be the author of any deception. But I have an irresistible belief that the experiences I have of bodies are imposed on me by the bodies themselves, and there is no way I can extricate myself from such belief. If this belief were not a true one, if they were simply dream-ideas implanted in me by God, He would seem to be the author of a universal and invincible illusion on my part, and this is incompatible with His perfect truthfulness. Therefore Descartes concludes:

Hence we must allow that corporeal things exist. However, they are perhaps not exactly what we perceive by the senses, since this comprehension by the senses is in many instances very obscure and confused; but we must at least admit that all things which I conceive in them clearly and distinctly . . . are truly to be recognized as external objects.[12]

We should not fail to note that Descartes' return of the external world to good standing is an extremely qualified one, and does not apply to all that common sense includes under the term "world." Since God would only be guilty of deception in the case where my convictions were invincibly erroneous, then it is only those features

[12] *Ibid.*, p. 154.

of bodies which clearly and distinctly belong to them which are certified as objectively real. Which are these? They are those properties which "are comprehended in the object of pure mathematics." This means *extension* and *motion*.

Whatever other features seem to belong to bodies either reduce to these or else lose the character of being clear and distinct. Such things as color, warmth, sound, pain, resistance, coolness, taste, and the like, are not so evidently properties of bodies that I am unable to dissociate them from bodies.[13] It is quite possible to realize that these things are subjective experiences which I attribute to bodies but which do not essentially belong to the clear and distinct idea of body. The only property which so belongs is extension, and therefore the world which Descartes' veracious God has underwritten is a geometrical universe of matter in motion. This is the source of the famous Cartesian dualism. It has now turned out that the essence of mind is thought, the essence of matter extension. Everything that is not real in the way that matter in motion is real, can only be real in the way that consciousness is. The repercussions of such a view are tremendous and multi-directional. Descartes' dichotomy cemented the mechanical view of the universe which made possible vast advances in science; but by treating the human self as a "ghost inhabiting a machine,"[14] it raised the mind-matter problem in an extremely exacerbated form.

DREAM AND REALITY

For our purposes, it is not necessary to follow out all the ramifications of Descartes' thought, but only those which are pertinent for the philosophy of knowledge. The main question which must be asked is about his point of departure: has he correctly described human consciousness? We will not be overly concerned about the

[13] *Ibid.*, pp. 116–117, 154 ss.
[14] Gilbert Ryle's phrase, *The Concept of Mind* (New York: Barnes & Noble), 1949, pp. 15–16.

The Critical Doubt

particular escape route which he found from his own subjectivist beginning, but about that beginning itself. Is Descartes' translation of the actual position in which human consciousness finds itself an accurate and adequate one? Is the first indubitable for human consciousness the experience of itself as an isolated and individual ego?

This question is a crucial one and upon the answer to it depends the rest of what happens in epistemology. In the philosophy of knowledge, everything depends on the point of departure. If Descartes is right in his point of departure, then we begin with him in subjectivism and then must decide whether he really overcame it, and if we think he did not, we must try to find our own escape route. This is what ensuing philosophy tended to do. If we wish to avoid the subjectivist difficulty, we must concentrate on the view of consciousness which produced it. This is what contemporary philosophy is doing. The question requires a full airing, and the entire next chapter will be devoted to it.

Some brief consideration may be given to the specific language in which Descartes couched his doubt as to the objectivity of the external world, in particular to his "dream doubt." Descartes really does seem to be asking "How do I know that I am not always doing what I ordinarily mean by dreaming?" And yet if this is what he means, his question borders on nonsense. Our ordinary dream state is identified by comparison with our waking consciousness. We only know it as dream by comparing it with the consistent, organized, coherent world in which we are veridically conscious of ourselves and reality. It would be literally nonsensical to ask: how do I know that waking is not what I ordinarily mean by dreaming, because if it were, I wouldn't know what I ordinarily mean by dreaming. It makes no *practical* sense to wonder if waking is dreaming; if I could make a critical examination of my experience in dreaming, it would cease to be a dream. Therefore, Descartes is not in the condition of the man who pinches himself to make sure that he is really awake; this man's problem is a practical one which is soluble in principle.

Therefore we should perhaps take Descartes to mean something a little less vulnerable. This can be put as follows. Suppose the waking state is just as shut off from reality as the dream is. Not that it is a "dream" in the ordinary sense, but that it is as purely subjective in its own way as the dream. Then our plight could be expressed as a kind of proportion: just as dream image is to sense object, so sense object is to x. And even diagrammed:

$$\frac{\text{Dream image}}{\text{Sense Object}} \text{ as } \frac{\text{Sense Object}}{\text{x}}$$

In other words, perhaps in relation to the "really real," the sense object is an illusion. Even this belief is not altogether precise. It might only be taken as emphasizing that there is something more real in a being than can be given to us by the senses, that sense perception is a pale and partial revelation of reality. But there is nothing particularly new about this way of regarding sense perception. Plato had done it long before Descartes; and in a way, anyone who subscribes to the superiority of intellectual insight would have to give some weight to it. Of itself this belief would not derogate the objectivity of the reality given to the senses—it would only consign it to an inferior place. From one standpoint this is what Descartes is doing. He differentiates between the sensible and the intelligible at the expense of the former; his criterion for objectivity is precisely intelligibility (clearness and distinctness). He must then be classified among those who espouse Plato's distinction between *epistemé* (knowledge of the intelligible and necessary) and *doxa* (knowledge of the sensory and contingent).

Thus far, Descartes is only distinguishing between the other as given clearly and distinctly to thought and the other as given obscurely and confusedly to the senses. Yet in the proportion diagrammed above, Descartes may equally well be taken as emphasizing the *subjective* status of the sense object and not merely its confused character. The comparison with the dream, in other words, could be used to stress the purely private character of sense awareness. On this basis Descartes is claiming not that the objec-

The Critical Doubt

tivity of the sensed entity is obscure, but that it is not given at all; the sensed entity is just as cut off from the independently real as is a dream entity.

But this would mean that our awareness of the reality of the other is purely a work of thought, and this view carries built-in difficulties. Even if we were to accept it as faithful to human consciousness that existence can be delivered to thought alone, we would immediately have the difficulty that an other delivered only to thought would tend to be an abstract and universalized other—since human thought is conceptual and abstract. Data which cannot be delivered in this abstractly intelligible manner would lose their objective standing. Existence thus conceived would be inevitably impoverished, reduced to its most abstract character: on the one hand, a purely mechanical nature, and on the other, a purely logical subject. Descartes himself progressed quite far in this direction. Human experience tends to be rich in the direction of obscurity; the knowledge of lived experience is quite obscure, and yet to sacrifice its cognitional value is to reap a doubtful advantage. The only way to avoid this danger would be either to make Descartes' criterion of intelligibility mean much more than it meant in his own hands (which in a way is what the phenomenologists are doing in their expansion of the meaning of the "given") or to refrain from stating the original condition of consciousness in his way.

3 THE POINT OF DEPARTURE

"INSIDE" AND "OUTSIDE"

Any evaluation of Descartes should center not on his methodic doubt but on the accuracy of his description of consciousness. Give or take a few nuances, the employment of the methodic doubt is inevitable in epistemology, for it is simply the critical method self-consciously used, and criticism is the business of epistemology. The real question is whether Descartes, in turning the light of criticism upon consciousness, has really succeeded in tracing its authentic outlines. Contemporary philosophers, who by and large disagree with the Cartesian viewpoint, concentrate their fire on his analysis of the structure of consciousness and the present chapter will follow suit.

By way of preface, we may begin with an admonition which is elementary, but whose usefulness extends much further than its application to Descartes' thought. For, concealed at the base of all subjectivism, including Descartes', is a false image of consciousness which thwarts all attempts to break through to realism. This is the image of consciousness as a container "in" which reality is present. Only rarely, of course, would things be stated quite this baldly, but the attitude is operative even when it does not find its way into verbal formulation. It is a perfectly natural attitude, as is evidenced by our everyday manner of stating the relation between consciousness and its object. What I am aware of, I am prone to say, is "in" my awareness; what I am not aware of is "outside" my awareness. Reality as present to me at any given moment is "within" my consciousness. Sometimes we go on to say that it is "in my mind." And sometimes the image is pushed to the clearly untenable limit of saying that it is "in my head."

However spontaneously we may fall into this way of speaking, it is nonetheless ruinous. For, having posed matters in this way, I am stuck with the image and with its consequences. The consequences are dire indeed. For the briefest reflection will give rise to an inevitable question. If what I know is "in" my consciousness, then how does it ever allow me to make contact with what is "outside" my consciousness. My consciousness is *my* consciousness, a subjective occurrence in me; hence if the reality which I know is "within" my consciousness, it is within me, and my knowledge therefore leaves me locked up inside myself.

There is no need to think that Descartes proceeded according to this explicit image (if he had, its shortcomings would have been more evident). The point is that his way of stating the problem, his way of describing consciousness, is only possible if the image is implicitly operative in his thought. His problem is that of winning through to the "other," and certifying the varied status of the "other." This must mean that he does not regard the other as a primitive datum for consciousness, and hence that reality as present primitively to consciousness is not present as other but as "within" the consciousness of the subject: its credentials of otherness have still to be verified. Many a modern philosopher has been trapped into a similar subjectivist beginning by this implicit conception of consciousness as a container. Once the image is identified, it may be summarily dealt with. For if anything is clear, it is clear that we cannot seriously compare consciousness to a container or receptacle.

To demonstrate this we need only contrast the manner in which a contained thing is literally in a container with the manner in which the known thing is "in" the knower. A literal relation of container and contained is a relation between two spatially external objects. When an orange is in a crate, it makes perfect sense to say that the orange is from one standpoint still *outside* the crate. That is, the orange is not within the wood of the crate; it is surrounded by it, but it is nevertheless still spatially juxtaposed to it. Orange and crate are touching one another, and hence externally related: it is perfectly possible to mark off the limits of each, to say just where the crate stops and just where the orange starts. Now obviously this is not so with the relation of consciousness to its object. When I am aware of the orange I cannot tell where my awareness "leaves off" and where the orange "begins." I cannot point to some point in space and say "Here I, as knowing subject, stop, and here the object as known begins."[1] My awareness is not juxtaposed in space to this orange, not touching it, not outside it. True, my head and the orange are spatially related to each other—but this only proves that consciousness is not going on "inside my head." My consciousness does not stop at the limits of my head, at my eyeballs, or halfway between my head and the orange. My consciousness is not spatially related at all to the orange.

This insight may be expressed in alternate ways. We may use it to bring out the non-spatial character of consciousness and the absurdity of talking as if the known object is "in" the consciousness of the knower. Or we may take the opposite tack and accentuate the interiority of known and knower. If we should like to continue to speak the language of "being in" here, we must recognize that this relation cannot be understood from the side of the container/contained relation, but that it is a totally *sui generis* interiority. The known is "in" the knower, if you like, but to the limit of interiority—which is identification. The known object is in the subject in such a way that it is impossible to distinguish the limits of knower and known; the knower in so far as he knows is identical with the known object in so far as it is known.

This is the line which Scholastic philosophy has traditionally taken, in an effort to emphasize the non-subjective character of knowing. Whichever way the position is phrased, and they are only verbally different, the fact remains that it is senseless to treat

[1] And this is so whether we are talking of perceptual consciousness or intellectual consciousness.

the relation of consciousness to its object through the distorting image of the preposition "in." This is no light observation, for many a philosophical problem has arisen just because of a philosopher's inattentiveness to the trap set by his own language. If we realize that any problem which arises in regard to consciousness from the direction of this image is a pseudo-problem, we will have made a significant advance.

THE BI-POLARITY OF CONSCIOUSNESS

As a matter of fact, much of the advance that contemporary philosophy has made beyond the Cartesian lines has consisted simply in reclaiming ground lost because of this image. Once we recognize that there is no problem of getting "outside" of consciousness, we have recovered an essential vantage-point. To be conscious is already to be outside oneself. We do not have to break through the container of consciousness, because consciousness is not a container. The circle of awareness includes the other. This is what various contemporary thinkers are saying in one form or another.

It is also what the Scholastic philosopher has traditionally said against Descartes' epistemology. Here is where the counter-analysis of consciousness begins. Descartes' analysis implies that consciousness is primarily self-consciousness and only derivatively consciousness of the other. The primitive indubitable is the cogito-self, and I must infer by means of the intelligibility contained in it the existence of the other.

Thomism has always held the contrary: the self is only known reflexively in the knowing of the non-self. If this does not precisely claim that the knowledge of the other is primary and self-consciousness derivative, it at least implies that knowledge of self and other are co-temporaneous and indivisible. I only know myself in knowing the other. In the consciousness of the objects which my awareness encounters, I am reflexively aware of my own ego; but my ego is not a datum given in any sense *prior* to the object—

neither temporally nor epistemologically prior. It is given along with it, and unless the object is given, the ego is not given. I *learn* to say "I"; and I learn to say "I" in distinguishing myself from what is other than myself. It is at least significant that even Descartes has to appeal to a hypothetical "other" in order to be the author of his own deception: the evil genius is the hypothetical other who causes me to be deceived universally.

It is the standard view of the Scholastic authors that self-knowledge cannot be separated from knowledge of the object. In speaking of the mind's knowledge of itself, St. Thomas consistently does so by regarding it as grasping itself as a potency in a certain order, the order of cognition. But, "Potencies are only known by reason of their acts, and acts by reason of their objects";[2] hence it is clear that the intellect only knows itself in knowing its objects.

For it is manifest that by knowing the intelligible object, [the intellect] understands also its own act of understanding, and by this act knows the intellectual faculty.[3]

St. Thomas often reiterates this:

The human intellect . . . is not its own act of understanding, nor is its own essence the first object of its understanding, for this object is the nature of a material thing. And therefore that which is first known by the human intellect is an object of this kind, and that which is known secondarily is the act by which that object is known; and through the act the intellect itself is known . . .[4]

St. Thomas makes it clear that when he speaks of his mind's knowledge of itself, he is thinking of it as knowing itself as a capacity for truth; this implies that it only knows itself in knowing itself as this capacity for truth, that is, as the capacity for reaching the other. Unless it had already reached the other, it could not

[2] *De Anima,* I, lect. 8, n. 111.
[3] *Summa Theologiae,* I, q. 14, a. 2, ad 3.
[4] *Summa Theologiae,* I, q. 87, a. 3.

The Point of Departure

know itself as this capacity for reaching the other. This is unmistakably implied in the famous passage from *De Veritate,* q. 1, A. 9.

Truth is known by the intellect inasmuch as the intellect reflects upon its act; not only inasmuch as it knows its act, but inasmuch as it knows the relationship of its act to the thing, which relationship cannot be known unless there is known the nature of the active principle, which is the intellect itself, whose nature is to be conformed to things; hence the intellect knows truth inasmuch as it reflects upon itself.

There is no question then of the intellect knowing itself as a purely private ego. It knows itself as an openness to the real, as an attainment of the real; unless it had reached the other, and thus transcended the status of a private ego, it could not know either the nature of truth or the nature of itself.

This is a theme which many a contemporary thinker echoes in his own way: the empirical ego is never given in isolation from an object and can therefore never claim a more privileged status in being than the object. Edmund Husserl's notion of "intentionality" was originally put forward to emphasize this very fact: the nature of a conscious act is such that the act is a reference to another. It in-tends, or tends out to its other; the intelligibility of consciousness is its intentionality.[5] In Husserl's words, all consciousness is "consciousness of." To be aware is to be aware *of* something, and that of which I am aware has a status irreducible to awareness and is just as indubitably real as my awareness. A purely subjective awareness is not empirically verifiable; we do not have to win our way out from subjectivity to objectivity, for we never find ourselves within pure subjectivity. Do not forget that Descartes' cogito-self was an *individual* thinking subject, and that he claimed in effect that I can be indubitably aware of myself as an individual thinking ego without being indubitably aware of the existence of anything else. This is exactly what seems to be unfaithful to actual experience.

[5] And this in turn is a version of the older Scholastic doctrine of intentionality.

I do not discover myself as an individual self except in *relation to* what is other than myself. Consciousness is *bi-polar*: it is essentially relational. To say consciousness is first of all to say self-aware-of-non-self.[6] Both poles are empirically given. Consciousness is given as this bi-polar relation. Then we cannot remove one term of the relation without eliminating the relationship itself. Descartes thought that he could call the existence of the objective pole into doubt and still have the existence of the subjective pole, but if the empirically given subject is essentially a relational subject, this cannot be done. To attempt it would be something like trying to eliminate convexity and retain concavity; the concave and convex are two sides of one relation, and are not separately intelligible. Subjectivity and objectivity are two sides of one bi-polar relation and are not separately intelligible.

In order to make his analysis stand up, it would appear to be necessary for Descartes to be able to give an empirical meaning to "ego" or "self" which excludes all reference to objectivity. If he is really thinking about the self of experience, then he should be able to *point* to this self in such a way that he is not simultaneously pointing to the non-self. The trouble is that it is not possible to do so. The empirical subject is not anterior to nor more indisputably real than the empirical object. I discover myself as subject by separating myself from the pole of the other; I come to consciousness of "self" by identifying it against "non-self." The "I" of experience is known reflexively by differentiating itself from the non-I. Therefore, in knowing a "self" I also know a "non-self" and hence Descartes' discovery of the "I" *could* not be a discovery of the self alone. If "I" means anything, it means it as designated against "non-I."

Once again, we must remind ourselves that these remarks hold good against Descartes, for he believed himself to be talking about the empirical ego (the "I" as actually experienced), and not about some postulated Absolute Ego, which others have speculated to underlie both the subjective and objective poles of experience, and

---

[6] Although it is, secondarily, to say self-aware-of-self-aware-of-non-self.

The Point of Departure

to produce them both by an act never revealed to consciousness. This is the view of Absolute Idealism, and it makes little difference in assessing Descartes. The "I" to which he assigned privileged status was not the Absolute Self of Fichte or Hegel, but what you and I mean by "I"—this individual experienced self. It is entirely relevant, then, to urge against him the point that the empirical object is contemporaneous with the empirical subject, that the very meaning of the statement "I exist" can be understood only by contrasting the I with the non-I, and that therefore the absolute privilege which Descartes gave to the individually experienced ego is not justified.

BEING-IN-A-WORLD

It is interesting to observe the manner in which contemporary thinkers tend, each in his own way, to surmount the Cartesian viewpoint. With Gabriel Marcel, the rejection of the cogito-subject forms one of the foundation-stones of his thought. He regards the cogito as an abstraction, a subject which is conceived as the limit of the evacuation of content from the experienced self—but not an existent. Man's being is a being-in-a-situation. This is what is empirically given; the only "self" that is ever vouchsafed me in experience is a self I find in this situation. The existential indubitable is the self as incarnate in the body and as manifest in the world. The first moment of my experience is what he calls an "exclamatory awareness" of myself.[7] "Here I am"!—this is one translation of the fundamental awareness. And this "here" does not refer only to my incarnation in a body. No doubt it is my body which primarily sets me down in a world of real beings; the body is not even to be thought of as something which I "have," for I only really have what is other than me. "I *am* my body": so Marcel translates the limit-experience of my incarnate existence.[8] But my being "here" means at this point of time, at this place,

[7] *The Mystery of Being,* vol. I, trans. G. S. Fraser (Chicago: Regnery), 1951, pp. 91–92.
[8] *Du refus à l'invocation* (Paris: Librairie Gallimard), 1940, p. 30.

with these parents, in these cultural surroundings, and so forth. The only ego which escapes this placement is one which I *think* of; purified of all empirical intrusions, the ego is contentless and empty, and therefore, in Marcel's view, inevitably tends to deteriorate into something purely formal, as it did with Kant. Such an ego cannot be said to *exist* at all.

What is given to me beyond all cavilling is the "I" of experience; but the "I" of experience is given as a focal point within an englobing situation, and hence the real indubitable is the "confused and global experience of the world inasmuch as it is existent."[9] What is real is the altogether. The cogito is discovered by a retreat from the altogether; far from being the primary datum, it is a derivative construction and in danger of being a mere abstraction. Pure subjectivity is contentless subjectivity; as existing subjectivity I am not pure subjectivity, but a being-by-participation. This is a key word in Marcel. I am not an existing subject who *also* participates in reality. I am not a being plus participation: I am a being-by-participation.[10] My existence may have more than one level, but at every level it is participation which *founds* the experience of subjectivity. Marcel will not only distinguish a level of incarnation (actualized via sensation and the experience of the body as *mine*) but more significantly a level of *communion,* in which I come to myself as spiritual subject through my participation in a communion of spiritual subjects. "Esse est co-esse" is true above all on the level of spiritual being: I am only an I in the face of a thou. The proper beginning of metaphysics, he says, is not "I think," but "we are."[11] The experiences of love, hope, and fidelity, which are the actualizations of my participation in communion are not intelligible on Cartesian terms. Finally, Marcel allows that I am a being-beyond-a-situation, that my existence con-

---

[9] *Metaphysical Journal,* trans. by Bernard Wall (Chicago: Regnery), 1952, p. 322.

[10] *The Mystery of Being,* vol. I, ch. VI.

[11] *The Mystery of Being,* vol. II, trans. by René Hague (Chicago: Regnery), 1951, p. 9.

tains a vector of transcendence; yet even here it is participation which is decisive. For the acts which found me as subject-in-communion are also the acts by which I experience the pull of transcendence.

Perhaps no one has carried the rejection of the cogito-self farther than Martin Heidegger or made a greater attempt to found philosophy on a new basis. The terminological obscurity for which he is famous is actually a consequence of his striving to express the totally unique mode of existence which belongs to human reality. Heidegger has in common with Marcel the conviction that the starting point for philosophy cannot be located within knowledge; that is, if the self is conceived along purely cognitive lines, it always tends to become a purely thinking subject and hence a world-less subject for whom the existence of the other becomes problematical.[12] What is wanted is a recognition of the reflexive activity as appended to the profounder reality which Heidegger has named *Dasein*. Instead of talking first about knowledge, we should talk about the human reality through which there is the ground of the possibility of knowledge. Man is *Dasein*, there-being, the there of being, the being through which being is revealed.

We should not pose man's knowledge as a problem of knowing the world, for man's knowledge comes to itself as the cognitive side of a being through whom there is world. There is no question that man's being is open to the world, for it is only his being that allows the question of world to be raised. As soon as there is *Dasein* there is world, for *Dasein is* being-in-the-world. This phrase is hyphenated, says Heidegger, because we are dealing with a unitary phenomenon. The world is a correlate of *Dasein,* and *Dasein is* this openness to the world. We should not speak as if there are two entities, alongside of each other, between which some relation has to be validated.[13] The world itself is not an entity which can be designated as could an item within the world.

[12] *Being and Time*, p. 86. A full discussion is on pp. 78–90 of this work.
[13] *Ibid.*, p. 81.

The world is a primary phenomenon, which is always there in its totality for *Dasein*; the world is a referential totality of meaning, and it is there in every relation of *Dasein* toward any and every specific worldly item.[14] Every object which my action employs incorporates in it a totality of meanings, the reference to which is already there for me as an acting being and which allows me to perceive this object as "something to be employed." This relational totality of significance cannot be discovered or verified within the world, for it *is* the world. *Dasein* always finds this world as already-here. And it finds itself as the correlate of the world. A world-less subject is never given. It is therefore nonsense for *Dasein* to raise the question of the being of the world, for this implies that it discovers itself as a world-less subject.

Descartes did not have sufficient grasp of the uniqueness of the mode of being of *Dasein*;[15] he lumped it under the heading of "substance," treating it merely as a special kind of "thing" along with other things. He then had the problem of how this substance would make contact with other substances. But *Dasein* is not adequately grasped according to the notion of substance. *Dasein* is not a thing: "things" are only there for *Dasein* because *Dasein* primordially has a world. What comes first, then, is not a consciousness of things, nor consciousness of a thinking substance; but being correlated to world. Probably we should not even say that consciousness comes first, for consciousness always emerges onto a scene where *Dasein* and world are already correlated. Consciousness tends to translate this correlation into a cognitive relation between subject and object, but it cannot be represented by

---

[14] Obviously "world" here does not mean the physical universe. We should take it on its own terms, or if analogs are needed, think rather of the way we talk about the "world of sports," the "business world," or the "political world." It is something like the most inclusive use of the term in this manner: Heidegger's world is "the world of all worlds." This includes the notion of a physical world, rather than being included within it. See esp. pp. 79, 92 of *Being and Time;* a full discussion is included in pp. 91–148 of this book.

[15] *Ibid.*, p. 131.

The Point of Departure

this means. *Dasein* ex-sists; it transcends itself, it is always outside of itself.

All this is, ultimately, possible because *Dasein* is the bearer of the question of Being.[16] *Dasein* raises the question of the being of the entities it meets because it itself is a transcending in the direction of Being. The "world" is the gathering of entities under the aegis of Being. The absolutely primary word is the word "Being"; the existence of *Dasein* is the speaking of that word, and in speaking it, *Dasein* polarizes the entities of experience and inhabits a world. *Dasein*, then, is not first of all a knower or a reflective consciousness, but a mode of existing by which the Being of beings can be revealed. To know oneself thus is not to be aware of an individual thinking substance.

José Ortega y Gasset is yet another philosopher who breaks with the purely private self of Descartes. His fundamental concept is the category of "my life," and it is chosen because he feels it to translate the fundamental experience of human existence more faithfully than purely cognitive language and to bypass the maze which we enter as soon as we begin talking of "subject" and "object." For "life" is a border-notion. It is two-pronged and in no danger of giving rise to the subjectivist difficulties about how I get "outside" myself. For "to live means having to be outside of myself."[17] Life is inconceivable in purely subjectivist terms, since it is a commerce or exchange between self and non-self. This is clearly borne out in biological life, although naturally there is no question of conceiving the meaning of the notion with primary reference to this. Ortega simply insists that if philosophy wants to discover the most radical reality of human existence as its point of departure, it ultimately discovers the self as the dynamic exchange with the other.

---

[16] On this, see *Being and Time*, pp. 244–252. See also his *Lettre sur l'Humanisme*, texte allemande traduit et présenté par Roger Munier (Paris: Aubier, Editions Montaigne), n. d., pp. 57, 59, 63.

[17] *Man and People*, trans. by Willard R. Trask (New York: W. W. Norton), 1957, p. 48.

I am not a "thinking substance," for having said no more than that I have not yet comprehended my mode of existence as I actually undergo it: a "substance" could be conceived as closed in on itself, completed in its own borders. But I simply do not experience myself in these terms. I am an out-going existence; for me, says Ortega (in words almost identical with Marcel), "existing is first and foremost co-existing."[18] The world and my thought are in active correlation. The consequence of this, for Ortega, is that I am not able to claim that I know reality as it is "in itself"; the world is not my thought, yet it is not given as independent of my thought. The primary fact is not the self or the world, but myself as open to the world, or the world as delivered to my unfolding existence.[19] My life is exactly the clashing of these two cymbals. I may burrow into my consciousness as deep as I like, but I will never find anything more than my life; and my life is never pure subjectivity or pure objectivity, but always encounter, always the clash of the two cymbals.

With these sentiments, Maurice Merleau-Ponty is in profound agreement. Against Descartes, he holds that human consciousness is not "self-contained"; no matter how deeply we penetrate into ourselves, we always find a reference to the other.[20] Nor is this relation to the other merely cognitional: it is a relation of being; it is a pre-conscious and ontological intentionality. For this reason, he also agrees with Ortega that it is futile to try to discover the world as it is "in itself." Revelation of reality is made to the human subject, and the human subject is always a *situated* subject. Specifically, it is a *body-subject*. Merleau-Ponty here uses practically the same words as Marcel: we are our own body.[21] Reflection seeks to discover the authentic lineaments of the real, but reflection is always upon the unreflected. The opacity present in

---

[18] *What is Philosophy?*, p. 208.
[19] *Ibid.*, pp. 197–202.
[20] *Sens et non-sens* (Paris: Nagel), 1948, pp. 143 ss.
[21] *Phenomenology of Perception*, trans. by Colin Smith (New York: Humanities Press), 1962, p. 206.

The Point of Departure

our finite and bodily mode of existence is never banished by thought: my knowledge is always conditioned by my existence, and hence when we speak of the real we will always be speaking of what it is as being-for-us.

Obviously under these conditions it is also futile to try to discover a "pure subject." My thought and my subjectivity are embedded in a situated existence: man and the world form the most radical sort of *gestalt*.[22] The world is my field of existence and my subjectivity does not transcend my existence. My existence is bodily existence, and my body is a dialog with the world. The cogito-self of Descartes is not something that can be pointed to in experience. It could only be pointed to if our thought were totally transparent to itself, but this is just what the obscure character of human existence precludes. The pure thinking subject could only come forward if thought could totally banish the unreflected, but this human thought cannot do. Actually, Merleau-Ponty will hold that even if it could do so, it would be contentless, since it is from the side of our existence that meaning originates. Our existence is an openness to the world, and meaning is the face which the world presents within the openness which we are. The subject enters the world as a question, and the world always has the character of a reply.[23] We *are* this questioning existence; the body itself is inserted into reality as a living question. Therefore the self which discovers its own source in a questioning existence has discovered *more* than a subject.

One of the most interesting of the alternatives to Descartes' point of departure is that proposed by Father Auguste Brunner. A purely private ego, he agrees, cannot serve as the initial indubitable in the philosophy of knowledge, for it is not experienced but is simply an abstraction. On the other hand, merely stressing

---

[22] *Sens et non-sens*, pp. 170–172. For an excellent presentation of this, see Remy C. Kwant, O. S. A., *The Phenomenological Philosophy of Merleau-Ponty* (Pittsburgh: Duquesne Univ. Press), 1963, pp. 64–69.

[23] Again for an excellent presentation of this, see Kwant, *op. cit.*, pp. 21–27.

being-in-a-world or "intentionality" is not sufficient either. The intentionality of consciousness is also an abstraction; it is a pale and partial apprehension of the concrete reality which is *really* the primary conscious experience: the fact that I exist in dialog with a community of persons. Here is where Brunner begins: with dialog.[24] The self which reflection discloses is a self already involved in a dialog with other persons. The reflection which discloses the self has already disclosed the "thou," for the self of experience is an "I" in the face of a "thou" and never anything else.

Even Descartes, after all, had to use language and should have recognized that language is essentially *social*. It is ironic that Descartes, in wondering whether perhaps he alone existed, used language to do the wondering—and that language is empirically not a creation of my private cogito-self but a bequest of other persons whose existence I am trying to use it to question. Language is clearly a border-reality; it is not the property of any particular self but exists on the frontiers of dialog. It is a phenomenon of dialog. The first indubitable, therefore, is not that I exist, but that dialog exists. My doubt itself is framed by dialog, for it is framed by language which is a product of dialog. Empirically, I find myself within language. Therefore, the thou is already given to me. It is empirically given that language is not a product of my individual self; hence, if the individual expresses his own existence in dialog, he has expressed more than his own existence. Dialog, Brunner holds, gives me the thou as a primary phenomenon. It also gives me the existence of the world as that about which dialog is carried on: dialog contains the address of the "I" to the "thou," but it also contains the "other" of the "I" and "thou," to which dialog refers. The "other," the world, then, is met as a "third" in respect to which a dialog beween persons is held.

[24] *The Fundamental Questions of Philosophy* (St. Louis: B. Herder), 1937, pp. 18ss. For a fuller treatment see Brunner's *La connaissance humaine* (Paris: Aubier), 1943; and the exposition on Van Riet, *op. cit.*, pp. 613–621.

THE EPISTEMOLOGICAL CIRCLE

This review could be prolonged, but enough has been said to suggest why Descartes' approach to consciousness is defective. It is not that he should be accounted wrong in his insistence on the indubitability of the "I exist," but only that more is contained in this certitude than he was willing to allow. In so far as the statement really *asserts* something, in so far as the "I" has meaning and is not simply equivalent to an empty "x exists," it asserts more than Descartes believed, for the meaning of the existing "I" includes the reference to the other which Descartes felt required to go on to validate.

Yet have we done something basically illegitimate here? Have we pretended to "solve" the epistemological question of the truth-value of our knowledge simply by assuming that in certain privileged cases it *has* such truth-value? The question is whether our awareness reaches a non-self. We seem to have answered it by listing cases where it does—and thus to assume rather than justify the truth of our knowledge. Or, to put the objection another way: Epistemology is an attempt to assess and, where possible, validate our conviction that we know reality other than the self. Have we begun this assessment simply by the declaration that we *do* know reality other than the self? If so, why isn't this a *petitio principii*?

The difficulty is that the question of the philosophy of knowledge is itself based on the realization that in respect to human knowledge it is possible to make the distinction between appearance and reality. Once we recognize the possibility of this distinction, however, there is a puzzle as to seeing how it can ever be surmounted. Do we simply declare that it *is* surmounted in this or that case and that is the end of it? Or do we search for a criterion which we can use to determine when it is successfully surmounted? This latter would be the search for the point of departure, which has been carried on since Descartes. We are moved to search for some kind of starting-point impervious to attack, in order to assure ourselves that our later conclusions will not be vitiated by a suspect premise. This urge of philosophy to establish its own foundations has driven certain thinkers like Edmund Husserl to an indefatigable and perpetual beginning-over. For the dilemma seems to be that if we begin with pure awareness as our basis, we seem to beg the question, and if we begin with anything other than pure awareness, we seem to introduce immediately the appearance/reality distinction, and to place awareness always at one remove from its object. Thus we may be thought to be condemned either to answer doubt by appealing to a place where it is already answered, or to make the answer to it impossible.

In reply to this difficulty, one point may be briefly made. Perhaps the charge of "begging the question" is not entirely to the point in a philosophical arena. Somewhere along the line, philosophy is probably inevitably going to beg the point. For instance, if we ask "How do I know what I think I know?" it is not really reprehensible to reply that in this or that case I really do know. For if the answer to this question is possible at all, it must already be present to my experience. Therefore, when I appeal to the privileged portion of my experience to demonstrate that in this case at least I really do know what I think I know, I am not really begging the question—or if I am, it is inevitable. The answer to such a question must either be already available or it is not available at all. Obviously I cannot go outside of my knowledge in order to justify my knowledge, and so the ground for the justification of knowledge must already be implicitly present to my knowledge. And in calling attention to it, I do not commit a fallacy.

Thus, in answering the question "How do I know that I am not the only existent?" I am not proceeding fallaciously when I say "I know it because I know that other persons exist." I am bringing into full focus a datum which is *there,* but whose obscurity has made the question possible. Somewhere along the line, *any* attempt to deal with the epistemological problem is going to have to assume *some* privileged instances where my knowing does put me in indisputable touch with reality (or it is not going to get an

The Point of Departure

answer at all). The only valid objection would be that a thinker has found this where it does not really exist. For example, if I were to make the scientific world-view the absolute beginning for my review of knowledge, if I were to treat this as an instance of where knowing achieved an original and primary contact with the real, it would not be hard to show that this was erroneous: for the scientific picture of the world derives from and presupposes a whole prior contact of my awareness with the real and cannot be used as an original justification of the truth value of awareness.

Nor is there any initial necessity to think of the search for a beginning or for a privileged contact with the real in the *singular*. We cannot decide beforehand that there is only *one* such contact, for consciousness may in a plurality of instances reach a privileged datum in which the appearance/reality distinction is surpassed. At least, we have no reason for ruling out this possibility. The beginning of epistemology does not have to function as a premise from which ensuing truths are deduced. Some tend to treat it in this way, which explains their anxiety to discover an absolutely unquestionable premise. The "beginning" of epistemology need be singular only if truth is delivered deductively; if it is the product of direct encounter of thought and the real, there is no reason why the encounters should not be multiple.

THE QUESTION AS IRREDUCIBLE BEGINNING

The need to find a unified beginning is felt by the philosopher not so much because of the nature of knowledge as because of the nature of his own critical pursuit. He wants to bring the bewildering variety of questions with which he is forced to deal back to some kind of unity. He wants to see knowledge whole, and thus is driven to bring it back to its own foundations. The search for foundations is not actually a search for some privileged item of knowledge, but for the ground of the possibility of knowledge. There must be something about knowledge which makes it possible to answer the question of its truth-value. Knowledge, which makes the distinction between appearance and reality possible, must also contain the ground whereby this distinction is surpassed. It must, *as* knowledge, in its own foundations, already surpass the distinction between appearance and reality.

Now, human knowledge is also complicated by other factors, as we have seen. Human knowledge is the knowledge of an existing subject, a being-in-a-world; it is the knowledge of a being which is not pure knower. We must therefore reconcile two things: human knowledge must arise out of existence, out of an extra-cognitional source, and must yet *as* arising out of that source contain the grounds for surpassing it.

Human knowledge has its foundation in existence (which in man is extra-cognitional) and yet *in* that foundation must find the grounds for surpassing the appearance/reality distinction. This means that man's mode of existence must contain the grounds for surpassing that distinction. Man's existence, which seems alien and external to his knowledge, must itself be such that it is the ground of his knowledge and of any absolute which is attained by his knowledge. For to surpass the appearance/reality distinction is to reach an absolute insight. Here, then, we emerge to a surprising conclusion: man's contingent existence must be the ground for his contact with the absolute. This is unexpected. For we might think that our finite and situated mode of existence would, if anything, impede and prevent absolute cognition. If this were so, there would be discontinuity between our cognition and our existence, and our situation would be an accidental and inexplicable appendage to our knowledge. But if the foregoing reasoning is right, our situated and perspectival mode of existence does not exclude us from the absolute but is actually what provides access to the absolute.

We may approach matters in the following way. The epistemological problem is the problem of surpassing the distinction between appearance and reality and of justifying the hyper-individual value of our knowing. Now it may be taken as a cardinal principle that that which makes the appearance/reality distinction possible

The Point of Departure

is not itself dubitable. Here Descartes' view is beyond reproach: doubt cannot be ultimate, for doubt is generated because of the possibility of distinguishing between what appears to be and what really is. Doubt inhabits the chasm which is opened between these two. It might at first appear that once this chasm has opened for our knowledge, then nothing can close it. Yet this is not so. For there must be that in our knowledge which allows this appearance/reality distinction to appear, and the ground of the distinction cannot itself fall on the side of appearance.

For Descartes, the appearance/reality distinction is sufficiently grounded in the experience of myself as an individual thinking subject; that is, the intelligible paradigm for "reality" is that contained in my reflective grasp of myself as a thinking being, and the reason that the reality of other things may be called into doubt is that they do not exhibit this same intelligibility. The notion of appearance, on this view, arises because I apprehend everything besides my individual thinking self as a falling-away from the paradigmatic mode of reality which belongs to the self. Thus, we may say that the self is unconditionally real, for it is the ground for the distinction between appearance and reality. But if the criticism of the Cartesian viewpoint is well taken (and that is the present contention) this will not do. The cogito-self cannot sufficiently ground the appearance/reality distinction, since it is not itself an irreducible beginning. We must go back behind it. The self of experience is not a private thinking substance, but a self which is transcendentally related to a world, a fundamental *gestalt* in which self and other are configurationally united. What then is the irreducible cognitional beginning, in terms of which the distinction between appearance and reality is both raised and surpassed?

It is the *question*. It is my existence as a questioning being which generates the appearance/reality distinction. If I get down to the core of my knowing, to the foundation upon which my existence as a knowing being is built, what I find is the question. At the absolute center of knowing, there is the *question*. Nothing can go back behind this—no doubt, no scepticism, no error can conjure it away; nor can any subsequent knowledge be grasped except as a reply to the primordial question which I *am*. As a knower I inhabit the question; I exist questioningly. Only because I can call experience into the light of the question can I distinguish between appearance and reality. *Before* this distinction comes my existence as a questioning being. But this means that the question takes precedence over the appearance/reality distinction, that whatever intelligibility is contained in the question is contained *indubitably*.

The importance of this can be overlooked because we are in the habit of regarding a question as something merely negative: I do *not* know something, and therefore I question. As such, the question seems to be the pure absence of cognitional value. It seems to occupy the terrain of ignorance, to have no more intelligibility than a negation. What is proposed here is that this is not so, that the question is actually the primordial form of cognition. Meaning is first given to us in the form of the question; man's existence is this question. The question is not, as we usually picture it, a blank negative posed in the face of a solid block of reality. To picture it thus is to empty the question itself of value, to represent it as a cipher oriented towards a fullness. Because we do this, we find it hard to grasp what one could mean who assigned cognitive value to the question as such. One only knows, we feel, what he can *assert*; that is why epistemology is often thought to be a review of propositions or judgments: a proposition is the public form of an assertion, and only assertions are cognitional. Questions express what I do *not* know. But in putting things thus we neglect to advert to the fact that underlying all assertion is the need to assert. Why do I assert anything? Because implicitly I have previously questioned. The primordial question is the ground for the existence of any assertion whatsoever. This is what we overlook. As Ortega y Gasset says, the ultimately astonishing thing is that man has problems at all. Why should we have problems, why should we question? In asking this question, thought sees that it can go no further. Man has problems because he exists questioningly.

The Point of Departure 65

If the question is the primary form of cognition, then whatever is contained in the question is indubitably real. But the question contains much more than the Cartesian cogito. Surely it contains the self, but not in an exclusive or even prominently thematic way: it contains the self as open towards the other. The self which comes to itself in the question comes to itself as openness to the other. The other is just as present in the question as is the self. That is the justification for Heidegger's and Ortega's viewing of the world as the correlate of my existence. Being is present to me questioningly: what is given in the question is being in its questionability. This is not playing with words, for this presence of being in its questionability is my ultimate assurance of intelligibility. Reality is given to me as correlative to the question: then, in inhabiting this question, I inhabit meaning, and there is no escape from it. I *am* this dwelling in meaning, because I *am* the question. The revelation of the world as questionable is its revelation as intelligible: this is *cognition,* primary cognition, and it is given in the question. The world is the correlate of my existence because the world is the totality of entities as incorporated into the question: because my thought is open to Being in its questionability, it is the correlate of the world as included within the question of Being. Self and world are the two sides of an experience which is questioningly open to Being.

More than this, what is given in the question is the fact that *we* question. The question comes to itself, utters itself, in *language.* Then it is we who speak and we who question. As the questioner, I am part of a community of questioning beings. *We* exist questioningly. Thus Heidegger will say that "language is the house of being":[25] man, as questioning existence, raises the question of the Being of the beings he meets, but he raises this question in language, and thus Being dwells in language. Conversely, man dwells in the intelligibility of being by dwelling in language. Here Brunner is right. Where thought starts is with the question; but the question finds voice in language. The full intelligibility of the question in-

---

[25] Heidegger, *Lettre sur l'Humanisme,* p. 24.

cludes the community of questioning beings who give voice to it: it includes dialog. In inhabiting the question, I am open to the "thou" who addresses me and who dwells with me in language. Contained in the question is much more than the thinking substance of Descartes: the appeal and response of the "I" and "thou," being in its questionability, the world about which I raise the question of its being. It can now also be pointed out how my existence may be the foundation of my relation to the absolute. For even on a pre-cognitional level, I exist questioningly: human reality is inserted into the world as a living question. As he comes to the consciousness of himself, man grasps his existence as a questioning existence. But a questioning existence is turned to the absolute. It *is* the presence of the absolute, the presence of being in its questionability. Then man's properly human mode of existence *is* this openness to being.

If these contemporary thinkers are right, it might be wondered why Descartes saw things so differently. In so far as such questions can be answered, the answer probably is that he did not carry his examination back far enough. He remained too much within what Husserl has called[26] the "natural view" of things which regards the human entity as simply one among others, even while trying to subject this view to criticism. When he got back behind the "natural view," he still had not modified his conception of the knower, and when he resuscitated the self it was the self of the "natural view" with the other entities omitted—an isolated "thinking substance." If we carry reflection back to its ultimate ground in human reality, we discover human reality as a unique openness to being: both as existent and as knower, I am a question inserted into reality. My privilege is not to be a thinking substance, but to be this unique openness to reality. My claim to a privileged status consists in my being the scene for this disclosure of reality.

Descartes did not sufficiently recognize that the question is more

[26] Edmund Husserl, *Ideas; General Introduction to Pure Phenomenology*, trans. by W. Boyce Gibson (New York: Macmillan), 1931, pp. 101–106, 125–127.

than the revelation of the subject. He grasped the privileged role of thought, but he grasped it as questioning *activity,* and thus reconfined this questioning activity to a separate thinking substance. He thus considered consciousness as the act or function of a "thing" in the same way that the activities of the entities which consciousness encounters are activities of "things." Consciousness, however, as the disclosure of all activities is not an activity of a thing in the same way that these activities are. Birds fly, fire warms, plants grow, man is conscious, so would run the list of activities. But consciousness is not the activity of a subject in the same sense as these others: it is the questioning existence which brings to light all these other activities and cannot be comprehended in terms of them. Descartes' essential mistake was that he had not sufficiently liberated himself from the conception of thought as a "thing." Man's unique mode of existence was apprehended by him as the existence of a "thinking thing," a conception not only terminologically inappropriate but philosophically misleading, since it introduces more problems than it solves.

4 THE PROBLEM OF PERCEPTION: I

NAIVE REALISM

Any philosopher of knowledge will have some kind of problem about perception. For the general realization of the bi-polar nature of consciousness does not settle every question that can be raised about the objectivity of the whole range of data present to consciousness. The area of perception is especially replete with perplexities.

At the start we all stand in the comfortable assurance of common sense, which proceeds on the assumption that the world presented to us through sense perception is purely and simply "there," even when we are not sensing it. It is there as such, in the exact manner it is sensed, in complete independence of our conscious awareness. Thus, when my auto speeds over the highway and I tranquilly behold the panorama of sights, sounds, and smells which make up the countryside, it does not occur to me to think anything else but that I am perceiving what is there as such when I am not perceiving it. I am aware of the green of the grass, the solidity of the hills, the blue of the sky, the noise and clatter of other cars, the drone of an airplane overhead, the resistance of the road against the car-wheels, the gigantic collective shape of the trees, the motion of clouds, the heat of the July sun, the mingled scent of pine and gasoline fumes. And all of this is there for me as extended in space, as a dense distance—as far as I can see, there stretches the voluminous expanse which seems to surround and contain me and my awareness. This panorama is a successive one, for the speeding car keeps introducing me to new vistas and leaving others behind. But it does not for a single moment enter my head that as I leave each vista behind, as the scene which I beheld a moment ago vanishes from my view, that it ceases to exist. I assume just the opposite. I assume that the scene upon which I looked a second ago still stands there in a way in which it stood there for me, ready to be presented to someone else (or to me, if I choose to return).

"Assume" is even a poor word, for I do not consciously assume this at all; it is hardly a cognitional act of any kind. The objectivity of the landscape is a kind of habitation for my own being. The scenes which are up ahead on the road loom up for me already; my present consciousness is a kind of living-towards the impending future, so that the objectivity towards which I live is at the base of my present consciousness. The absent other is still there for me, whether it is the other I just beheld or am yet to behold. The naive consciousness (which simply means lived consciousness, unreflective, non-theoretical consciousness) is sustained by the pure "thereness" of that amongst which it moves and consequently does not dream of questioning this thereness; its own self-presence would slip away if it did so, for it finds itself out-there, among things.

"Naive realism," as it is called, is simply this lived acceptance of total objectivity—or the philosophical affirmation of the cognitive value of this lived acceptance. It is often said that naive realism holds that the precise qualities which we sense are *formally* there independent of sensation, but this may be a wrong way of putting it. The language of "qualities" is probably not apt for expressing the position of lived naive consciousness, for the latter is primarily an *acting* consciousness, and moves among things, not qualities. A thing is, for it, a unified center of action which is set over against my action; it is that against which I act, and which reacts upon me. It is both the condition for and obstacle to my action. Those philosophers are doubtless right who, like John Dewey and Max Scheler, ascribe our original conviction of objectivity to the feeling of the "resistance" of the world. My action and my will do not flow freely. I meet impediments, and that is how I first become aware of myself; an actor meeting counter-actors. As an actor, I am a unified center, and things as counter-actors are unified centers met by me. As resistant, their reality is not conferred upon them by me; therefore as resistant, they are unqualifiedly real and objective.

Since this is the context in which naive consciousness meets the world, then all features of that world tend to share the pure "thereness" of the world towards which action thrusts. As soon as we begin to talk about "qualities" and to wonder whether these are objective or not, we have taken a step back from action, for quality is a theoretical term. Action does not advert to qualities. For it, the separate features of the world are not met as separate features, but incorporated into the unity of the resisting thing. Green, rough, smooth, warm, blue, solid, sweet, shrill, soft, round, large, loud, are experienced as imbedded in the resistant matrix which is the field of my action, and not experienced as "qualities." When naive consciousness goes on to distinguish an "I" from the other, it automatically includes these features on the side of the independent other. The first reflective consciousness is only a regularization of the situation in which the acting consciousness finds itself. Whether this is justified or not, is a question that may well be raised, but it would seem that we must at least realize what underlies naive realism.

LOCKE AND REPRESENTATIONALISM

As it happens, when critical reflection got around historically to posing the problem of reflection, it quickly forsook the realistic outlook of common sense. Consequently, some of the points now to be made in the course of an examination of the problem of perception as it arose historically may seem to be somewhat in the nature of back-tracking from the insistence on the bi-polarity of consciousness contained in the last chapter. This is inevitable, since the thinkers who initiated the discussion of this problem did not begin with an acknowledgment of the bi-polarity of consciousness. On the contrary, it was they who gave the subjectivist outlook its most popular formulation, the so-called "image" theory of perception. Nevertheless, it is useful to begin the examination of the problem historically with these thinkers, rather than in a directly analytic way, and this not only because of the intrinsic interest to be found in their writings. For the truth is that their viewpoint is not merely a contingent historical peculiarity of their own, but it is one which recommends itself to any human mind when operating at a certain stage of reflection.

It is the version of the British philosopher, John Locke[1] which defined the status of the discussion for those who followed. We shall have to concentrate on the most cursory presentation of a small segment of the thought of a man who was extremely influential—influential, it may be, out of all proportion to the profundity of his thought, and apparently because he expressed so well a viewpoint inevitable in reflection.

His aim is similar to Descartes': to justify the use of understanding, and to set knowledge on a firm footing. His aim, like Descartes', is to carry thought back to its own foundations. But he does not accept the elevation of the intelligible over the sensible. Rather, he regards all intelligibility as derivative from the senses. His famous comparison of the mind of man at birth with a *"tabula rasa,"* a blank tablet upon which nothing has yet been written, is meant not only to dispense with any recourse to "innate ideas," but to prepare the explanation of how meaning is put together by an elaboration of sensory data. We know nothing which has not been derived from the senses; the only original writing upon the tablet of the mind is that which is inscribed by the senses. Locke is thus an "empiricist," in the most familiar philosophical meaning of that word: a sense empiricist, one who holds that all content of thought is eventually reducible to a sense-reference.

[1] 1632–1704.

While many interesting contributions to the psychology of knowledge are made in the course of Locke's attempt to trace out how we build up our complex thought-meanings from simple sense-beginnings, it is his way of conceiving the objects of this sense experience which provides the key to his epistemology. What we know, according to Locke, is an "idea." This is a highly significant word with which to begin, for it immediately gets us entangled in the image theory of perception. Most people would say they are aware of *things*. For Locke, however, the object of awareness is an idea. No more than with Descartes does this mean exclusively a "concept." Rather it is: "the object of understanding whenever a man thinks; I have used it to express whatever is meant by phantasm, notion, species, or whatever it is which the mind can be employed about in thinking . . ."[2] An idea, again, is "the immediate object of perception."[3] The premises here seem to be those which are operative in all such beginnings: that of which I am aware is present to my awareness; it is therefore present within my awareness; if it is within my consciousness, it is a mental datum; therefore it is an idea. So, data like white, round, cold, moving, solid, sweet, painful, extended, are all ideas.

Now obviously, one who begins here with Locke has the immediate problem: if what I am immediately aware of in perception is an idea, and if an idea is a mental event and hence subjective, then in what sense is my perception a revelation of anything other than myself? Is reality at all like my idea? How do I know it is, if I never know extra-mental reality, but only ideas? The experience of seeing blue, feeling something smooth, tasting something sweet, hearing a shrill noise, feeling heat, are experiences going on in me—but how do I know that they reveal anything of the ways things are in themselves? When I am not sensing things, are they really blue, smooth, sweet, shrill, hot, solid, extended, shaped?

---

[2] *Locke Selections*, edit. by Sterling Lamprecht (New York: Scribner's), 1928, p. 95. All references to Locke are to this volume. (Quotations are from his *Essay Concerning Human Understanding*).

[3] *Ibid.*, p. 205.

The Problem of Perception: I   73

Here is Locke's problem. It is an acute one. How do I know that my ideas resemble things? Are bodies really like the ideas I have of them? We cannot simply assume that they are—

. . . we may not think (as perhaps usually is done) that they are exactly the images and resemblances of something inherent in the subject; most of these of sensation being in the mind no more the likeness of something existing without us, than the names that stand for them are the likeness of our ideas, which yet upon hearing they are apt to excite in us.[4]

Ideas are my ways of subjectively reacting to the influences which bodies bring to bear on me. They are the representations in my consciousness of bodies outside me, mental copies or images of these bodies. But are they good copies? How far do they resemble the original? Here Locke distinguishes. What I *directly* know are ideas, but in respect to some of these ideas, I can infer that they really do resemble qualities which are found in the objects themselves. There are certain qualities which belong essentially to bodies, and which are inseparable from them, so that a body could neither be conceived nor exist without these qualities: such are solidity, extension, figure, motion or rest, and number. These Locke denominates "primary qualities," and he concludes that our ideas of such qualities represent what is found as such in bodies themselves. Not all ideas are so objectively well founded. Such features as color, sound, taste, are not essentially contained in the concept of body; they are simply sensations caused in us by the primary qualities and by no means on an equally objective footing.

The ideas of primary qualities of bodies are resemblances of them, and their patterns do really exist in the bodies themselves; but the ideas, produced in us by these secondary qualities, have no resemblance of them at all. There is nothing like our ideas existing in the bodies themselves. They are, in the bodies we denominate from them, only a

[4] *Ibid.*

power to produce these sensations in us: and what is sweet, blue or warm in idea, is but the certain bulk, figure, and motion of the insensible parts in the bodies themselves, which we call so.[5]

If we wish, then, to speak of color, sound, taste, as being "objective," the most we can mean is that there is a power in objects sufficient to cause these subjective impressions in me. There is some reason why we see the grass as green, rather than red; taste sugar as sweet and lemon as sour; hear a grating noise rather than a melodious one. But apart from our conscious experience, these things are not there as such:

Take away the sensation of them; let not the eyes see light, or colours, nor the ears hear sounds; let the palate not taste, nor the nose smell; and all colours, tastes, odours, and sounds, as they are such particular ideas, vanish and cease, and are reduced to their causes, i.e. bulk, figure, and motion of parts.[6]

What Locke leaves us with, then, is a geometrical universe, in which the "objective reality" of the world is reduced to the bulk and motion of extended bodies and everything else is relegated to the subjective. He was by no means alone in this way of seeing things. Descartes, as we saw, said essentially the same thing; Galileo, Hobbes, Newton,[7] all concurred, and this view became in fact the standard scientific and philosophical belief throughout the 18th century. It is not too much to say that it is the view which is most immediately superimposed by our culture on the primitive naive view; with the permeation through every educated and quasi-educated mind of the scientific way of conceiving the world, many people tend, at the level of their expressed beliefs, to assume the truth of this outlook. Every high school student knows that "of course" the sky isn't really blue, sugar isn't "really" sweet, water

[5] *Ibid.*, p. 207.
[6] *Ibid.*
[7] On this, see E. A. Burtt, *The Metaphysical Foundations of Modern Physical Science* (New York: Doubleday Anchor Books), 1954.

isn't really warm (in fact isn't really "water" but H_2O). It is all a matter of refracted light, cortical reflexes, molecules in motion. This is the "bifurcation" of nature which Whitehead decries[8] and which is exhibited in its most accessible form by Locke: the splitting of nature down the middle into the geometrical "real world" of extended bodies in motion and the "mental world" of our sensations.

From the foregoing it is easy to see why Locke has been called an "indirect" or "representative" realist. His starting-point is actually that of the epistemological idealist: what my act of awareness immediately terminates in is an idea. But in respect to *some* of these ideas (those which represent primary qualities) we may infer that they correctly *represent* a feature of reality which is there independent of our awareness, and so *indirectly* may vindicate realism's belief that consciousness reaches the non-self.

An evaluation of Locke's theory is really contained in Berkeley's rejoinder to it, but one or two separate remarks may be made. First of all, it seems correct to say that Locke was really assuming a sort of realism from the beginning, in spite of the apparent idealism of his starting-point. His question really was: how do we know which of the ideas we have correspond to qualities present in bodies? He never seems to have asked himself how he knew that there *were* bodies. That he simply assumes. This is not only a felicitous demonstration of that balance which enables British thinkers to allow down-to-earth considerations to hold speculation in inconclusive counterpoise. It is also an inevitable concomitant of any brand of representationalism. For it amounts to the failure to examine thoroughly the consequences of one's own assumptions. Representationalism holds that ideas are caused by bodies, but are themselves subjective data; it overlooks the issue of how we may know the causal property of bodies if we do not know bodies but only ideas. This dilemma is fatal to representationalism, and it was left to Berkeley to develop it.

[8] A. N. Whitehead, *The Concept of Nature* (Cambridge: Cambridge University Press), 1920, Chapter II.

BERKELEY

The term "refutation" should be used sparingly in philosophy, but one case where it is clearly applicable is to Berkeley's rebuttal to Locke. It certainly seems just to say that if we begin where Locke began, we should logically finish where Berkeley finished. George Berkeley, bishop in the Irish Anglican church,[9] was prompted by the highest spiritual motives in his philosophizing. Views like that of Locke might not be as directly reprehensible as those, say, of the materialist Thomas Hobbes (who reduced mind to the motion of atoms), but they played into the materialists' hands through their granting a mysterious "material substance" co-equal autonomy with the reality of mind. He who undertakes to overthrow materialism may make out a splendid case for himself if he can simply show that what the materialist means by matter does not exist; this is what Berkeley proposed to do. Locke's "material substance," supposed to be independent of mind, is a myth. If genuine reality is spiritual, then all specious objections to the existence of God and the immortality of the soul fall away. And it is the easiest thing in the world to show that reality is spiritual.

Let us just take Locke at his own word: what we know directly are ideas. Berkeley does not quarrel with this—he emphasizes it to the utmost degree. What we know directly—color, sound, taste, resistance, pain, pleasure, joy, desire, sorrow, extension—all these things are contents of consciousness. They are, as consciously known, ideas. But if this is so, then the ground is cut from under Locke's ensuing reasoning. Berkeley will first ask Locke upon what ground he makes anything significant out of his distinction between primary and secondary qualities. Is this distinction based upon experience? When did I ever experience a body which had the primary qualities without the secondary? The answer, clearly, is never. Then this is not a difference between ways of experienc-

[9] 1685–1753.

ing: all qualities as *given* are on even terms—they are all ideas. What reason, then, is there to give one type of idea a privilege not accorded to another?[10]

Not only is there no basis in experience for Locke's granting a privileged objectivity to ideas of primary qualities, but what he is defending is simply unthinkable. For, if what we know directly are ideas, then what can it mean to discover which ideas "represent" things as they are "in themselves?" How would we ever discover which ideas are good copies of reality?

The way we ordinarily go about deciding whether something is a good copy or not is by comparing the representation to the original: this photograph is a good copy of John Smith if it really resembles him, and this we learn by comparing photograph to man. But the difficulty of proceeding like this with our perceptions leaps to the eye: how can we compare our ideas to the originals if we never perceive the originals but only ideas? Not only this, but what do we even mean by asking whether this idea resembles the original? For what could an idea resemble except another idea? Locke's whole program, then, is illusory, for it is trying to do the impossible.

Again, I ask whether those supposed *originals,* or external things, of which our ideas are the pictures or representations, be themselves perceivable or no? If they are, then *they* are ideas, and we have gained our point: but if you say they are not, I appeal to anyone whether it be sense to assert a color is like something which is invisible; hard or soft like something intangible; and so of the rest.[11]

Berkeley will go still further. Existence, he states, is actually inconceivable except in terms of ideas. For whatever we know we know in terms of experience. Every assertion we make can only have meaning for us if it applies to something in our actual

---

[10] *Berkeley Selections,* edit. by Mary Whiton Calkins (New York: Scribner's), 1929, p. 129. All references to Berkeley are to this volume. (This quotation from *Principles of Human Knowledge*).

[11] *Ibid.,* p. 128.

experience. Grant, however, that experience always terminates in "ideas," and then the statement that anything else exists becomes empty. All we can mean by existing is what we directly experience as existing. What we experience is psychic, mental. Therefore, says Berkeley, "esse est percipi"—the only *meaning* for "being" is "being perceived."[12] Actually his complete formula should read: "esse est aut percipere aut percipi"—to be is either to perceive or to be perceived; for he allows that there are two ways of being: as a mind or as the object of mind. I exist, and the objects of my conscious experience exist (my ideas). But that is all I can mean by existence.

To mean something by a word, I must be able to use it to point to some item of my experience; but the word "existence" must either point to an experiencing self or to the ideas which it is experiencing, and in either case we are in the realm of the spiritual. The conception of something called "matter" which is completely outside of mind, which exists in a way other than mind and independent of it, is a pseudo-notion. If we do not believe this, let us make the effort to conceive of something existing unperceived. To imagine things existing unperceived is simply to imagine oneself perceiving them, and thus still to confine their reality to what it is for perception.

But, say you, surely there is nothing easier than for me to imagine trees, for instance, in a park, or books existing in a closet, and nobody by to perceive them. I answer, you may so, there is no difficulty in it. But what is all this, I beseech you, more than framing in your mind certain ideas which you call *books* and *trees,* and at the same time omitting to frame the idea of anyone that may perceive them? But do not you yourself perceive or think of them all the while? This therefore is nothing to the purpose: it only shews you have the power of imagining, or forming ideas in your mind; but it does not shew that you can conceive it possible the objects of your thought may exist without the mind.[13]

[12] *Ibid.,* p. 126.
[13] *Ibid.,* p. 136.

No wonder, then, at Locke's conception of material substance as an "I know not what" underlying experienced qualities—for a material substance is in principle unknowable. Locke should have noticed that his reasoning involved him in the strange result that matter as such turned out to be an unobservable; it always remained an "I know not what," a useless appendage to what was directly given—mind and its ideas. Once we see that matter, considered as an independent entity, is a ridiculous fiction, than all sorts of foolish problems are avoided, such as the worry over whether my ideas correspond to anything other than themselves; the reason is that there is no "external" world independent of ideas for these ideas to "correspond to."

Much confusion is sometimes aroused in a first acquaintance with the doctrine of Berkeley. It is thought, for instance, that he is declaring that the world is an illusion, life a dream, and so forth. This is not really the point at all. He is not denying that the world exists, that things are real. He is really asking what we mean by the statement that the world is real. When I say this apple really exists, that it is real, what do I mean?[14] What do I mean by the "apple" about which I am so sure that it exists? The apple is this red, round, firm, smooth, fragrant, sweet, crunchy thing here before me. But every attribute I apply to it in this description, Berkeley would insist, is an idea, a way in which I am consciously experiencing. Therefore, all I mean by the apple is a set of ideas (experienced data) which form a constant constellation in my experience. If I insist that the apple is real, that it exists, Berkeley is far from denying it. He will only ask me to point out some feature which is contained in the term apple which is *more* than an idea.

That is why Dr. Sam Johnson was missing the point when, stoutly championing the interests of common sense, he kicked the stone and exclaimed "Thus do I refute Bishop Berkeley"! His point, of course, was that the stone was a massive material thing,

[14] *Ibid.*, pp. 124–125.

stubbornly there in spite of Berkeley's abstruse attempts to dissolve it into the thin air of ideas. This would not have fazed Berkeley in the slightest; he would merely have asked, "What did you experience when you kicked against the stone? A feeling of resistance, which I declare is an idea; a feeling of pain, which everybody admits is an idea. You saw, visually, a gray shape, felt a rough surface, and heard a thudding noise. All ideas. Therefore the stone you contend is undoubtedly there is (undoubtedly) there. But what is it but the experienced unity of diverse ideas—so that you have not refuted me but confirmed me." Berkeley was very definite in arguing that he has no quarrel with what the plain man meant by matter, matter as actually experienced (which could be regarded as a facet of experience, and therefore a facet of mind); his only quarrel was with the mythical material "substance" of philosophers which was supposed to be some totally unthinking and unthought "x" apart from experience altogether. This was not only an unverifiable—for, how could we verify in terms of experience what is in principle beyond experience—but it is actually inconceivable.

I deny therefore that there is any unthinking *substratum* of the objects of sense, and *in that acceptation* that there is any material substance. But if by *material substance* is meant only sensible body—that which is seen and felt (and the unphilosophical part of the world, I dare say, mean no more)—then I am more certain of matter's existence than you or any other philosopher pretend to be.[15]

The objection is also raised that if Berkeley identifies being with being perceived, then he is implying that when things are not perceived they do not exist. Does this mean that when I walk out of the room, the perceived objects which fill it simply cease to be? Not necessarily, for they can be perceived by some other mind. Berkeley is not contending that my individual mind confers reality on things. But suppose no one is there? What about the building

---

[15] *Ibid.*, p. 309 (*Three Dialogues Between Hylas and Philonous*).

The Problem of Perception: I

when it is vacant at night, deserted by everyone, with no perceiver there at all? Does it still exist? Berkeley could still say yes, for he allows not only the possibility but the necessity that there is an absolute mind which is at every moment perceiving the data which I perceive, so that even if no finite mind is perceiving them, they can still be said to exist.

As a matter of fact, the quasi-independence of sensations is the basis of Berkeley's "proof" for the existence of God. He certainly does not hold that my ideas derive their origin from me: they are not in my power but rather impose themselves upon me regardless of my own will. This incidentally, is why those persons also err who accuse Berkeley of being unable to distinguish dream and reality. He distinguished these in about the same way as anybody else distinguishes them: the dream-world is disorganized, arbitrary, subject to my control; the real world is orderly, predictable, fundamentally beyond my volitional control.[16] I am not at liberty to experience anything I like, and this is the sign that my ideas are imposed upon me by some superior source.

> . . . sensible things cannot exist otherwise than in a mind or spirit. Whence I conclude, not that they have no real existence, but that, seeing they depend not on my thought, and have an existence distinct from being perceived by me, *there must be some other Mind wherein they exist.* As sure, therefore, as the sensible world really exists, so sure is there an infinite omnipresent Spirit who contains and supports it.[17]

To Bishop Berkeley, reality appears as a community of spirits, (thinking beings) among whom one spirit is primary, the source of the experience of the others. We may still use the word "matter"

---

[16] *Ibid.*, p. 141 (*Principles*).

[17] *Ibid.*, p. 276. It might be wondered what would happen to Bishop Berkeley's philosophy if he did not bring in the existence of God but confined himself to what is directly given in experience as he conceived it. In a way, phenomenalism is the working out of the answer to this question: it is Berkeley with the absolute removed.

if we like, but if this is to have real meaning, it is simply the term for certain aspects of the experience of spirits: the aspect under which experience has the features usually called quantitative. Far from being independent of mind, matter is simply one aspect of mind.

In evaluating Berkeley, we are faced with the central difficulty of deciding how to interpret him. He may mean either:

1) That of which I am directly aware is *my own* idea. This is certainly what Berkeley first seems to mean. And if this is taken as his consistent position, then he has all the difficulties of a strict subjectivism. If *all* my consciousness terminates in myself, how can I use *any* item of that knowledge to get beyond myself? It might be suggested that his view applies only to sensations, and that he could do what Descartes did: use an intelligible argument for God to extricate himself. Yet he himself argues against the existence of abstract terms, and is quite sensist in orientation. He does not develop the argument from intelligible evidence, although he accepts unquestioningly the concepts of cause and substance (the latter when applied to spiritual substance). We might defend him by saying that he is simply relying on the immediate primacy of the experience of the self and using the self as the norm for the assertion of any existence, but this would be more an argument offered in his behalf than a reasoning he himself developed.

As matters stand in his own writings, he cannot be absolved from the charge that, on his own theory of knowledge, he cannot use God to find his way out of subjectivism, for on the subjectivist assumption, his idea of God also has only subjective value. Beginning with the assumption that all of my perceptions are ideas, I do not yet have an "other," and I urgently need some means to bestow the coefficient of otherness on these ideas. Even if Berkeley thinks he has succeeded in reaching this in respect to the absolute, this only validates *one* "other"; at this stage there is still the alternative of conceiving himself to be alone in the face of an absolute who imposes his ideas upon him. The reality of other human selves and the multiple reality of the non-human is, to say the least, not coercively established. Since to exist entails either perceiving or being perceived, it is fairly clear that no meaning can be attached to the independent existence of inanimate things or plants; the status of animals is more ambiguous; the existence of other human selves is thinkable but not clearly demonstrable on Berkeley's assumption that we know directly only our own ideas.

2) That of which I am conscious is *God's* idea. On this interpretation, the same thing that exists outside my perception is *also* perceived by me. Sometimes he speaks like this. If this is what he means, then I really do know the non-self, and Berkeley is not an idealist at all, but a *realist*. The essence of epistemological realism is that my act of knowing puts me in touch with a non-self. The fact that Berkeley calls that non-self an "idea" and denies that it is "matter" seems to be more a metaphysical point than an epistemological one. The primary epistemological question is: in knowing, do I know what is other than myself? On this second way of taking him, Berkeley would be saying that I do—and simply adding that the real nature of what I know is that it is still mental; it is God's idea (the idea constantly perceived by God) now imposed on me.

CONTEMPORARY VIEWS

a) SCIENTISM

The universal confirmation of the accuracy of the portrait of reality as it is painted by science has had the side effect of aggravating the epistemological problem of perception. For it has pressed home to reflection the seemingly either/or choice between the outlook of science and the outlook of common sense. What is the structure of reality in itself, apart from its relation to human consciousness? If it is really like the picture which the scientist paints, then the spectacle present to common sense does not faithfully represent it—and the features which present themselves to immediate perception are not really there independent of perception; if they are not, we are prone to ask "where" they exist, and to conclude that they must be subjective experiences of a perceiving subject.

Reflection on the findings of either physics or biology could easily give rise to this sort of consideration. Sir Arthur Eddington's famous parable of the "two tables" is a vivid presentation of the difficulty as it is engendered by physics (although he himself does not accept it as insurmountable). Here he sits, he tells us,[18] beginning his task of writing his book on the nature of the physical world. But troubles arise immediately, for, strange to say, he is simultaneously sitting at and leaning on "two tables." The table at which he sits is, for common sense, a rather bulky black object, hard and resistant, extending continuously in space for a distance of about three feet, solid and still, quite filling the space within its surfaces with a matter called wood. But the scientist, when he looks, sees no such table. The table of the physicist is mostly empty space, within which atoms of infinitesimal size are swirling about in incredibly rapid motion without ever touching one another. Which is the real table? If the table of perception is real, the scientific table is unreal; if the scientific table is real, the table of perception is unreal. Prompted by the unprecedented practical success of the scientific view, many infer forthwith that it is the scientific table which is really there, and that the features presented to perception are not objective data. Not only is color, in Eddington's phrase, mere "mind-spinning" but so are the other secondary qualities, and so, in a true sense, are even extension and the continuous character of the perceived table, which do not correspond to a state of affairs obtaining outside of me.

A similar difficult dilemma could be reached on the basis of the conclusions of biology. For what the physiologist has to tell us about the nature and origin of perception does not seem very easy to reconcile with the conviction of the man in the street that he perceives a public world which is independently there. Perception, and this means all perception, and not merely optical awareness, we now know to begin with a stimulus which derives from a physical body, moves through an intervening medium, and impinges on a nerve ending. An impulse is then transmitted to a

[18] A. S. Eddington, *The Nature of the Physical World* (New York: Macmillan), 1929, p. ix ss.

cortical center and a modification set up on the brain-cells. As an accompaniment of this cortical activity, sensation occurs. Various questions for the epistemology of perception are raised. Obviously the cortical activity of the brain-cells is nothing like the molecular activity of the body which transmitted the original stimulus; it is not even like the light-waves which caused the neural reaction. But then how can my sensation, which is simply the accompaniment of a cortical activity give me the awareness of something which is completely unlike itself?[19]

The difficulty does not stop here. For the physiologist knows that by an artificial stimulation of my brain-cells he can cause me to perceive colors, hear sounds, experience scents, when there are actually no objects present at all. Does it not then begin to seem as if what I *always* am actually experiencing is a sensation which accompanies a brain-state? On this basis, sensation is so far from putting me in touch with what is other than myself that it does not even take me outside of my own body.[20]

With this sort of evidence we may feel ourselves to be faced with a somewhat harrowing dilemma: we either relegate science, with its unparallelled store of verified fact, to the status of a useful fiction; or we consign the rich and variegated display of perception to the cenacle of our individual minds. It is sometimes overlooked how far reaching the second alternative would be. For in attributing to ourselves what perception attributes to the world, we would have to say not only that the table is not "really" solid, the sky not "really" blue, the melody not "really" sounding, but also that the sunset is not really splendid, the symphony not really majestic, the painting not really beautiful. If the "secondary" qualities are subjective, then surely what have been called the "tertiary" qualities (beauty, goodness, and the like) are also subjective. What the sun "really" is, is a gaseous assemblage of molecules, the

---

[19] Some might even begin to talk as if I am really conscious of my own brain-states, but a little further reflection would reveal the foolishness of this, for my own brain is never the object of my awareness.

[20] For a review of the physiological opinions, see R. J. Hirst, *The Problems of Perception* (New York: Macmillan), 1959, pp. 145 ss, 279 ss.

symphony "really" is a series of disturbances of the air, the painting "really" is a collection of chemicals. It can hardly be denied that a certain depression settles on the spirit when the obligation is felt to talk in this manner. And this depression is not irrelevant to the epistemological question. For it should begin to be clear that the question of objectivity cannot be raised apart from the exigence of the inquiring consciousness. If the aesthetic consciousness is dissatisfied with a certain way of conceiving the nature of reality, this dissatisfaction must be reckoned with, for to shunt it aside would not silence its demands.

More to our immediate point is the quandary in which scientism finds itself directly upon the enunciation of its own thesis. Scientism is obviously one version of representationalism; it is representationalism brought up to date. As such it suffers from the fatal weakness of inconsistency to which all representationalism is subject. What scientism contends is that my sensations are purely subjective, caused in me by the real objective entities—bodies conceived as science conceives them. But the difficulty just will not down: if my sensations are subjective, then how do I know that there really *are* bodies independent of them? If scientism is right, then its position vitiates the evidence upon which it claims to be right. For example, the physiologist says that I perceive this table the way I do because certain light-waves are refracted from the table, impinge on my retina, and cause a cortical reaction. Therefore the table as I actually perceive it is a subjective collocation of sensations aroused in me because of brain activity; what I am actually aware of is my own sensations, and nothing independently objective.[21] But when the physiologist says the light-waves are refracted from the table, impinge on my eye, and so on, he is talking about the table which I perceive: this table right here. This table, however, precisely as it can be experienced and pointed

---

[21] Some will go so far as to assert that what I am aware of is inside my head, which is obviously nonsense. We have only to ask ourselves what is the comparative size of the table which I perceive and my head to convince ourselves that the perceived table is not inside my head—if we are not convinced by the immediately given externality.

to, is, on his own theory, simply a collocation of subjective sensations. Then his position amounts to the absurd claim that sensation arises because a collocation of sensations causes me to have sensations.

There seems absolutely no way out of the representationalist predicament. For representationalism is actually founded on a premise which nullifies its own conclusions. The representationalist assumes not only that there are things independent of experience, but that I really do experience them, at least to the extent that I can call them "bodies" and can know how they interact with my body (also assumed as something independent of sensations) in order to give rise to sensations. But he then turns around and declares that all I directly know are my own sensations. Then the external body which he declares to be *causing* his sensations is itself a sensation. And the anomaly does not stop there. The physiologist says that sensations are simply accompaniments of brain-states. But what is the brain, on his premise? All I know about the brain I know through perception. Perception is of subjective sensations. Then the brain itself, in the only way I ever come into contact with it (through my perception), is a collocation of sensations. In other words, the scientific representationalist, or any representationalist, is in the impossible position of holding that I both do and do not know more than my own sensations.

Because of the patent untenability of representationalism, it must be regarded as a halfway house on the road of epistemological speculation. Most contemporary philosophers so regard it, and tend to move either to a position of complete phenomenalism or back to a more direct realism. We will look briefly at some of their positions.

b) SENSE-DATUM APPROACH: A WAY OUT?

1) *Moore, Russell, Broad*

One avenue of escape from the impasse of both representationalism and Berkeleyan idealism might seem to be to question the starting point which they both take for granted. That is, the belief that what we are directly aware of is our own idea. This assumption immediately places the discussion on a subjectivist footing and causes most of the ensuing trouble. A valiant attempt to bypass it and to carry the whole discussion back to a more unquestionable basis was made by those who espoused the epistemological primacy of the "sense datum." The notion of a sense datum was introduced by George Moore and Bertrand Russell as a kind of "neutral indubitable" upon which both epistemological realist and idealist could find common ground.[22] Prior to any decision as to whether the "patch of red" of which I am aware was an idea or an independent material object, all disputants might at least agree that I am immediately aware of the red patch and that it certainly exists. We do not have to ask yet whether it exists as an idea or a material object, for the distinction between idea and material object is not cognitionally primitive; it comes later, after I begin to discern the differences among the data which really are primitive.

What is primitively given to awareness is that I am aware, and aware *of* something (a red patch, a shrill sound, a sweet taste); the precise status to be assigned to that of which I am aware is only determined posteriorly. What Moore thought to be beyond doubt was that awareness reaches something and that what it reaches is not identical with awareness. Thus, he argues against Berkeley, in his "The Refutation of Idealism," that rather than the "esse" of the perceived datum consisting in its "percipi," the datum of which I am aware necessarily has a status not reducible to my awareness of it.[23] My awareness of blue, green, yellow has something in common: awareness; but it has something which differentiates it: the objects in respect to which awareness takes place, blue, green, yellow. There is therefore a distinction between awareness and its objects, and hence it is impossible to claim as

---

[22] George Moore, *Philosophical Studies* (New York: Harcourt, Brace), 1922; Bertrand Russell, *The Problems of Philosophy* (New York: Henry Holt), 1959 (first published in 1912). For a brief discussion of sense-datum theory, see Hirst, *op. cit.*, pp. 26-73.

[23] Moore, *op. cit.*, p. 13.

The Problem of Perception: I

Berkeley did, that the very *being* of the datum is the being of awareness. At the very least, Moore contends, there is no way to show that the existence of the datum logically implies awareness of the datum; and he ends his essay by adopting a strongly realistic position: "awareness is and must be in all cases of such a nature that its object, when we are aware of it, is precisely what it would be, if we were not aware."[24] Russell concurs with this (in his earlier works), holding that it is perfectly conceivable that the sense data which we perceive exist precisely as such when we are not perceiving them, and inventing the term "sensibilia" to denote such unsensed sense data.[25]

It is evident that the original intention of the sense-datum theorists was strongly realistic. They thought that they had discovered a way to cut straight through the subjectivist thicket and affirm that consciousness reaches immediately and directly something other than itself. In this vein, Moore exclaims that there *is* no question of how we get outside the circle of sensation; to be conscious is *already* to be outside that private circle.[26] Consciousness is transcendent from the start. But an interesting development occurs in later sense-datum theory. It is somewhat foreshadowed in the use to which the sense datum was very quickly put. For it cannot escape us that what the sense-datum theorist says in regard to perception could just as well be said of hallucinations and dream-experiences. In these, too, consciousness can be analyzed into an act/object correlation. This, in fact, was felt by many to add to the strength of the sense-datum view; it not only derived support from but helped to make intelligible what occurred in delusive perceptions. Thus, in a relational experience (the round penny from a certain angle looks elliptical) or in hallucinatory experiences (seeing pink elephants) it was felt that two things could be said: I am not seeing a physical object,[27] and yet I am seeing something. What I am seeing is not nothing, hence there

[24] *Ibid.*, p. 29.
[25] Russell, *Mysticism and Logic*, pp. 143–145.
[26] Moore, *op. cit.*, p. 27.
[27] In physical reality there is no elliptical penny and no pink elephant.

is a meaning to saying that it really exists; *it was regarded as a sort of "epistemological object" of awareness and named a sense datum.* From here it is a rather short step to the belief that what I am seeing in *all* cases of perception is a sense datum. Delusive experiences are, as subjectively undergone, qualitatively indistinguishable from veridical experiences: the red I dream about and the red I see are identical; if there really were pink elephants they would look to those who perceived them the way they now look to those who suffer from hallucinations. So it was concluded that the *immediate* object of both delusive and veridical experience was the same—a sense datum. Whatever I go on to say about "material objects" I must say on the basis of that of which I am directly aware—sense data.

But see what has happened here. If a sense datum is common to both veridical and delusive experience, it evidently cannot underwrite an immediate contact with a world of independently existing material objects. In later theory, the sense datum begins to function as a kind of "third thing" interposed between awareness and physical objects. In this manner, many of the difficulties it was introduced to eliminate filter back into the theory. Some of these appear in a famous proponent of the doctrine, C. D. Broad.

Broad attempts a continued adherence to realism, but has difficulty fitting it into his sense-datum assumptions. He is sure that we are justified in ordinary language in saying that we know the truth of such statements as "I hear a bell" or "There are rats in the attic," since the situations in which they are justified clearly sometimes arise. Yet the notion of the bell as a "material object" contains hypotheses which are not and cannot be verified through direct perception. Common sense assumes that the bell as a material object is a unity, a completed entity, that it endures through a stretch of time, that it is publicly available to other observers. None of this is perceptually verifiable. What are given to perception are sense data, multiple, momentary, and fleeting. The notion of an object is constructed upon the basis of these indubitable but fugitive givens, but not verifiable purely in terms of them.[28]

2) *Ayer and Phenomenalism*

Alfred Ayer carries this a considerable distance further, and winds up in a kind of phenomenalism which has had considerable influence.[29] Ayer treats the sense-datum *vs.* material object dispute as mainly one of language. There is, he contends, no substantive quarrel between the two camps, for no matter which side of the dispute we adopt, it gives rise to no different empirical expectations on our part. That is, if the common sense defenders say, "I directly see the car as a material object in the garage" and the sense-datum people say "I directly see a collection of sense data out of which I construct the notion of a permanent unity, car," no real quarrel arises since each would act towards the perceived datum in the same way and entertain the same expectations with respect to it. The dispute is therefore linguistic, not real. The parties are really disputing as to which is the most appropriate language in which to speak about their experience; each experiences exactly what the other experiences, but each refers to it in a different way. One way is not "wrong" and the other "right" since there is no possible test which will ever turn up any difference between them.

If I say "The car is in the garage," and you say "The car is not in the garage," one statement must be true and the other false, since they are asserting different things; but if you say that the car is a material object and I say that the car is a name for a collection of sense data, neither need be false for they do not refer to differences in experience, but only to different ways of talking about

---

[28] C. D. Broad, *Mind and Its Place in Nature* (London: Routledge & Kegan Paul Ltd.), 1925, Chapter IV.

[29] A. J. Ayer, *Language, Truth and Logic* (New York: Dover, n.d.), (first published 1936). Some modification of Ayer's earlier views are in evidence in his later writings, particularly *The Problem of Knowledge* (New York: Penguin Books), 1956, pp. 124–125.

experience. Each language may have its appropriate use, but the question of utility is not a question of truth. It may be more useful to measure in meters than yards, but that does not mean that one who describes a distance as one meter is "right," and one who describes it as 39.37 inches "wrong." Ayer leans to the belief that for ordinary purposes the material object language is perfectly satisfactory, while for technically exact philosophical purposes, the sense-datum language has the advantage.

At first sight, this may be considered as an attempt to dismiss the whole issue as a pseudo-problem; a not unwarranted attempt, for there does seem to be something tantalizingly unreal about the problem of perception. If we look again, though, Ayer may appear to be open to the charge levelled against him that he really believes that the sense-datum theory is factually right.[30] Does he not really believe that what we actually perceive are sense data? Only on this basis could it be claimed that there is no difference between the beliefs of the material-object theorist and the sense-datum theorist. Only if we already believe that there is no more in the meaning of material object than what the sense-datum people find there could we contend that their assertions are indistinguishable. Ayer ultimately seems to hold that material object statements can be exhaustively translated into sense-data statements and hence are reducible to sense-data statements. His "linguistic phenomenalism" amounts to the view that what we mean by "physical object" is simply constant "patterns" of sense data. Knowing that certain data are conjoined in a systematic and recurring manner, we signalize this recurring pattern by a name and regard it as an object. But there is no more in the meaning "object" than in "recurring patterns of sense data." Hence, Ayer is still in the older tradition of phenomenalism, even though he tries to state it in a more unexceptionable manner. And it can even be averred that of its own nature the sense-datum theory tends equally well to either total realism or phenomenalism, that in fact the two are rather hard to distinguish, given the sense-datum assumption.

[30] J. L. Austin, *Sense and Sensibilia* (Oxford: Clarendon Press), 1962, pp. 56, 59, 106–107; and Hirst, *op. cit.*, pp. 116–117.

In general, *phenomenalism holds that the notion of an object is a logical construction of thought, rather than something in any way directly given to experience.*[31] What is directly given is a stream of discrete experience, which usually turn out to be a stream for sense: either sensations, in the older, more subjectivist, view of John Stuart Mill; or sense data in the neutral manner of the contemporaries. For Mill a "material object" was simply a "permanent possibility of sensation":[32] thought discovers constancies and predictability in our subjective experiences and attributes this to an independent ground or grounds, which it calls an object. The object, then, is the conceived foundation for the orderly occurrence of my sensation. Thus, to say that "the other side of the moon exists when no one is looking at it" just means that "If I went through the series of sensations which I call traveling through space in a certain direction, I would have the series of sensations I call seeing the other side of the moon." Ayer's earlier theories are in principle quite close to this, although of a more linguistic turn.

The phenomenalist's contention is that he can sufficiently describe all that is truly given to experience in his terms and that every other way of speaking is superfluous, since it must reduce to phenomenalist terms in order to be significant. The rebuttal to phenomenalism would have to rest on asking ourselves whether this claim is true. 1) Can he successfully reduce all statements to an *exclusive* reference to sense-data? 2) Can he assert in his language everything that object language wishes to express? The rebuttal to phenomenalism on both counts is quite strong.

R. J. Hirst's objection, in particular, seems well taken.[33] Hirst argues that phenomenalist language always turns out to be "tainted" by realistic material-object language. That is, the phenomenalist always surreptitiously utilizes language which reintroduces material-object assumptions back into his own descriptions.

---

[31] For a good exposition, see Hirst, *op. cit.*, pp. 74–110.
[32] John Stuart Mill, *An Examination of Sir William Hamilton's Philosophy*, Ch. XI.
[33] *Op cit.*, pp. 90–94.

The phenomenalist, after all, has a rather imposing task: he must translate the meaning of "object" completely into sense-datum language without relinquishing any part of what the material-object statement means to assert. Now, the *public character of the object, its permanence, and its causal efficacy do not lend themselves easily to such translation.*

If reality consists exclusively in sense data and the awareness of them, it seems incredible that the continual agreement between the sense experience of different observers is possible. The only sufficient ground for the harmony of the experiences of different observers seems to be that there is a common *object* different from the sense data themselves which is the ground for the experiencing of the sense data; dreams of different people cannot be so harmonized, precisely because there is no common object. Even to talk of "observers," as the phenomenalist continually does, is to introduce object language, for the observer is not reducible to sense data. When he says that the statement "There is a car in the garage right now" is equivalent to "If you were experiencing garage-like sense data, you would be experiencing car-like sense data," he has not totally laid the ghost of the object, since the "you" he still requires is not reducible to sense data but remains as an inexpungible vestige of an object.

Finally, and most pressingly, the phenomenalist is faced with the seemingly insurmountable fault that his way of speaking loses contact with the character of actuality which the ordinary object-language statement unmistakably exhibits. For when I say of an absent object that "There is a car in the garage right now," I mean to refer to something which *actually is,* an actual member of the world as it here and now exists. But the phenomenalist must translate categorical statements about objects into hypothetical statements about sense data—and thus he loses the thematic actuality which attaches to the former. This defect would be especially glaring in the case of an assertion about the state of the world before man existed.[34] "Dinosaurs existed before man

---

[34] See D. M. Armstrong, *Perception and the Physical World* (New York: Humanities Press), 1961, p. 53 and Hirst, *op. cit.,* p. 107.

The Problem of Perception: I

lived on earth," an ordinary material-object statement, would have to be converted into a contrafactual conditional: "If man had existed before he did, he would have had dinosaur-like sense data." But this obviously loses the whole character of actuality in the original statement, which wants to state not what would have been but what actually *was*. It therefore appears that the phenomenalist claim to be able to render the *whole* meaning of ordinary statements in its own terms cannot be sustained. The phenomenalist might take refuge in the alternative claim that this untranslatable additional meaning is not legitimate, but there are few who would be prepared to accept this way out.

c) LINGUISTIC ANALYSIS

1) *Stebbing's Paradigm Argument*

By now, many a reader will be inclined to agree with the solution to this problem offered by certain analytical philosophers who see the whole thing primarily as linguistic muddle. Their approach is in some ways similar to Ayer's but they are more content to rest in the primacy of common sense and to allow the various ways of speaking about the data of experience to stand side by side, rather than contending that they can be translated into each other.

One of the liveliest presentations of this view is contained in the vigorous reply of L. S. Stebbing to the "two tables" fable of Sir Arthur Eddington.[35] She accuses Eddington of an intolerable raddling of language in this and other instances. For his famous "problem" is generated solely because of his failure to exercise requisite caution in applying a vocabulary proper to the speech of common sense to the inappropriate area of scientific inquiry. The primary issue is, what do we mean by "table?" What sort of word is this? It is a word which derives its meaning from ordinary perception, and has application only to that realm. It is wrong for Eddington to make silly jokes about "two tables," for the silly jokes lead to solemn though equally silly philosophical problems.

---

[35] L. S. Stebbing, *Philosophy and the Physicists* (New York: Dover), n. d., (originally published 1937), p. 54 ss.

There is only one table, for the meaning of the word table is derived from the world of direct perception; I cannot ask whether the table of direct perception is real or not, because if it isn't, there aren't any real tables. There is no scientific table, for "table" is a word for which science has no use and no application; science may talk of atoms or electrons, but nothing it says about these can cast doubt on the reality of tables as I perceive them.

The *paradigm* for the reality of such objects as "tables" is found in the world of direct perception. It is altogether misleading to apply the vocabulary of one realm to another. This would be easily seen in the reverse case if someone were to try to cast doubt on the reality of atoms and electrons on the ground that they cannot be perceived. The "reality" of atoms and electrons is the reality they have for scientific discourse; their use in science is the paradigm of their reality and it would be foolish indeed to reprobate them because they are not real as are objects of perception. Conversely, it is absurd to reprobate language about the reality of perceptual objects on the ground that science does not find it appropriate.

Stebbing's point is easy to see and she reiterates it enthusiastically. Language derives its meaning from ordinary usage; the fact that it *has* such meaning is given in its usage and the fact that it must apply to something is also clear, since it derives its meaning from so applying. I *must* mean something by "chair," "table," "house," "red," "sweet," "solid," etc., for I use the words, and the reality of the referent is given in this use of the word. Therefore, the word cannot be used to cast doubt on the reality of its object. Thus Stebbing roundly rebuts Eddington's amusing account of the difference between the experience of the ordinary man and the scientist in the adventure of walking through a doorway:

I am standing on a threshold about to enter a room. It is a complicated business. In the first place I must shove against an atmosphere pressing with a force of fourteen pounds on every square inch of my body. I must make a landing on a plank travelling at twenty miles a second around the sun—a fraction of a second too early or too late, the plank would be miles away . . . The plank has no solidity of substance. To step on it is like stepping on a swarm of flies. Shall I not slip through? etc.[36]

This is mere obfuscation, in Stebbing's eyes. For what we mean by "solid" is precisely derived from our experience of such things as planks as solid. If they aren't solid, then what do we mean by solid? The question of the "solidity" of anything lives off the paradigmatic perceptual experience and it is nonsensical to try to question whether it really applies to the objects of that experience. I do not even know what I am talking about, if it does not apply.

2) *Ostensive Signification*

This view could apparently be generalized to the assertion that I cannot consistently question the "reality" of the objects of ordinary experience, for the paradigmatic meaning of reality is discovered in perceptual experience, and if they are not real, then I do not even know what I mean by reality. Something like this is done by other writers, of whose views the version of Martin Lean is a good and convenient representative.[37]

His counterattack is against Broad's claim that we never experience objects, but only sense data, and that ordinary language contains unverifiable hypotheses about the items of experience. Lean will have none of this, contending that it is simply based on an erroneous view of language. What we directly perceive is just what common sense believes us to perceive—public, independent objects. He insists that language is completely ostensive and can contain no unrecognized hypotheses and point to no unobservables. Its meaning is in its usage: a word in itself is only a sound, and we confer meaning on it by the way we use it. Therefore, the word "physical object" must have a valid reference, for it is a word in perfectly good English usage. Nobody can question the common-sense conviction that we really perceive objects unless he

[36] Eddington, *op. cit.*, p. 342.
[37] Martin Lean, *Sense Perception and Matter* (New York: Humanities Press), 1963, pp. 16–24.

thinks he has some privileged meaning for the word "object." But if object means anything, it means something that can be pointed to in experience, for the whole meaning of language is conferred on it by its pointing to experience. If it were not to point to experience it would have no meaning; if it does have a meaning, it does point to experience—and hence its mere use validates the reality of that to which it points.

There is no doubt a very genuine attractiveness about this way of stating things, for the tantalizing nature of the problem of perception does at length generate the thought that there is something fishy about it. We are prone to say, "Well, after all, what would an object be which did carry the earmark of its own objectivity? Where do I get the privileged idea of objectivity by means of which I can question the objectivity of that of which I am now aware? If these tables and chairs are not objective, what would it mean for me to be aware of what is objective?" There seems, then, a genuine component to this view. And yet there are marks against it. For one thing, it is clear that a version such as Lean's rests on a completely ostensive theory of language. It is questionable whether such a theory can mean anything more by the word "object" than the phenomenalist means. In order to do so, it would have to be able to *point* to more than the phenomenalist can point to. The argument between Lean and Broad would seem to turn on the unresolved, and in effect unrecognized, dispute as to what exactly the notion of a physical object entails and how much of it can be simply verified in sense perception. Broad is equivalently holding that there are conceptual elements involved in the notion of an object and that therefore what is given to the senses is not an object but something (sense data) on the basis of which we infer or construct the notion of an object. Lean simply begins with the common-sense conviction that we do perceive objects and tries to defend this conviction, while remaining within the confines of his ostensive theory of language. He will say, against Broad, for instance, that we do not merely see a surface or a temporal slice, we see "something which" has a surface and duration. The question is, however, in what way it can be claimed that we *see* a "something which." Actually a completely ostensive theory of language would find it hard to distinguish its meaning for object from the phenomenalist's.

If the analyst preferred to put his emphasis not on the validity of the word object, but simply on the appropriateness of the two vocabularies, he might avoid making the claim that the word object means more than the phenomenalist means, but he would do so at the penalty of allowing the two vocabularies to stand side by side in a completely unresolved manner. This gambit has the effect of suppressing the problem altogether. For now there is no problem of how the world of science and the world of common sense are compatible; there are no longer two "worlds" or two kinds of entity, but one experience described in two languages. This treats language as purely conventional and neglects the extra-linguistic reference. But the language through which we refer to experience under the name "table" and "atom" may not seem to all to differ only conventionally. The difference seems to have a real foundation, and the question of the relation between them to be a real question. To allow them to coexist in a merely juxtaposed manner seems more a matter of refusing to raise the question of their relation than proving that there is no question.

As a matter of fact, Stebbing really does specify further the nature of the relation between the two languages. For she treats, as do many others, such things as "atoms" and "scientific laws" as conventional statements about the formal relations of perceived entities.[38] Atoms are not special kinds of perceptual entities but pegs on which to hang perceptual statements. On this view it is scientific language which has a somewhat secondary status. For the objects of science turn out to be not invisible "things," which causally generate the perception of the perceived data (as representationalism holds) but formalizations introduced to facilitate the expression of the orderly connection between perceptual enti-

---

[38] Stebbing, *op. cit.*, pp. 65/66, 78–91.

ties—constructions. They must have "reality" in a way parallel to the reality of physical objects: They are meaningfully utilized in language and are real to the exact extent and in the exact manner that the language employing them requires. Perceptual language is ostensive, and so perceptual objects are "real" as ostensively indicatable; scientific language is formal, and scientific entities are "real" as constructions which make the formal laws of science possible.

But I immediately bog down in confusion if I think of the reality of perceptual objects by the methods of science, or try to validate the objects of science by means of perception, or if I try to compare the two. I cannot compare the incomparable. I cannot compare the color blue to the formula πr^2, for the one is a perceptual entity and the other a formal rule. Note that this approach tends to regard perceptual objects as more primarily real, and to consider scientific entities as abstractions. While it has found considerable favor among scientists themselves, one cannot escape a certain queasiness in accepting it as the definitive solution.

3) *Wittgenstein, Ryle, and "Ordinary Language"*

Perhaps the best known and most fascinating attempt to deal with philosophical problems in terms of the primacy of "ordinary language" is that of Ludwig Wittgenstein. Wittgenstein agrees that problems like the difficulty about perception arise out of language and he views philosophical analysis principally as a "therapy" which will bring to light and dissolve these linguistic neuroses. In this therapeutic process, ordinary language must occupy a place of primacy, for it is from it that our words derive their meaning. Yet he cannot rest content with a simple "ostensive theory" of meaning, which is entirely too short-sighted. No doubt meaning derives from use and a word means just what we use it to mean. But the "uses" of words go far beyond simple pointing; try grasping the meaning of "if" or "but" ostensively, for example. To ask what a word *is* is similar to asking what a certain piece *is* in the game of chess.[39] A pawn simply *is* what it does in the game of chess; it has no properties occult or latent besides the ones which fit it for its role in the game. Analogously, a word *is* what it does in the game of language.

Of course, one could think of variant language-games, and Wittgenstein amuses himself by doing so, but ordinary language has a primacy because it is the game we all play. Words are more complicated pieces, just as language is a more complicated game, but the bewildering diversity of their uses is no more mysterious than the fact that things which are all equally "tools" can do such bewilderingly different things.[40] "The" meaning of a word—even of a single word—is a chimera: a word is everything it does.

Wittgenstein's view has relevance for the problem of perception, since this can be regarded as arising from a failure to appreciate the diverse manner in which words signify. One who imagines that ordinary-language words and scientific words "signify" or mean in the same way will find himself faced with the exasperating problem of which ones signify the "real" object: the words (and their presumed targets) will be in *competition* with each other. But once we realize that the language-games of science and of common speech are quite different affairs, we will be no more inclined to feel that we must decide between them than to feel that we must decide which is the *real* queen of spades—the poker, pinochle, or hearts queen.

In a similar manner, Gilbert Ryle denies the right of the scientist to derogate the reality of secondary qualities and to claim that reality can be described only in terms of the primary qualities which he himself finds useful.[41] For the truth of the matter is that

---

[39] Ludwig Wittgenstein, *Philosophical Investigations*, trans. by G. E. M. Anscombe (a bi-lingual edition) (Oxford: Basil Blackwell), 1953, p. 47.

[40] *Ibid.*, p. 6.

[41] Gilbert Ryle, *Dilemmas* (Cambridge: Cambridge University Press), 1960, pp. 82–85.

scientific words do not function in the same manner as ordinary-language words. They do not *describe* at all. A physicist's view of nature differs from the ordinary man's in somewhat the same way that an accountant's view of a university differs from the undergraduate's.[42] If the accountant is thorough enough, everything in the undergraduate's world will be referred to by him, but this does not make them competitive, and certainly doesn't turn the undergraduate's world into a bubble compared to the true reality. Thus, there are not two books, the librarian's and the accountant's, side by side. A balance-sheet must be constitutionally speechless about some things; it does not *describe* at all, and what is reached descriptively must remain inaccessible to it. Just so, the physical theorists neither describe ordinary tables and chairs nor rivals to them—they don't describe at all. Actually the language of the physicist presupposes the world of the ordinary man, and the real question is not which is real, but "How are the concepts of physical theory logically related to the concepts of everyday discourse?"[43]

It must be said in favor of approaches like Wittgenstein's and Ryle's that they seem to afford a breath of fresh air, and one that often does seem to come from the mouth of an escape-tunnel. Some genuine promise is undoubtedly held out by linguistic analysis. And yet of themselves they do not impress as sufficient anyone who is not prepared to regard the entire problem of perception (and indeed of philosophy at large) as a matter of the way in which we use words. Not many would be prepared to concede this much, for language in some way is felt to be a window opening beyond itself; these approaches tend to pull the shades and turn it inward. Even after we untie the linguistic knots, the question is still left over: what is the character of the reality which allows itself to be the subject of such diverse references?

[42] *Ibid.*, p. 75 ss.
[43] *Ibid.*, p. 91.

5 THE PROBLEM OF PERCEPTION: II

SCHOLASTIC SOLUTIONS: PRELIMINARY

Before considering some typical Scholastic opinions on sense perception, we may briefly re-iterate the position of naive realism. The latter holds that in perception we are immediately aware of objects other than ourselves; that these objects are "public" in the sense that numerically the same object is perceptible by an indefinite plurality of observers; that these objects are permanent entities which exist as such when we are not perceiving them; and finally that in their independent existence they have the same qualities which they present to perception. The habitual presumption is, then, that my act of perceiving makes no difference at all to the perceived object, that it has no hand in constituting what I perceive, but that it reaches this object just as it is in itself. The features of extension, motion, resistance, color, sound, taste, warmth, and so forth, which I perceive, are there when I do not perceive them.

Now while there are philosophers who defend most or all of these convictions of common sense, it probably would not be accurate to refer to these philosophers as "naive realists." For the essence of philosophy is reflection, and the essence of naive realism is unreflecting taking-for-granted; so that even when certain statements about experience coincide, the philosophical realist is always a "critical" realist in the sense of not being "naive." But consequent upon their critical scrutiny of common sense, some Scholastic philosophers find it necessary to make more emendations than others in the naive realism of our everyday convictions. Certain basic points are common to the standard Scholastic treatment of this subject, however, and as a preliminary to the main issue, they should be noted.

First of all, there is the elementary observation that the problem cannot be argued in terms of the "errors" of the senses, for the senses do not "err" at all. The question of the truth or falsity of perception is a question which takes us beyond sensation itself. For the same reason that the senses do not, properly speaking, contain "truth," they cannot be charged with falsehood. Sensation does not judge—it merely reports on data immediately present to it. The possibility of error only arises with judgment, for judgment asserts something about the datum immediately present to sensation, and what it asserts may be either so or not so. Until there is assertion, there is not, in a full sense, any "deception." We speak of the senses "deceiving us"—in the case of optical illusions, or shades of color, for example—but this is an abbreviated way of speaking. If I *judge* that one line is longer than another, and it is not, I err; but my senses, which simply grasp the visual appearance, do not err. Error will be found to consist in going beyond immediate data of sensation and falsely going beyond.

A judgment which confined itself to a mere expression of what was immediately present to sensation would also be immune from error. If I were to content myself with reporting that "this line appears longer than the other to me," this would be no error but simple truth—it really does appear longer. When the color-blind person is charged with having defective sensation, the charge is really levelled against his judgment. His sensation merely reports what he is now experiencing. He really is experiencing a red datum. But when he judges, he spontaneously goes beyond the immediate report of the senses and declares "This patch of cloth is red"; this means that he talks about an *object* which is public and which possesses for everyone the property which he is experiencing. If he were to confine his judgment to the datum itself, he would say "I am now experiencing a red datum," and he would not be wrong. The point is that our judgment always spontaneously takes us beyond the immediate, our assertion outruns the sensation, and the gap between the scope of the judgment and the report of the senses is what makes error possible. This is an obvious remark, but it quickly calls our attention to the fact that the whole question about the "objectivity" of sense perception cannot be settled in terms of perception alone.

Of course, we may still charge the senses with "error," meaning that they present us with data on the basis of which we are misled into judging erroneously. It is with this in mind that a second standard point is usually made by Scholastics regarding the "conditions" of a reliable act of perception. Given the physico-physiological setting of sensation, it is suggested that we must recognize that certain requirements have to be met before we can rely on our sense experience to give trustworthy testimony. Sensation appears to involve a stimulation of a bodily organ, by a physical object, through a medium of action, and certain conditions are requisite on the part of all these elements. The object must be properly proportioned to our kind of senses: infra-red colors or microscopic objects are not so proportioned; nor are sensible objects which are too distant or otherwise unfavorably given. Secondly, the organ of sense must be a normal and healthy one. Flagrant failures to fulfill this condition are found in the case of blindness, deafness, or color-blindness; but there are more moderate damages possible, including temporary aberrations, such as the morbid state of a sick man's palate because of which his taste sensation is distorted, or the abnormal condition of an eardrum which has just suffered a heavy blow. Finally, since the object is perceived through a medium, the proper medium for this perception must be present: color is properly perceived in sunlight, rather than under a photographer's red-lamp, sound, in the open air rather than underwater. Oddities like the bent appearance of a partially submerged oar may be explained from this direction: the oar is being perceived through a duality of media—air and water—in which the behavior of light varies.

As a third preliminary, we may cite the familiar distinction between proper and common sensibles. Proper sensibles are those data which are perceived by one sense alone: color, sound, odor, for example. Common sensibles are those which can be presented to more than one sense: extension and motion (which can be perceived by sight and touch, and perhaps other senses). This distinction is deemed to be useful in explaining various common sensory illusions. For when we perceive and judge of a common sensible by employing one sense alone, we seem to be quite liable to error. Thus, the man who "perceives" that the railroad tracks converge on the horizon is judging about shape (a common sensible) by means of sight alone; so, too, with the perception of the oar bent in water. That is why the child who plays the game of closing his eyes and guessing what objects are by means of their "feel" alone is easily mixed up. The correction for these errors is correspondingly simple, since if we deliberately test our single-sense observations by bringing the other senses into play, we soon set things to right.

Considerations like this serve a purpose in clearing the air of a certain initial confusion. But it must be emphasized that they by no means advance the philosophical understanding of perception very far. For they all take place within the common-sense conception of sensation and its object, and they leave quite untouched the question of the *status* of the object which is reached in sense perception. Reference to the conditions required for perception or to the distinction between the proper and common sensibles may help to explain some practical puzzles which arise for common sense, but it bears within it assumptions of a quite obscure sort. What exactly is meant by a "normal" organ, or a "proper" medium? Does this refer to anything more than the way a standard observer perceives? Why is the standard observer convinced that the green he sees in the carpet is really there and the red which the color-blind person sees is not? Because his organ of sight is normal. Which means what? That most people see things the way he does? Yet this does not touch at all the question of the status of what is seen.

The phenomenalist could make the same distinction between normal and deviant within his framework: what is perceived is not independent of the perceiver, but most perceivers see things in this way, so this consensus is used as a standard. What is "objective," on phenomenalist grounds, is decided by what agrees with this usual way of perceiving things. But then this distinction doesn't advance us one inch towards validating the independent existence of perceived data; it is a distinction which could be made either within the phenomenalist or the realist assumption.

The same thing can be said of the distinction between proper and common sensibles. This amounts to little more than an admonition of how to avoid being led into certain errors based on perception. But the avoidance of sensory error is a practical question, not a philosophical one. It only becomes philosophical when the existence of error recoils upon the status of the "correct" datum. By seeing how certain errors arise, I further very little my philosophical grasp of perception (I am benefited only to the extent that I am freed from the worry that the railroad tracks really do come together, if that happened to be bothering me). The philosophical question is: if the datum which is given to me in perception is susceptible to this kind of deviant presentation, then precisely what is its status?

This question can be raised about the data given in "correct" perception, as well as erroneous perception. When I claim that my color perception is right and the color-blind person's wrong, am I merely rejoicing in the support I get from the views of the majority (and scorning him as a non-conformist) or am I saying something about the reality of color? What exactly is the proper medium for viewing the color of an object? Normal sunlight, we may say. But does that mean sunlight at noon, at dawn, at sunset, at three o'clock on an overcast day, at 10:52 on a windy morning, or what? Some might say that the variations are negligible, but they can only mean by this that they make no practical difference, which is not in dispute. We are all familiar with the series of paintings which the impressionist Monet made of the cathedral of Rouen, depicting the wealth of subtle color-changes which the cathedral exhibited as the day progressed. Now *which* of these was the *real* color of the cathedral?

VIRTUAL REALISM

Questions like the foregoing arouse the suspicion that we are putting things wrongly. Maybe in dealing with something like color, we should not even be asking which is the "real" color of the object. That might involve us in the seemingly impossible attempt to single out which of our numberless color-perceptions of a certain object was "right," all the others being presumably not quite right. There is something very dissatisfying about this way of speaking. This dissatisfaction leads many a philosopher to the conclusion that in dealing with such data as color, we are not dealing with intrinsic properties of the object at all, but with data which are essentially *relational*. On this view, we should not ask what color an object is "in itself," because the datum of color already entails a reference to an observer and to the conditions under which his observation occurs. "The" color of an object is an abstraction: there is only the color viewed in some relational context by a viewer situated at a certain perspective within that context. When we have said "color," we already have spoken of a reference to a perceiver and of the conditions of his perceiving; therefore we should not go on to ask which is the "real" color of an object. This seems to be like asking how this object would look to an observer who was situated nowhere and for whom there were no conditions of his seeing—a question of doubtful validity. Color, say these philosophers, is a relational reality. It is the face which the world presents to a given observer under given conditions.

As with color, so with other sensible properties. What shall we say of sound, taste, warmth, odor? Very much the same thing. They are not intrinsic properties of an object in total isolation from an observer, but data which are present in the interaction of object and observer. Sound is a datum which is there for the consciousness of an observer in interaction with the world. Then the lamented tree which falls in the middle of the forest falls soundlessly, since sound is the consciously experienced side of an interaction, and where the interaction is missing, sound is missing. Such is the view of those philosophers, among them many Scholastics, who hold what may be called "critical virtual realism." This is the position that sensed qualities are fully objective only for consciousness, and only virtually objective independently of consciousness. This is to be contrasted with naive realism and with "critical formal realism," which holds that sensed qualities are formally objective independent of all conscious experience. The latter holds that the precise formality of color, sound, taste, extension, motion, and the rest, are present even when consciousness is not going on. Now this is what virtual realism denies. If the full meaning of color or sound entails a reference to an observer, then it cannot be formally realized apart from that reference.

On this view, we would have to say that the grass is not formally green outside of experience, stones hard, flowers redolent, sugar sweet, or sounds loud. What this view does should be clearly understood. It reduces the world outside of consciousness to a qualitatively barren state. It does not, however, introduce complete arbitrariness into perception. For it holds that while these qualities are not formally present beyond perception, still they are *virtually* present. That is, there is a power in the object independently of perception which accounts for the formality which is present when perception occurs. Why do I perceive grass as green, lemon as bitter, roses as sweet-smelling? Obviously this is not a matter of whim. Then there is some determination in the object which, in interrelation with my sensory organ, gives rise to my experience of these data and not to others. It is quite conceivable, however, that this same objective determination might, in interrelation with an observer with different sensory organs and under different perceptual conditions, generate the experience of a formally different datum for his consciousness.

One or two explanatory points should be made. First, let it be remembered that virtual realism wants still to be regarded as an *immediate* realism, and in no way an indirect realism. That is, it is not denying that in knowing we immediately know a non-self. There is no pretense that I first know my own "idea" and then have to argue to the fact that an object corresponds to it. What I know is not a subjective modification of myself. It is an object. This rose here, red, soft, and sweet, is an object, not a collection of my ideas; the green of the grass is objective, and so is the sound of the locomotive. In knowing, then, I am immediately beyond the sphere of my own individual self. True, the data under discussion are only formally objective for perception, but they *are* formally objective for perception. To say that color, sound, taste, odor, are relationally objective is not to say that they are subjective.

This is where virtual realism differs from the theory of John Locke. Locke held that the secondary qualities were, as experienced, "ideas," and hence subjective, and he then had to cope with the problem of how well these ideas resembled the quality in the object. Now this may well have been a deficiency in his own way of stating things, and he may have been driving at a point quite similar to the virtual realists. But the fact remains that on his view as expressed in his own language, he does not think that we immediately know objects. The critical virtual realists hold that awareness is always of the other and does not reach this other inferentially. Nor do they have to ask whether the sensed data "resemble" the object as it exists un-sensed; formally objective qualities do not resemble virtually objective qualities. What is real apart from sensation is an object which is determinate and sensible (able to be sensed) and a determinate subject which is capable of sensing: consciousness is the actualization both of the capacity of the subject for sensing and the capacity of the object for being sensed. As such, it is not something "subjective," but the actualization of an object's presence to a subject.

Secondly, and very importantly, attention must be called to the way in which this position has been presented. The reader will

The Problem of Perception: II

have noticed that the entire discussion has centered around the secondary qualities or "proper sensibles." It is these qualities which the virtual realist has declared to be only virtually objective. The natural question is why he has made this statement exclusively in respect to them, and exempted the primary qualities from his conclusion. Why does he allow formal objectivity to these independent of consciousness, and refrain from extending his reasoning to include them? Two points may be made in answer.

a) The feeling is that the relational character of a datum is only a reason to doubt its intrinsic objectivity if there is a relation of *heterogeneity* between perceiving organ and perceived object. In such a case, where the organ is different in nature from the object, then this difference will be a cause for distortion and militate against the intrinsic character of the perceived datum. Thus, the datum of color is perceived by the eye and neural apparatus; but there is no likeness between the color-datum red and the optical apparatus: the eye, nerves, and cortex, are not red. Or a sound as heard has no similarity to an ear-drum, which is not itself "like" a sound. But in the case of extension and motion, there is no such heterogeneity, but rather a homogeneity between perceiving organ and perceived object. Thus, the hand by means of which I perceive the extension of the table-top is extended in the same general way as is the table-top. Therefore the fact that I perceive extension by means of an organ introduces no distortion into perception, for there is a homogeneity in respect to the perceived quality. This homogeneity introduces an invincible conviction of objectivity into my perceptions, for I can run my hand along the table-top and perceive a continual coincidence between organ and object. Therefore, although these data, too, might in a way be said to be "relational," the relation does not detract from their formal objectivity. That is why Van Steenberghen, who makes a great deal of this point, will say that not every conceivable knower would have to experience objects with the secondary qualities they present to us, but that for any and all knowers, the primary qualities would be in the object: even for an angelic knower, there would objectively be a *distance* between Louvain and Brussels.[1]

b) Secondly, some Scholastic authors rely on the fact that science gives us no reason to doubt the objectivity of primary qualities. This is in contrast to the view of science on secondary qualities, which it finds quite dispensable. What underlies this second view is the recognition that for immediate consciousness many, if not all, qualities are experienced as objective: the green of the grass is experienced as just as much a quality of the object as its extension, for example. Therefore, the only reason we have to doubt the objectivity of *any* quality is that this doubt is imposed upon us by some other facet of our knowledge or experience. But science has succeeded in demonstrating that phenomena of color, sound, and the other secondary qualities can be understood by considering bodies as atomic structures in contact through an electromagnetic medium with my physiological body; at no point do the secondary qualities enter into this description. They are causally explained as arising from the interaction of entities which are sufficiently conceived without their aid. And so many philosophers draw the conclusion that there is nothing to be said against the objectivity of primary qualities and a great deal to be said against that of secondary qualities. They accept the scientific picture as hard-core philosophical datum. Fr. Gustave Weigel will say, for instance, that the scientific view makes speculation in this area unnecessary.[2] R. J. Hirst is not inclined to put forth much effort in behalf of secondary qualities because "science has no need of them."[3] Other authors tell us[4] that science gives no ground to doubt the objectivity of primary qualities, implying the decisiveness of the scientific outlook for epistemology.

[1] Van Steenberghen, *op. cit.,* p. 217.
[2] Gustave Weigel, S.J., and Arthur Madden, *Knowledge, Its Values and Limits* (Englewood Cliffs, N.J.: Prentice Hall), 1961, p. 19.
[3] *Op. cit.,* p. 318.
[4] Joseph D. Hassett, S.J., Robert A. Mitchell, S.J., J. Donald Monan, S.J., *The Philosophy of Human Knowing* (Westminster, Md.: Newman Press), 1955, p. 151.

EVALUATION OF VIRTUAL REALISM

Critical virtual realism decides the problem of perception by holding that in spatial qualities I know what formally belongs to the object as it is in itself apart from perception, while in secondary qualities, I know what is only virtually in the object apart from perception. The virtual realist will be seen to begin habitually with the assumption that perception is the work of a bodily consciousness, that it takes place by means of the causality of sensory organs. Now whoever begins with this as an assumption is not so much validating the objectivity of primary qualities as he is *assuming* it. For a sensory organ is a spatial organ, and if we begin by assuming that perception is *caused* by spatial organs, then our question has been answered before it has hardly been raised.[5] Some might protest that this is a justified procedure, since there is no way of getting behind the role of the sensory organs in consciousness; in epistemology we must begin somewhere, and that will turn out to be with the role of the organs in sensation. Without even striving to settle the legitimacy of this stand, we only wish to point out that any one who does begin here has obviously already granted spatial qualities a formally real status: if spatial organs are at the *origin* of perception, then they must be formally real independent of perception.

Consequently, it is not even necessary for these apologists to go on to raise arguments in favor of the formal reality of the primary qualities. One who believes that sensory organs play a causal role in perception must be referring to the sensory organs that we are all familiar with—and these are spatial. Given this, it is not at all necessary to show that because there is homogeneity between organ and object no distortion is introduced into perception. For

---

[5] Of course, the problem of secondary qualities might also be regarded as finished with at this point, since our meaning for "sensory organ" normally includes secondary qualities, and hence an assertion of the role of the body might be thought to include as part of its meaning the contribution of the secondary qualities involved in identifying a "sensory organ."

once consciousness is seen as *originating* in an interaction between organ and object the formally spatial character of both of these is assumed. Otherwise, when Van Steenberghen shows[6] the homogeneity between hand and table in respect to extension, he would merely be correlating two objects of consciousness; that two objects of consciousness have a homogeneity would of itself prove nothing about what is true independently of consciousness. In order for his point to have weight about a reality "in itself" apart from consciousness, he must already believe that consciousness originates in this spatial contact, that the hand of which he speaks is not simply an object of consciousness but an organ by which consciousness is generated—and hence he must *assume* that this spatial organ is real, independent of consciousness. Likewise, when he speaks of the lack of homogeneity between the eye and color, this could only be evidence against the objectivity of color if he assumes that the eye of familiar conscious experience is causally involved in the production of vision; but this assumes *at least* its formally spatial reality. In other words, the virtual realists are posing the whole question of sense qualities within a context which simply takes for granted extension as a formal reality independent of conscious experience altogether.

Sometimes it appears that the virtual realists are exerting strenuous efforts to prove that the objects of *perception* are formally extended—a fact which does not need proving at all. It is evident that the desk, the piece of paper, the rock, which is the object of my perception is in itself, as such, extended. No argument is needed to bring that out. But it is also evident that the objects of perception are colored, sounding, and odorous. This piece of paper which I *perceive* is not only rectangular but *white;* this grass which I perceive is not only two inches high but *green*. No argument either proves or disproves that, since it is given. Then what has Van Steenberghen proved which warrants his statement that not every knower would have to perceive this grass as green, but that

---

[6] *Op. cit.,* pp. 215–217, 222–223.

The Problem of Perception: II

every knower would have to perceive it as extended? What grass is he talking about? If he is talking about *this* grass, the object of perception, then it is a tautology to say that every observer would have to experience this grass as green, for part of the reality of this perceived grass is its greenness. Anyone who does not perceive that is not perceiving this grass but something else. Does he, perhaps, mean not this perceptually present grass but the object independent of perception which presents itself to me perceptually as green? In that case, perhaps there is no assurance that this object as unrelated to consciousness is green—but is there any more reason to think that it is extended? Just because, as given to consciousness it is extended, seems no guarantee that, as not given to consciousness, it is extended. The hand which I perceive and the desk which I perceive are both objects for consciousness; that they are both extended does not apparently prove anything about either hand or desk apart from consciousness. If he pleads that this takes too disembodied a view of consciousness, that perceptual consciousness is the work of a sensory organ, then he is no longer arguing but treating this as an irreducible beginning.

It would seem that the virtual realist must make up his mind either to go the whole way with his view or else to treat it not as a conclusion but as an irreducible premise. That is, if the data given to perception are really relational data, then perhaps there is reason to think that they are all relational data, and do not inform us at all about how objects are apart from their relation to consciousness. There is no compelling reason to stop with the secondary qualities which does not already assume the right to stop with the secondary qualities. It therefore comes down to a question of which "object" the virtual realist is talking about. If he is referring to the perceived object, then *all* qualities are formally in the perceived object precisely as they are experienced as being; if he is talking about the object independent of perception, there seems to be no sufficient reason for saying that *any* perceived quality is there.

In other words, if virtual realism goes to the end in its reasoning, it is very likely to wind up in the position of Immanuel Kant.[7] Kant's view is based on his distinction between noumena and phenomena. The noumenon is reality in itself, the phenomenon reality as it presents itself to consciousness. Since human knowledge is not *in toto* creative of its object, Kant assumes that it is legitimate to speak of reality as it is in itself, apart from all relation to consciousness. But every conceivable consciousness (human or otherwise) is a definite kind of consciousness, with a determinate structure. Reality as it presents itself to a knower must, then, present itself according to the conditions under which he can know. Whatever determines his manner of knowing also determines to that extent the manner in which objects are known by him. Turning to human knowledge, Kant found that the *a priori* forms (or structural determinations constituting my consciousness independent of all actual content) which specify my kind of knowing are the forms of space and time. What determines my way of knowing is that whatever I know I must know spatially and temporally. Any reality which cannot be present in this way, *is* never present to my consciousness, and so is never known; conversely, any reality which is present to my consciousness must conform to the conditions under which something *can* be present, and hence *must* be known spatially and temporally.

Underlying experience is a noumenal subject and a noumenal objective ground. Experience is the product of a relation between these two (which must forever remain inexplicable). Everything present to my experience is phenomenal. This word must not mislead us. Kant does not mean to signify that it is "illusory" or "deceptive," but only that it is reality as present according to the conditions of my manner of knowing. In knowing phenomena, I know *objects,* not illusions, or merely subjective occurrences. The rocks, trees, water, animals, people whom I experience are real, just as real as the self of my experience, but they are phenomenally real. That is, the qualities which I find in them are objective, not

[7] Without, of course, necessarily subscribing to the full range of Kantian philosophy, in particular his metaphysics.

subjective—but they are objective in them as phenomena. That is why the accusation of some that Kant has a "subjective" theory of space is misguided. Space is subjective as a *form* of our knowing, but it is objective in the sense that it informs every object of my experience. Space is real in the sense that it is a qualification of human experience: the objects I experience really are spatial. What about noumena? Here no answer is possible. The noumenon is the trans-experiential objective ground of my experiencing things the way I do, and because it is trans-experiential, I can say nothing about it. What I mean by space is this indicatable feature of my phenomenal experience; as long as there is human experience, there is space. Whether the noumenal ground which is experienced by me in a spatial manner could be presented in another manner to another knower, I cannot say.

Once experience is viewed as phenomenal in this way, the distinction between primary and secondary qualities loses much of its point. What is given to me perceptually is experienced as fully real: this grass is green, sweet, smooth, extended, moving. All these properties are real exactly as they are experienced as being real: *formally* where they are experienced as being. What about the grass apart from experience? This is a confused question. *This* grass precisely is the grass as experienced, and it makes no sense to ask about it apart from experience. If I mean what about the noumenal ground of this perceptual experience, apart from experience, then there is no more reason to think of it as extended than to think of it as having the secondary qualities.

There is no clear reason why the virtual realists should check their reasoning short of a Kantian conclusion. If experienced data are relational, then it would appear correct to view them all as relational. No argument seems to prevent this, but only the conviction that our experience of ourselves as spatial is a rock-bottom inexplicable which reveals a datum that is real independent of all consciousness. Everything stands or falls on the truth of this conviction.

The other reasoning which is at the basis of virtual realism's conferring of formal reality on the primary qualities may be more briefly handled, i.e., the scientific evidence which seems to lead in this direction. It cannot be too often reiterated that scientific data cannot be decisive on this issue, for reasons which have already been pointed out. No scientific statement can provide an ultimate ground for judging the nature of perception, for every scientific statement is built upon a perceptual foundation. It can have no more objectivity than perception has, and cannot be used to test the fundamental objectivity of perception. The fact that science has no need of secondary qualities and can confine its description of reality to the quantitative language of the primary qualities does not establish either that secondary qualities are un-real or that the world independent of consciousness is characterized formally by primary qualities.

The long-entrenched opinion to the contrary is now increasingly recognized as the hypostasizing of an abstraction. Because science left aside all secondary qualities and attended only to the quantitative aspect of reality, there grew up a propensity to treat this quantitative aspect as a "thing" or "collection of things" existing in itself. Part of the epistemological advance within science itself in recent times has consisted in recognizing the abstract character of its own way of conceiving reality and repudiating the projection of this abstraction as an autonomous reality. This repudiation was facilitated because the progress of scientific theory had finally reached the point where not only had science been able to dispense with the secondary qualities in its description of reality, but it now found itself denuding the object even of the primary qualities. Thus, Werner Heisenberg could say of the atom as it was conceived by a physical theory which he himself had been influential in bringing into being, that it had neither color, sound, nor extension, nor any of the qualities which the bodies of perceptual experience have.[8] It is now a matter of the most extreme perplexity to decide just what is the status of such an entity. Some regard it

[8] Werner Heisenberg, *Philosophical Problems of Nuclear Science* (New York: Pantheon), 1952, pp. 38, 86.

as simply a logically conceived "x" which serves as a term of reference for a set of mathematical equations. The "scientific object," on these terms, is not a special entity, but a special way of regarding the familiar objects of experience. Far from providing a sure basis for solving the problem of perception, this special procedure retains all the puzzles of perception, and stirs up a hornet's nest of its own.

SUMMING UP

As some contribution towards the unravelling of an extremely tangled skein of puzzles, we may make the following basic suggestions:

1) The fundamental obstacle to the decision as to whether "material objects exist unperceived" is that the meaning of that assertion is multivalently obscure. Strange as it may seem, after centuries of speculation, it would not be possible to get anything approaching a consensus of opinion as to what this statement means, much less whether it is true or false. Every single word in the statement contains an obscurity. We will concentrate principally on the notion of "object" which is at stake. In order for this statement to be true, what is it which the asserter thinks would have to be true about the "object" which is involved? What is this "object" which he claims to exist unperceived? Several points seem secure:

a) For judgmental consciousness, *every* datum is objective and independent. That is, my judgment experiences itself precisely as a complete self-effacement in favor of its object. The judgment is an awareness of itself as making no difference whatsoever to what is judged about.[9] Whether I say "The table is round," "Two and two are four," or "I have a pain," the judgment effaces itself

[9] On the self-effacing character of judgment, see Maritain, *op. cit.*, p. 87, and a quite different kind of realist thinker, the English philosopher H. A. Prichard, *Knowledge and Perception* (Oxford: Clarendon Press), 1950, pp. 63, 204.

altogether before its object. My *pain* is just as much objectively there independently of my judgmental consciousness as is a table or a chair. We are in the habit of thinking of pain, joy, sorrow, and the like, as subjective experiences, but for the *judging* consciousness, they are found, there, other than itself as judging.

b) For perceptual consciousness, every quality is just where it is experienced as being. This is a matter of direct experience. The green is, for perception, just where it is experienced—in what I call grass; the blue is in the sky; the gurgling in the brook; the scent in the rose. The only question that can be raised in this area is the psychological one of whether I am sure where I experience these qualities, and this is often obscure. Do I really experience the sweetness in the sugar—or do I experience it in my tongue, or do I experience it in the encounter between sugar and tongue? This is a factual question which may often be hard to answer. But wherever I do experience the quality, that is where it is, and nowhere else.[10]

From here on, things become less clear. For, my habitual conviction is not simply that everything is objective in respect to judgmental consciousness, but that the objects of perceptual consciousness are completely objective. Whence do I derive this conviction? What appears to happen is that my lived consciousness is integral, and that I assimilate the perceptual data to the independence of the objects of judgmental consciousness. That is, just as the object judged about is altogether independent of the act of judging, so the perceived object is posited as altogether other than the *total* consciousness which is aware of it. I assimilate perceiving to

---

[10] Suppose I experience the pain in an amputated limb? Even so, one of two things: 1) I really do experience it there—which cannot be declared an impossibility except by *assuming* that I cannot feel a pain where a bodily appendage no longer exists, which is only an assumption and exactly the assumption in question. (For a forceful exposition of this, see E. A. Burtt, *op. cit.*, p. 315.) 2) I am psychologically mistaken in thinking that I experience it there: I really experience it elsewhere and immediately *interpret* its location through past recollections.

The Problem of Perception: II

judging, and then the perceived object has the same independent status as the judged object. I then come to believe that if my individual perceiving consciousness were not there, the objects which I perceive would still be there exactly as they are for perception.

Endless difficulties are raised by this belief. Rather than attempting to deal with them, let us only try to specify what is involved in this claim for the independence of perceptual objects. If I claim that tables, rocks, chairs, clouds, are there independently of individual perception, what do I want to assert? Are they there as they are for consciousness? But then I am hypostasizing the pure "outside" view, which is the one which is there for an observer. Are they there *for themselves*? But then they are not there as they are there for consciousness—for, for consciousness they are there for us. Furthermore, to speak of these things as being there "for themselves" is difficult to do in the case of tables, rocks, and clouds. The only way of being "for itself" that is clear to me is my own way—consciousness's way; surely, though, I don't quite mean that these objects are there for themselves as consciousness is there for itself. But how can they be there independent of all other consciousness without being in any way "for themselves"?

We now begin to realize that the epistemological assertion overflows into metaphysical territory. In order to assert fully that perceptual objects are independent of all individual consciousness, we ought to know what we *mean* by this assertion. Yet as soon as we try to spell out what we mean by it, we must theorize as to the nature of their independent existence. Are they something analogous to conscious selves, à la the monads of Leibniz? Are they data for an absolute experience, à la Hegel? Are they substances, à la St. Thomas? The dire uncertainty in the face of all these questions may be utilized in bringing us to the realization of the limits of the self-contained character of the epistemological inquiry. To a large extent, we can separate the epistemological question from others, such as the metaphysical, but we eventually reach the limits of this separation. Unless I know what I mean by saying that "material objects exist unperceived" I cannot be said to know the truth of that statement in anything but a most rudimentary way. But in order to know what I mean, I must make an attempt to conceive the mode of existence of these independent objects, and then I am in a theory of being, rather than a theory of knowledge.

It is not too much to say that the problem of perception remains the most unresolved in the whole of epistemology. In fact, it would be somewhat disingenuous to say anything else. A perpetual starting from scratch seems to afflict our inquiries here. This should not be taken as a defeat for thought, however, since the recognition of this plight and the restless effort to surmount it is rather an indication of the genuinely philosophical limit-situation which we reach here. If we were to sum up what can be salvaged as epistemological currency from a very fluid situation, we might list the following:

1) Perceptual consciousness is never pure subjectivity. It always contains an actualization of the presence of a non-self as well as our own presence to ourselves.

2) Perceptual consciousness never stands alone, but is always incorporated into the total relation to the other which includes elements which go beyond perception.

3) Perceptual data always exist just exactly where they are experienced as existing.

4) Perceptual consciousness seems to put us in contact with a multiplicity of non-selves; in so far as it is incorporated into a total *acting* consciousness, it presents us with multiple centers of resistance.

How much further than this we can go with security is debatable. A quite consistent picture of reality can be presented by a view which regards all perceptual objects as existing in their full and formal reality *only* for human consciousness. This could be done either in a Kantian manner, or by regarding perceptual objects as "events" which are there at the boundary of a subject-object encounter. There is a common tendency to do just that on the part of many contemporary thinkers. Some, like Merleau Ponty, will say that there is no sense contending that we reach the world as it exists "in itself," since the objects of experience always contain a reference to our experiencing selves. A familiar view among Scholastics that through perception we know "objects as they affect us" could be fitted into this framework. One simple way to hold that we *do* know the world in itself, of course, would be to hold that the world as it is "for us" *is* the world in itself: that reality is relational to its very foundation, and that therefore the very question of a search for the "object in itself" apart from all relations is an empty search.[11] Relational properties are only defined *against* intrinsic properties if one fancies that the reality of an object can be conceived in total abstraction from its relations. If this is not so, then there would not be the same difficulty in conceiving the qualities of the object as at the same time totally relational and totally intrinsic.

There still remains the other alternative of simply stopping with the irreducible givenness of the bodily experience of consciousness with all that that entails. We might confine this irreducible thereness to extension, as do the virtual realists, or maintain a similar irreducibility for the secondary qualities. We could claim what some do, that just because science correlates color with light-waves or warmth with molecular motion, this does not by any means prove that the secondary qualities do not *also* exist objectively.[12] Heat may be an objective concomitant of molecular motion, color an objective concomitant of light-waves; or they both might be co-equal objective properties, discernible from different vantage-

[11] This is the view of the later Husserl; in a quite different way it is the view of quite different idealists like Hegel, Leibniz, or Bradley, and of an "organic" realist like Whitehead.

[12] This seems to be the basis for the defense of the objectivity of secondary qualities made by P. Coffey, *Epistemology*, 2 vols. (New York: Longmans Green), 1917, vol. II, pp. 127–137 and by Reginald O'Neill, S.J., *Theories of Knowledge* (Englewood Cliffs, N. J.: Prentice Hall), 1960, pp. 41–47.

points. It really seems to be only a prejudice which throws the secondary qualities out of reality. Illusions are not conclusive, either, since they only prove that these qualities are conditioned by circumstances, not that they are un-real. When we see a round penny from a certain angle as elliptical, the explanation is again the relational character of the datum. We are seeing a round-penny-turned-at-a-certain-angle-to-my-eye: a total circumstantial datum. What would be amazing would be that the penny from this angle still looked round, for this would nullify the reality of space and of the whole context of relations which the penny has to other entities. I am never perceiving the penny, but a whole contextual relation, out of which I concentrate on a single member. To exist spatially is to exist *perspectivally,* but that is only confusing if we fail to see that perspective is itself an objective datum. True, it is not a property of an object apart from a viewer, but neither is it a property of a viewer. It is a property of an object-as-viewed-from-here. The *intelligibility* of perspective implies a reference to a determinate object and is therefore a revelation of that object. The same can be said about the perspectival character of secondary qualities.

To hold that sensory perception puts me in touch with qualities which exist formally in an independent object, we would have to hold several things: a) The conception of an object as it exists in itself, apart from all relations, is a meaningful conception. b) The conception of primary and secondary qualities existing apart from all relation to consciousness is a meaningful conception. c) There is nothing in experience that would eliminate this possibility. It may be safely declared that sensory illusion and scientific evidence, the only two reasons usually adduced for the elimination of objectivity are not conclusive. Therefore the decision on this question comes down to our stand on the first two points. Even if the possibility of the first two points is denied, there is at least one more alternative that one could adopt who wanted to hold the strict reality of sensory qualities. That is the belief in an Absolute Consciousness transcending our own in which all these qualities are perpetually held fast; on this view, one way to sustain naive realism would be by espousing Absolute Idealism.

PUZZLES ABOUT "OBJECTIVITY"

Two more points may be made in conclusion. First, the question of objectivity is usually discussed in complete neglect of the consciousness which *asserts* this objectivity. We too easily overlook the fact that every assertion of objectivity is in function of a certain *exigence* of the consciousness which makes it. Consequently we overlook the keen dissatisfaction felt by certain realms of consciousness in the face of the Kantian or virtual realist disposal of secondary qualities. Specifically, what would the *aesthetic* consciousness feel if it were told that secondary qualities were only virtually objective? Suppose we were to tell Marcel Proust, remembering in ecstasy the taste of his aunt's madeleine cake, the azure Veronne River, the long-ago peal of the church bells, and the scent of the hawthorn blossoms along the lanes of the childhood village of Combray, that secondary qualities were not as formally real as extension and motion—would that make contact with the reality of his experience? And if it did not, in what way is it a satisfactory view of perception?

The aesthetic consciousness seems to experience itself as a profound, though stammering, affirmation of a splendor it *finds* in the most irresistibly objective manner. The world which it celebrates is, for it, gloriously there and it will just not take no for an answer. Now the exigence which this consciousness feels to assert absolute reality cannot be brushed aside by a consciousness operating at a different level or in a different way. The scientist just cannot tell the artist that the sunset is not really a riot of color nor a benediction of beauty; nor can the "neutral observer," the sensory knower, the down-to-earth man, or any other than a poetic consciousness. The assertion of reality is always a function of a certain exigence, and the tendency to overlook this introduces a fantastic confusion into the problem of "perception." What reflection can do is to mediate and harmonize the various exigences and the various realms of consciousness, but it can do this only if, as reflection, it inhabits these realms and feels these exigences. Up to the present day, epistemological discussions about the objects of perception have not done this. Progress in this quarter is urgently called for.

Secondly, reflection must also apply itself to the continued exploration of the meaning of "object" which is at stake in this discussion, something never quite clear. Even the aesthetic consciousness is not sure what it means when it says that it wants its world to be *there,* to be there-for-itself; it wants, somehow, to affirm the glorious and overriding reality of the objects it encounters, but it is not really sure what it means by this yearning. Philosophical reflection must delve into the inarticulate yearning of this and other levels of consciousness. For consciousness must recognize something puzzling and elusive about its conviction of the "reality" of perceptual objects. Not only is a perceptual object an amalgam of an indefinite number of perspectival views, but it is involved totally in time. No one has yet fully incorporated time into the discussion on perception. I feel that I experience objects and that these objects are real independent of my perception. But each object is a temporal unfolding, and therefore in demanding that the object be real, I am demanding that each temporal perspective be relatively unreal. I want it to be for-itself—and yet how can I conceive the for-itself reality of a rock with an infinity of possible spatial perspectives and a continuity of real temporal moments? It would seem that in asserting the reality of objects, I am always asserting more than perspectives: I am asserting the ingathering of perspectives into a unity which is somehow there in and for itself. Yet how can this apply to non-human things? Perhaps a clue may be gotten by considering the non-conscious unitary aspects of consciousness, such as the way our bodily experiences are there for us. Physiologically our body is not a datum for consciousness; what does it mean for the body to be there, and yet not consciously there? The possibilities for questioning along this line seem limitless, and it is to these questions that philosophical speculation about perception must press on if it is to be fruitful. Only by continually turning the problem over and subjecting it to the whole range of conscious exigences will we ever do much more than mark time in the same place.

6 THE SEARCH FOR THE UNCONDITIONAL

THE PRIMITIVE ASSERTION

Although the objectivity of sense perception can be placed upon firm grounds, there is no denying that there is a residue of uncertainty in this area. If nothing else, it is clear that the objectivity here vindicated is compatible with a relatively vast amount of error; sensory illusion of one kind or another is familiar to everyone. Therefore it makes obvious sense to say that the objects of sense perception may often *appear* to be other than what they really *are*. That which is known in sense perception is not given in such a way that it can underwrite an unconditional certitude about reality apart from the immediate perception.

The mind finds itself restive under these circumstances, for its ineluctable urge is the urge to the absolute. We are not at all satisfied to rest with the rather adulterated brand of sensory objectivity, but wish to press on to an area in which we can leave all qualification behind. Is there present in human experience any knowledge about which we will no longer have to fear that things may be other than they seem? Is the security of unconditional assent forbidden to us? Or is there not open to thought an affirmation which it can make with altogether unqualified assurance?

Now if there is such assurance, it can only be founded on a datum in which the distinction between appearance and reality is surpassed. If there is to be absolute certitude, there must be an absolute datum, one given in such a way that with respect to it

The Search for the Unconditional

we need not, even cannot, ask whether things be other than they seem. As long as it is thinkable that things be other than they seem, then it is thinkable that our knowledge of them be not true to what they really are. The search for the unconditioned therefore resolves itself into the search for the absolute datum.

Such a datum is given to us through the idea of "being." By the term "being," we designate all that is and all that can be. We designate the totality of reality, whether actual or possible. Man, star, stone, amoeba, are all beings; red, sweet, hard, loud, are beings; satyrs, unicorns, mermaids are beings (beings of fantasy); numbers, lines, points, are beings (beings of abstraction); thoughts, acts of will, emotions are beings. The idea of being applies to everything which is and to every *difference* between everything which is: daisies and grasshoppers are both beings, and whatever makes a daisy different from a grasshopper is also a being. Thus, green, leafy, with a yellow and white flower, containing chlorophyll, are modes of being; brown, many-legged, winged, are modes of being. The notion of being applies to every whole individual and to every part of that whole. There is no exception whatever to the idea of being: God is a being, and so is a gamma-ray. Absolutely nothing falls outside the scope of this notion. Whatever is not nullity, is being.

Suppose there are things which we have never known and never will—planets forever unseen, types of life never encountered, Descartes' evil genius, or some peculiar thing so foreign to us that we cannot even begin to imagine it. Even so, we know one thing about it in advance—the idea of being applies to it. Whatever we do *not* know about it, we do know that if it is at all, it is included within our concept of being. The idea of being is not, then, limited to experience. It applies to every being which participates in experience and to anything that could participate in experience but also to things which could never be part of our experience. This idea is absolutely universal, and no exception to it whatsoever is thinkable. Moreover, in respect to it, no distinction between appearance and reality is possible. It may make sense to say "maybe this only looks red and isn't really red," but it makes no sense to say, "maybe this red only *seems* to be being, and really is not." The idea of being, then, provides the fulcrum upon which absolute certitude turns.

We have already suggested that the absolute unconditional underlying thought is the reality of the question itself as the ground of all knowledge, and what is said here is not meant to controvert this. Being is delivered to us fundamentally as question. What we are seeking now is, as it were, the first irruption of the question into the order of affirmation. And we cannot go far wrong if we begin by saying that one thing we may affirm unconditionally is our *right to affirm*.[1] This is not playing with words, for it is a way of recognizing that that which allows the question of the truth or falsity of individual assertions to be raised is of a different order from the object of these assertions. That which allows the distinction between the truth and falsity of assertion is the questioning grasp of experience. But the question, as turning to experience, is immediately diffracted into a duality in the order of assertion. For it grasps experience as at a certain "distance" from its own ultimate and inexpressible intelligibility. That upon which assertion bears is twofold: it is not a sheer existent, which would leave no distance between itself and the question and thus obliterate the latter.

This distance of experience from the question is rendered in the order of assertion as a distance of experience from itself, and expressed in the primitive assertion that "something is" or "something exists." No assertion may escape that formula, and that formula entails the diffraction of the intelligibility of the question into a "what" and a "that." In the order of assertion the identity

---

[1] This point is strongly made by one of the major thinkers of the modern Thomistic movement, Joseph Maréchal, S.J., in his monumental six volume work, *Le point de départ de la métaphysique*. See Cahier I, p. 35, and Cahier V, p. 377. For an exposition of Maréchal's thought, see the exhaustive and remarkable survey of 19th and 20th century Thomistic epistemology by Georges Van Riet, *L'épistemologie thomiste*, pp. 263–300.

The Search for the Unconditional

of the what and the that (essence and existence) is impossible. Hence the unconditional in the order of assertion derives from the primitive fissure which underlies and makes possible this order. Experience as answering to the question always renders a twofold reply: something . . . exists. Neither of these can be reduced to nor deduced from the other, and the search for the unconditional in this area must lead through the distance which separates them.

FIRST PRINCIPLES

Now in the recognition of the irreducible value of the primitive assertion, that "something exists," there are contained a plurality of principles which derive their standing from this recognition. The unconditional certitude of these principles is rooted in the unconditional value of the primitive assertion itself. They are traditionally stated as follows:

1) Principle of Identity: What exists, exists; what does not exist, does not exist.

2) Principle of Sufficient Reason: Whatever exists has a sufficient reason for existing.

3) Principle of Efficient Causality: Whatever begins to exist, requires an efficient cause.

A detailed justification of the unconditional value of these principles is now called for.

1) To many ears, this principle sounds like an empty tautology, and it is not hard to see why. Even when we express it in this existential way rather than in the purely formal logical manner (A is A; non-A is non-A), the expression is so basic that it seems futile to go to the trouble of asserting it. But while it may be regarded as a truism, it is a truism upon which all thought turns. Unless we recognized this principle, we would be able to recognize or assert nothing whatsoever. What the principle asserts is simply that there is a radical difference between existing and not-existing; to be is not the same thing as not-to-be. Being and nothing are distinct, or better put, being is not equivalent to the absence of

being. One who thought himself capable of denying this principle would obviously have surrendered all right to think at all. The principle is readily converted into the Principle of Contradiction: Nothing can both exist and not exist. Once again, the recognition of this truth is involved in the recognition of any truth whatever: the very possibility of asserting is grounded in the realization that to assert and deny are not identical. We cannot both assert and deny the truth of a proposition. But what is asserted or denied is being. The ground, therefore, for the recognition that an assertion and denial of the same proposition is impossible, is the recognition of the impossibility that what is asserted both exist and not exist.[2]

2) This principle is equally indubitable, once its import is clearly understood. What is asserted is not some relatively shapeless confidence, such that "Everything exists for a reason," or "God created everything for a purpose," which piety may fairly accept (and perhaps consequent thought lend credence to) but something much more basic. "Reason" in this principle has nothing to do with "purpose" or "goal" and therefore carries no connotation either of God's providence or the benevolence of "Nature." "Reason" here means "ground" or "account," and what is asserted is just that thought must apprehend a sufficient ground for the fact that something exists. Upon inspection this principle will be found to be as irreducibly intelligible as the first. If there is a difference between being and not-being, then wherever we have being, there must be that which sufficiently accounts for the

---

[2] This principle is often formulated to include a reference to time: "Nothing can both be and not be at the same time and in the same respect." Although this seems just as unexceptionable, it introduces into the pure intelligible clarity of the principle some of the opacity of our knowledge about time itself. In order for the principle so formulated to be directly intelligible, it might be thought to include an assumption of the extremely suspect notion of a "point" or "instant" in serial time, at which simultaneous existing and non-existing are deemed impossible. It was Hegel who directed attention to the limitation of the principle when temporally applied, treating the process of becoming as founded upon a sort of dynamic violation of this principle. There is no need to take up his reservations here, although they are very much to the point in metaphysics.

The Search for the Unconditional

fact that here there is being and not nothing. Anything else would be absurdity. If there were not that which sufficiently distinguished being from nothing, then being would *not* be sufficiently distinguished from nothing (an obvious violation of the insight contained in the principle of identity). But if being *is* different from nothing, then there is that which sufficiently differentiates it. If the absence and the presence of being are not identical, then where we have presence of being rather than the absence of being, there must be a ground or reason for the presence of being rather than its absence. Once again, to say anything else would be to regard existing and non-existing as identical.

Since the principle of sufficient reason amounts to the demand of thought that the order of existence be intelligible, there is a sense in which it might be applied wherever there is an act of existing. Thus, it might even be thought of as applicable to the infinite being, God. Even here we could say that if the infinite being exists, then there must be a sufficient reason why He exists. If He is distinct from nothing, there must be that which sufficiently differentiates Him from nothing. God is said to exist *a se,* of himself; His nature is to exist. This does not exactly mean that in the real order God's essence is the ground of his existence. It means that His existence is not distinct from His essence, and that it is grasped by us as an intelligible terminus in which thought may come to rest. Of course, from our standpoint, we could express this by saying that for our knowledge, we see God's essence as the sufficient reason for His existence; but that only means that if we understand *what* God is, we cannot ask *why* He is. This could be put in more Thomistic terms: since in God essence and existence are identical, He *is* "esse." Then our thought which raises the issue of the sufficient reason for the existence of God recognizes that the nature of God *is* existence. As supremely actual, there is no severance of the ground of His existing from His existing; He exists because He is existence. So that God is grasped by us as His own sufficient reason for existing.

Yet this same statement cannot be made about contingent

beings. We cannot say of man, stone, tree, animal, or any other familiar object that they are their own ground of being. They come into being and they pass out of being; they begin to be. Whatever begins to be obviously does not exist of its own nature. What exists of its own nature exists necessarily; what exists necessarily cannot not-exist. Therefore, what begins to be does not exist necessarily. It is said to be contingent, indifferent to existence, meaning simply that its nature is compatible either with existence or non-existence. John Jones does not exist *because* he is John Jones—for it is not only thinkable but predictable that one day he will not exist (just as one day he did not exist). Therefore existing as John Jones is compatible with the possibility of not-existing. Certain types of being are susceptible of existing or not-existing: then when they *do* exist, the sufficient explanation for their existence cannot be that they are this *kind* of being (or this kind of individual). But the fact remains that there must be some sufficient reason why this being which *could* not-be here and now *is*. It is not its own sufficient reason for existence; nevertheless it requires that which accounts for its standing outside of nothing.[3]

It has become increasingly common among Thomistic writers to disparage the value of the principle of sufficient reason, on the grounds that it is an intrusion of "essentialism" into a metaphysical terrain which should be reserved for a properly "existentialist" thought.[4] The principle, there is no doubt, does not go back in its explicit formulation to St. Thomas, and Thomists who are con-

---

[3] Not only beginning to be and passing away in a complete sense, as the appearance and disappearance of individual unities, but any state of change gives the same reasoning. For no being insofar as it is changing is its own ground of being. Every state of a changing being is contingent: it was not a moment ago and will not be a moment from now. Therefore the grasping of a being as changing is the grasping of it as not intelligible in itself—as essentially *referred* to something other than itself.

[4] See, for instance, Joseph Owens, C.Ss.R., *An Elementary Christian Metaphysics* (Milwaukee: Bruce), 1962, f.n. pp. 76–77. A history of this principle as well as a criticism of its rationalist character is contained in John E. Gurr, S.J., *The Principle of Sufficient Reason in Some Scholastic Systems, 1750–1900* (Milwaukee: The Marquette University Press), 1959.

The Search for the Unconditional

cerned to uphold the primacy of the act of existing in metaphysics do not take kindly to a principle which derives at least verbally from the rationalist tradition of Leibniz and Christian Wolff. Those who make use of it seem to them to be asking that the existence of an entity be either "implied" or "not implied" by its essence; but this procedure confers a certain priority on essence. It is held to suggest that the ultimate principle of intelligibility is essence and thus falls afoul of the anathema passed in Thomistic circles on this viewpoint.

The cogency of this objection, however, is not easy to credit. For the principle of sufficient reason which is here in question is not the principle of Leibniz, which admittedly was put to highly suspect use. It is a thoroughly existential principle. What it amounts to is simply the application of the demand for intelligibility to the order of existence itself. This does not mean that existence must justify itself by an appeal to the order of essence. On the contrary, it means that it must justify itself *as* existence. An existent which did not leave room for the distinction between what and that to be made would so justify itself; an existent which does leave room for this distinction does not so justify itself. As existent it points beyond itself. Someone might like to question the right to make the essence-existence distinction, but one who concedes the right cannot easily question the principle of sufficient reason. Furthermore, the very fact of an existent which *begins* to be is evidence of the fact that in this case the affirmation that "this exists" cannot be an intelligible termination. For in thinking such a beginning-to-be, I am thinking an existence which contains *as* existence a reference to a *not,* and therefore a reference beyond itself. An existence which begins-to-be is not a self-terminating intelligible in the order of existence. To contend otherwise would be to contend that negation as such is intelligible.

3) This consideration leads directly to the principle of causality, which could be looked upon as the explicitation of the principle of sufficient reason in the area of contingent being. This third principle states that every contingent being requires an *extrinsic* suf-

ficient reason for its existence. Since it is not its own sufficient reason, and since, nevertheless, there must be one (or negation as such would be an intelligible terminus) then it refers itself to another as to the ground of its own existence. Then an "efficient cause," within the purview of this principle, is simply an extrinsic sufficient reason for the coming-to-be of something (or of any feature or state of a thing). This exact meaning must be kept in mind, for "cause," as will be seen, is sometimes taken to mean something quite different. Ultimately, what the metaphysical principle of causality amounts to is that the order of becoming and existence must be *intelligible*; that no phase of the process of contingent existence is intelligible in itself; and that therefore contingent existence is always *relative* existence, essentially referred, *qua* existing to another.[5]

THE PRIORITY OF THE FIRST PRINCIPLES

In view of what has been said, it should be clear why the traditional way of speaking about "first principles" is well founded.

a) They are called "principles" in keeping with the philosophical conception of a principle as "that from which something else flows or derives." What derives from these principles is thought itself. They are the sources from which the possibility of every specific thought arises.[6]

b) For that reason it is only a matter of nomenclature whether they be called first principles or "last" principles. They are the beginning of thought, the source (*principium*) from which thought arises; but they are also ultimate, in the sense that every particular assertion can be reduced to them as resting its ultimate intelligi-

---

[5] Note that the principle does not state that "every effect requires a cause," which would be an empty tautology (since we do not know what an effect is except by already conceiving it in relation to cause) but that "every event requires a cause," or "every process of coming-to-be requires a ground in another."

[6] They may be called first principles of thought for that reason, but they are also first principles in *respect* to being, since they hold good of being.

bility upon them. There is no claim that they are "first" in a chronological sense, as if the first judgment a child made were that "Nothing can both be and not be"; the point is only that the intelligibility of these principles is present in every judgment, including the one which is chronologically first.

c) They are often called self-evident, in the sense that they neither can be nor need to be justified in terms of further evidence. With these principles, thought reaches an ultimate ground, and it would be nonsensical to speak of justifying these principles in terms of sense perception, induction, or anything else. This "self-evidence" need not mean that these principles arise in abstraction from experience, but only that they are the ultimate light in terms of which experience is apprehended by thought. They are, of course, not self-evident as purely verbal utterances but as immediate transpositions of the direct encounter with being. There is no way to "prove" or "demonstrate" them, for every demonstration would presuppose them. Normally, demonstration consists in educing reasons for belief in a proposition which is relatively less known than the evidence which is brought forward to demonstrate it. But if this were attempted in the case of the first principles, the absurdity would soon appear. For the recognition of the principle of identity, e.g., would be involved in recognizing the cognitive value of any premise offered to "prove" it. Any premises offered to demonstrate the first principles would already implicitly contain them.

That is why it is sometimes said that these principles are "virtually innate." They are virtually there prior to any judgment whatsoever, including the first formed by an individual mind. This naturally does not mean that we are born with the words "Nothing can both be and not be" inscribed on our souls. But the point is that we are born with minds, and that part of the very structure of the mind is the power (*virtus*) of recognizing the truth of the first principles. Mind would not be mind without this native endowment.

Suppose someone suggested that these principles could be

formed by induction. That is, by realizing that "A cannot both be and not be," "B cannot both be and not be, "C cannot both be and not be," . . . I finally conclude to the generalization that "Nothing can both be and not be." Here we must distinguish: no doubt the *explicit* principle of contradiction, as a *universal* formula, is derived by a quasi-induction from experience in this way. There surely must be many people who live and die without making this explicit reflection and hence without knowing the universal principle. St. Thomas's insistence that we know even the first principles from experience must be interpreted in this way: the explicit assurance of these first principles is won from experience itself. Yes, but on the other hand I could not even make the individual judgments from which I induce the universal principles unless I already implicitly recognized the truth of these principles. What appears to be true is that I recognize, implicitly, in individual cases, the truth of these principles; if I did not, I could not even make the individual judgments. I would always have to be worrying that the individual judgment could simultaneously be true and false. Thus, in any individual assertion (the child's "This is my mother," "This dog bites," etc.), there is already operative the principle of contradiction in which it is recognized that asserting and denying are not equivalent.

It is also entirely plausible that the intelligibility even of these first principles cannot be justified simply as a universal, as perhaps a rationalist might contend; perhaps, I cannot claim that they are indisputably evident, without implicitly referring them back to the experience from which they were originally drawn. In this manner some seek to vindicate the indispensable role of sense perception in our knowledge.[7] The vindication has point if the claim simply is that we discover even absolute intelligibility through direct experi-

---

[7] Peter Hoenen, S.J., *Reality and Judgment According to St. Thomas*, trans. by Henry Tiblier, S.J. (Chicago: Regnery), 1952, makes a great point of insisting on the fact that the first principles are rooted in *sense* experience. Now, that these principles, as any principles, arise out of our existential encounter with reality (and not vice versa), there is no need to contest; but as Hoenen himself admits, the *intelligibility* of the principles derives from the light of the mind itself (p. 20). On this basis, it is hard

ential contact with being, but it leaves intact the non-sensory source of their intelligibility. To say, therefore, that the first principles are already there in sense perception is to speak in a rather misleading manner, for the light according to which they are grasped is not derivative from sense but an original work of thought. In respect to this, as well as in many other ways, the hoary formula that "Nothing is in the intellect which was not first in the senses," is either completely misleading or must be amended in such a way as to cast serious doubt on its usefulness.

One or two further clarifications are in order. When it is said that these principles are "first," it should not be thought that they are assumed simply as "postulates" or "rules of the game" of thought. A postulate is neither true nor false—it is assumed for the sake of lending consistency to what follows. A postulate always has the character of an hypothesis and it derives its strength solely from the body of consequent propositions which it makes possible; no matter how consistently articulated these propositions become, the postulate itself always has a lingering air of the tentative and the arbitrary about it. But the first principles are not assumed for the sake of argument; they are *known*. They are not simply positions which thought occupies when it has reached a certain stage of evolution; nor are they expressions of some kind of "faith" in reason. If they were regarded as useful results of an evolutionary process, in the manner that the pragmatists regard them (just as a man's hand is a useful result of that process), their value would be strictly factual, for a further development of the evolutionary process might generate a thought in which the first principles would no longer be true.[8] Even to think this eventuality as possible, however, we would have to employ the principle of contradiction in asserting its possibility. And more than this: in order

---

to see how much is at stake in tying them to sense. No doubt Hoenen is on a firm basis, too, in declaring that we cannot justify the first principles by *beginning* with their universal character (198); but it is not contended that they are primary *as* universal.

[8] For an explanation of and rebuttal to this, see Daniel Robinson, *The Principles of Reasoning* (New York: Appleton-Century-Crofts), 1947, pp. 367–368.

for what we are asserting to have meaning it must be possible for us to conceive already a thought for which the first principles would not be true. But such a thought is inconceivable, and therefore the assertion of its possibility is meaningless. The first principles, then, are absolute in a rigorous sense; they are absolute as *cognitive,* and not merely factual. The attempt to deny them would reaffirm them. No doubt this indubitability is still subject to the existential structure of our human condition, but this does not make them objects of "faith." They are cognitional absolutes apprehended by a being which is not an existential absolute; this apprehension may always necessitate an effort to close the gap between existence and intelligibility, but this is not "faith" in any useful sense of the term.

CAUSALITY AND DETERMINISM

Perhaps the most important philosophical requirement with respect to the principle of causality is that it be distinguished from the similarly denominated "law of causality" as this is often conceived by both common-sense wisdom and science. The scientific law of causality can be variously formulated. "Every event is necessarily connected with some antecedent event, given which it must occur"; or, "Every occurrence is the consequence of some antecedent without which it could not have occurred and given which it had to occur."[9] Sometimes this is conceived rather narrowly: the event of the breaking of the window is connected with the antecedent motion of the rock through the air (which is connected with the antecedent motion of the hand, and so on). Sometimes the conception becomes more sophisticated and it is assumed that the only *adequate* causal explanation of any given event is not some localized occurrence but the entire antecedent course of the universe. In either case, it is clear that the scientific law of causality is equivalent to the principle of determinism. For

[9] See Robinson, *ibid.,* p. 253. For a positivist's statement and criticism of this principle, see Philipp Frank, *Modern Science and its Philosophy* (Cambridge: Harvard University Press), 1949, p. 54 ss.

it holds that given the antecedents, the results will *necessarily* follow. In its ideal expression, it assumes the grandiose proportions of Laplace's declaration that, given the position and motion of every elementary particle in the universe at *any* moment of time, and given a mind sufficient to comprehend this, then the entire course of future history could be predicted for *every* moment of time.

Now this scientific principle carries built-in epistemological puzzles of its own[10] but the present intention is only to distinguish it from the philosophical principle of causality with which it could be confused. The philosophical principle merely insists that given any contingent entity or event there must be some extrinsic sufficient reason for its existence. It by no means says that this cause has to be a member of a temporally antecedent series, nor that it has to act *necessarily*. The notion of a "free cause" is not a philosophical contradiction, although it is a contradiction scientifically. A scientific "cause" is equivalent to a necessary antecedent, and therefore a free (non-necessary) cause would be a patent contradiction. This must be kept in mind, or the news that many contemporary scientists, under the influence of the Heisenberg principle of indeterminacy, repudiate the notion of causality would be startling indeed.[11]

THE CRITIQUE OF HUME AND KANT

The foregoing stipulation is also useful in considering David Hume's famous arguments against the validity of causality.[12] What Hume was primarily combatting was really the common-sense

[10] Especially when it is put in the form that *similar* consequents follow from *similar* antecedents, for here there is the question of whether an *exactly* similar antecedent ever occurs in nature.

[11] According to the principle of indeterminacy it is intrinsically impossible to assert that an electron has, simultaneously, a definite position and velocity; if this is accepted, strict deterministic causality cannot be held at the sub-atomic level, since the conditions upon which it rests are not fulfilled.

[12] *Hume Selections,* edit. by Charles W. Hendel, Jr. (New York: Scribner's), 1927, pp. 22–39. (From *A Treatise of Human Nature.*)

notion of a cause, according to which event A "makes" event B happen; for example, for common sense to say that the moving stone "caused" the window to break means two things: 1) there was a power in A (moving stone) which made B (breaking window) happen, 2) this connection was a necessary one, such that given a similarly moving stone, and a similarly constructed window, a similar breaking would occur. Now Hume, in keeping with his sensory epistemology, first asks where we get the notion of this "power." It is not drawn from observation and cannot be verified through observation. What we observe is the sequence of events, the moving stone and the breaking window (or the approaching fire and the feeling of heat); we do not *observe* some occult "power" which acts between one and the other. As for the "necessity" of this event, we surely do not observe this either. We observe the sequence, but not its necessity. Where, then, do we get the notion of necessity? We get it from the habit we develop of *expecting* event B to occur whenever event A occurs. We have observed such sequences many times before, and in each case event B follows event A—they are constantly conjoined. Because of this, whenever we witness event A, our mind automatically anticipates event B; we can't *help* anticipating it. This, however, is a psychological necessity in us, not an objective necessity in things. We project this psychologically inevitable expectation into the objective sequence and treat it as an inevitable connection in events. While understandable, this projection cannot be logically validated. For the two events are physically distinct, and there is nothing inconceivable about the consequent being different from what it normally is. What is there to prove, then, that the concept of cause has objective validity and is not simply a subjective category?

Immanuel Kant's answer to this reasoning is one of the most influential in the history of philosophy and actually forms the foundation for his own thought;[13] in following it, we must not lose

[13] *Kant Selections,* edit. by T. M. Greene (New York: Scribner's), 1929, pp. 122–130, 145–155. (Selections from *The Critique of Pure Reason.*)

The Search for the Unconditional

sight of the fact that Kant is attempting to defend the concept of causality which *Hume* attacked (and that this is still not to be confused wih the philosophical concept as defined above). What Kant attempted to do, in brief, is the following: He tried to show that the concept of cause *must* be applicable to objective reality, for it is only because of the applicability of such concepts as "cause" that we can even distinguish between objective and subjective reality. Hume, in asking whether this concept is really only "subjective" has distinguished himself as a subject from *objects*; if he could not do this without using the concept of cause, then obviously he cannot then turn around and question the validity of this concept.

Now, Kant holds that experience arises with the raw material of sensations. But the senses alone do not give us "objects." For this, the raw material of sensations must be molded by the formal categories of the understanding, of which Kant numbered twelve. Among these formal categories, "cause" is especially important. All our sensations are given as in temporal sequence; all our sensations are flowing. But what we notice is that some of our sensations flow in necessary order and that the sequences in which we experience them cannot be arbitrarily ordered: the ship flowing down the river cannot be experienced in any succession whatever, but must be experienced in a regular and orderly way.[14] The steps in this experience are uniformly connected. It is only because they are that I experience this as a ship flowing down a river and not a dream ship. Those of my sensations which are whimsical and disorderly do not form part of any necessary sequences; I consign them to the purely subjective status of illusion or dream. But it is only on the basis of the distinction between the lawful and the arbitrary that I distinguish between the objective and subjective. The objective realm is the realm of orderly phenomena.

Furthermore, I only become conscious of myself as a subject by separating myself out as a spectator of this orderly realm. A completely chaotic experience would give no ground at all for

---

[14] *Ibid.*, p. 124.

distinguishing between subject and object; in a completely chaotic experience, I could not even say "I" for there would be no ground to distinguish the "I" from anything else. Contrariwise, experience of objects just *is* the experience of the necessarily connected and orderly. Therefore, if one of the categories according to which my experience of orderly sequence is possible is the category of cause (necessary connection of events), then this category must necessarily apply to objects: it is the *condition* for the experience of objects.

Note what this reasoning of Kant's does, to his own satisfaction at least: it completely vindicates the validity of "cause" with respect to phenomena, but it also restricts the application of this category to phenomena. "Cause" for Kant means the lawful connection between phenomenal sequences; then if I am to have orderly phenomenal experience the category of cause must be valid—of that experience. But this is a very far cry from showing its validity in respect to what is beyond phenomenal experience. Its validity consists in being a condition for phenomena. Then to ask whether it applies apart from phenomena is to ask something absurd. Therefore, we cannot try to make noumenal use of this concept of cause—to prove by its means, for example, the existence of God or the free causation of will. To do so, would be to seek to extend beyond experience a notion whose entire meaning consists in being a tissue by which experience is bound together. Kant therefore denies all metaphysical value to the principle of causality.

What Kant holds, in effect, is that I only have genuine *knowledge* in respect to what is an "object," and that the complete meaning of object is a synthesis of sense intuition and formal concept. I "know" what I can integrally lay hold of. But the categories alone do not give me anything to lay hold of: they do not have any content. They are only pure forms or rules according to which things can be laid hold of. They demand completion through intuitive content and can only be filled in from the side of sense intuition. Then when I try to use these categories beyond sense experience, my thought is empty—I think nothing, I only "make as if" to think something.

The Search for the Unconditional

An evaluation of this position must attend to the exact meaning of the philosophical principle of causality. Kant does not really refute this principle because he does not really engage it. We may begin by allowing Hume's statements their proper desserts. It is true that we do not perceive causes; we only perceive sequences. The notion of cause is formed as a result of the demand which the mind makes upon experience; it demands that succession as such be intelligible, since, as mind, it is the insight that all being is intelligible. The philosophical principle of causality is simply this demand applied to temporal events, which results in the realization that becoming as such is essentially relative. It is only one who, like Hume, was prepared to deny the right of mind to make any demands upon reality and to reduce all experience to passive sense perceptions, who would be prepared to accept non-perceptibility as non-validity.

We must also distinguish the general philosophical principle from the realization of *what* is the cause of any specific contingent event. Hume would be on fairly secure grounds if he were merely pointing out the difference between our realization that every event has a cause and our decision as to what this cause was—whether an immediately prior temporal event or not. This is by no means as metaphysically certain. We can hardly claim to be able to identify the specific cause of an event with the same absolute certainty that we can assert that it must have such a cause. Finally, it goes without saying that any statement about the necessity with which that cause operates is completely outside the province of the principle of causality itself. Therefore, neither the reasoning of Hume nor Kant is conclusive against the philosophical question of causality. Hume's posture, in particular, is patently clumsy. His whole effort can be construed as a search for the *causes* of our belief in respect to the notion of cause—giving clear enough indication that he thinks there must be causes for it and thus sapping the life out of his own conclusions.

Kant is on somewhat more plausible ground when he contends that the categories alone do not give us an "object" or "thing" and hence that their metaphysical use does not provide knowledge in the same sense as phenomenal knowledge. This seems at least psychologically valid, although it does not justify the repudiation of metaphysics to which he went on. Even if we can use the category of cause metaphysically to prove a "first cause" of phenomenal being, we do not reach this way an "object" in a fully satisfactory sense. God is surely not an object for our knowing in the *same* sense as phenomenal objects. In one way He is much more intelligible, in another much less—but in any case He is not intelligible in the same way. Then, metaphysical knowledge is significantly different from phenomenal knowledge. So much may be conceded without surrendering the cognitional value of the first principles.

The answer to all philosophical doubt as to the validity of the first principles must invoke the absolute nature of the idea of being upon which they are based. With this idea, the distinction between appearance and reality is surpassed. So, likewise, is Kant's distinction between the noumenal and phenomenal. Whatever else the noumenal reality-in-itself may be, it must be such that the idea of being applies to it—and whatever intelligibility is based upon the idea of being. Far from deriving its meaning from the side of the phenomenal, the category of cause is an extension into the phenomenal of a trans-phenomenal category. It may well be that as this category is commonly employed it is hampered by intrusions from the imagination and that its metaphysical use is considerably vitiated;[15] to this extent the distaste of many contemporary philosophers for it has not a little justification.

The remedy for this, however, would seem to be its purification rather than its repudiation. The justification of the category of cause is the same as that of all metaphysical notions: the level of insight sufficient to *question* them is a level at which they are necessarily valid. We could not pose the question of the validity of the first principles unless we inhabited the absolute center of thought

---

[15] For one thing, the quasi-spatial externalization *vis à vis* one another of cause and effect, or again the tendency to picture the activity of non-phenomenal causality by strict parallelism with phenomenal activity, arriving at a kind of "ghostly mechanics."

The Search for the Unconditional

and called all reality into question. But we only inhabit that center by virtue of the idea of "being," and it is just the idea of being which necessarily implies the validity of the first principles. No attempt of scepticism or relativism will succeed in reducing these to a provisionary status, for they are the grounds for the asking and answering of all possible questions.

EVIDENCE, CERTITUDE, AND DOUBT

A few words on the question of evidence are in order at this point, since the analysis has been based upon the conception of an "absolute evidence" being contained in the notion of being. Certitude may be defined as "warranted assent"—an assent of thought warranted by adequate evidence. It was found that the certitude of the first principles was absolute because it was warranted by a datum present in such a way that the appearance/reality distinction was surpassed. Not all evidence is of this kind, that much is clear; and so, not all evidence can underwrite an absolute conviction. Still, wherever there is any certitude at all present, it will be seen to be directed towards a certain kind of evidence. This notion of "evidence" is hard to pin down, although recourse to it, patent or disguised, cannot be avoided. We may take it to mean "the way reality is present" or the "manifestation of being to thought."

It is easier to give examples of its role than to define it; and it is easier to make it conspicuous in its absence than its presence. If someone makes the statement "there are exactly 301, 614 fish in the Hudson River," what would be our intellectual response to this statement?[16] Surely, we would not merely nod and say "Interesting fact." We would be much more likely to lift an eyebrow at the temerity of the person who made such a remark. By no means could our reaction be described as one of "certitude." The possibility could not be ruled out, of course, that by some wild stroke the speaker had named the right figure, but it is so unlikely that we

---

[16] See Hassett, Mitchell, and Monan, *op. cit.*, p. 82.

find no difficulty at all in withholding our assent. Why is this? It is because the evidence sufficient to warrant the assent is clearly missing. Reality is not present to my thought in such a way that I can feel secure in an assent to this proposition. Whereas, if someone were to say of the room in which I sat, "There are exactly three windows in this room," my agreement or disagreement would soon be forthcoming. And this for the simple reason that the evidence to warrant the assent is easily available.

So with any possible type of judgment. The evidence may vary. The kind of evidence needed to warrant one assent might not be sufficient to warrant another, but every time I judge, I orient my thought in the direction of the way in which reality is present. I experience my thought as this attempt to take my bearings on the presence of being. This is the foundation for the frequently repeated declaration that being has dominance over thought. My thought experiences itself as essentially submissive, as an attempt to bow down to evidence. I do not decree what is, I discover it. My thought is, then, a pursuit, an openness to the real and not a pure spontaneity. Being imposes itself upon me and "coerces" my thought. There is clear justification for this way of speaking, although it raises some real difficulties, as we shall see later.

For the present, attention will be directed to the notion of the *range* of evidence. If evidence is "the way being is present to me," it clearly may vary greatly, and the sort of assent warranted by this varying presence will also vary greatly. Shall we reserve the name certitude for those assents which are absolutely warranted and regard every other assent as simply highly probable? This, in effect, is what Descartes proposed doing, and it is the inclination of anyone of a rationalist temper. Either, the feeling is, something is absolutely certain or it is not "certain" at all. This view has obvious merits, and yet there is a lot to be said for the familiar view which classifies certitude into various "types." Considered as "warranted assents," there seem to be various positions of the mind which are not unconditional and yet which are not satisfactorily lumped together as mere "high degrees of probability."

For one, there is some reason to speak of "physical certitude," which is an assent based upon the evidence of the habitual behavior of physical bodies, often formulated into the so-called "laws" of nature. Thus, what of the attitude of the outfielder who is waiting under the fly-ball, poised to catch it? It does not seem sufficient to describe the cognitional side of his readiness as an opinion that it is highly probable that the ball will descend. He is certain of it. Yet the evidence which warrants his certitude is not such that the opposite occurrence is unthinkable. For the evidence (the normal course of nature) contains a proviso not usually adverted to. As the positivist might state it, the proviso is: *if* the future resembles the past, this ball will descend; as it might occur to a believer: *if* God concurs and lets the natural ends of physical beings be achieved, then this ball will descend (but of course, miracles are possible). On either view the opposite is *conceivable,* and therefore physical certitude differs in kind from metaphysical certitude, where the opposite is strictly unthinkable. Thus the "laws' of nature, such as gravity, chemical combinations, or thermodynamics (even if they are interpreted in a completely coercive way and not merely as conventional generalizations, as is now the fashion), always retain a less-than-absolute character. There is always a certain distance between the nature or essence of things and their activities. While assent based upon this sort of evidence may be denominated "certitude," it is certitude against the background of a condition.

If we were to carry matters further and inquire into the force of such "moral certitudes" as my assurance that "The bus driver will not deliberately crash this bus," or the child's trust that "My mother has not poisoned my oatmeal," further hesitation might arise.[17] In some respects, we might wonder whether we should talk of certitude here at all. It is true that, from the point of view of lived conviction, these assents are not subject to active doubt. It is not a working question for me as I board the bus whether or

[17] Note that "moral" in moral certitude does not refer to the goodness or the badness of the act of the agent, but only to the fact that he is a rational agent, a responsible person, hence a "moral agent."

not the driver intends to crash it; it does not even occur to me as a conscious possibility to have an opinion about. Yet the motive for this kind of un-thinking confidence is simply the normal behavior of persons, and persons are free agents, and free agents are capable of deviating from norms. Even so, if I met someone as I came into class, who told me that he had seen an accident outside the building, and described it in shocked detail, my first reaction would not be one of suspicion ("Watch out for this fellow, he may be trying to put one over on me"). This way lies paranoia. My reaction would rather be one of belief. Warranted belief, we might say, for we are relying (without even noticing it) on the general principle that "People do not lie without reason." Still, this does not obliterate the implicit condition in such certitude: if this being behaves as a rational being normally does, I may rely on him. There are, however, pathological liars, and a trust in testimony must be duly circumspect.

An interesting situation arises in this area. We might be prone, at first, to regard "moral certitude" as a rather weak variety, and often rightly so. But there are special cases. One source of moral certitude is testimony, as has been seen. Normally this kind of certitude is rather diluted. Suppose, though, we were to ask ourselves what is our mental attitude as we express to ourselves such propositions as "There is in France a city called Paris," or "There once lived a man called Julius Caeser." How certain are we of the truth of such propositions?[18] As certain, it would seem, as we are of any possible propositions. Any proviso or condition has dwindled to the vanishing point. Most people would say that they are more certain of the truth of these propositions than they are, say, of the law of gravity. And yet this sort of truth is based exclusively on testimony (for one who has not been to Paris or been a contemporary of Julius Caesar). It is interesting that what seems like a poor sort of certitude can reach a conviction that

---

[18] On this, see John Henry Cardinal Newman, *An Essay in Aid of a Grammar of Assent* (London and New York: Longmans, Green, and Co.), 1903, p. 189ss. (Chapter VI, Section 2.)

The Search for the Unconditional

might as well be called unconditional. What is the explanation for this? It seems that the convergence of testimony in respect to these truths is so great and so unanimous they are practically subsumed into the principle of sufficient reason itself. The only sufficient reason for the existence of this convergent testimony seems to be the reality of what is testified to. Incidentally, this example also highlights the independently evidential character of convergence, which can confer cumulative strength on individual sources of evidence which, taken piecemeal, are not conclusive.

Allowing the title of "certitude" to all these situations, we still would hardly have touched the surface of the great bulk of cognitive responses given by man. For it is an unmistakable, if lamentable, fact that man for the most part is deprived of anything that can be dignified by the name "certitude" at all. Numerically speaking, the quantity of our judgments which we ourselves would care to go on record as classifying as certain is rather small; and the judgments of ours which others would admit as certain is, alas, even smaller.

Our life is passed under conditions which make impossible the kind of sifting of evidence that would allow us to certify many judgments as "certain." If we made the attempt in practice to withhold our assent and our action except on grounds adequately evaluated as "certain," we would be largely paralyzed. Most of our lives are spent in acting, and acting does not require and most often does not allow hidebound certitude. It can be satisfied with probability. What we most frequently act upon is *opinion*: a cognitive response to evidence not grasped as coercive but seen as sufficient to warrant action.

Action, so to speak, "fills in" what is missing in the evidential character of our convictions. The social, political, cultural, and interpersonal arenas are pre-eminently the scene of opinion, not certitude. It is of limited use asking whether this should be, since in the human condition it must be. The speculative and practical lesson to be learned by the epistemologist is simply the awareness of the difference between certitude and opinion. It is a fairly accurate definition of the fanatic to say that he is one who is certain about everything: he maintains his opinions as if they were certitudes and he treats differences from himself or from his "truths" (his "fixed ideas") as proof of the bad faith of others. In a democracy, especially, it is the first political virtue to acknowledge the ambiguous character of political truth and to commit oneself to a *positive* tolerance of the opinion of others.

Even opinion is sometimes forbidden territory, since there are innumerable questions in which our inability to render an opinion is complete. For example, in a modern complex society, issues of economy and finance can become so abstruse that the only proper cognitional response is *doubt*: a suspension of judgment. No obligation is laid upon us to pass a verdict on everything. This is a point which public opinion polls frequently ignore, assuming in their professional inquisitiveness that everybody has a right to an opinion about everything. Only evidence warrants a cognitive response, of either certitude or opinion. Lack of evidence (or largely inconclusive evidence) warrants only doubt. While this is, in one sense, a shortcoming of thought, the recognition of it is not a shortcoming, but something extremely salutary, perhaps even the indispensable prerequisite for genuine truth and authentic political virtue.

7 CONCEPTUAL KNOWLEDGE

UNIVERSALS

The first epistemological problem that some would like to raise in respect to concepts is simply whether they exist or not. It is a fairly spontaneous inclination on the part of the common-sense mind to abjure the reality of such "invisibles." If seeing (or sensing) is believing, then not seeing (or not sensing) is not believing; such is the initial state of mind, and such often remains the final state of mind. When this state of mind is raised to the level of a philosophical position, it is known as "pure sense empiricism," which is the contention that the only elements present to experience are particular sensory data and that "concepts" or "universals" either do not exist or are empty.

Those who speak of "concepts" or "universal ideas" do so in the opposite conviction that besides the momentary and individual data which are present for the senses at any moment of our experience, there are also present aspects of reality which are just as strictly "data" (that is, "givens," irreducible and indisputable presences), which are not equatable with sense data but which are unmistakably there.

Thus, when I am sitting at my desk, looking about the room and out the window, it is no doubt true that present to my consciousness are a whole stream of particularized sensory details: the particular shade of mahogany reflected in the particular light which is slanting through the window, the smoothness of the desk top, the uniquely shaped ink-blotches on the blotter, the delicious odor of the trees wet by the rain, the slightly distracting tapping of the window-blind moved by the cool breeze. All these data are present to my senses in a perfectly particularized way: it is always *this* color, *this* warmth, *this* smoothness, *this* shape, *this* motion which I perceive at any and every moment. These details are present to me before all naming and before any more complex act on my part; they could just as well be present, in their sense immediacy, and they are present, to a purely sensory knower such as a young infant or an animal. There is, then, a complex of transitory particulars perpetually present to my sensory organs.

But besides this, there is present to me the awareness of the fact that that upon which I lean is a "table," the shade is known as "shade," the "mahogany color" known and named as such, the cool breeze mentally hailed as "cool breeze." In brief, I have *names* for what my senses experience. My senses may not name them but I do. I name things "red," "white," "blue," "flag," "difficult," "easy," "sweet," "large," "pleasant," "painful," etc. My sensory experience is pre-nominal; as a child I experienced many or all of these things in a purely sensory manner without naming them. In naming them I am pointing to what the senses cannot point to but what is in a real sense "there"—because it can be (mentally) pointed to.

Every time I name something this name or word expresses a meaning which I grasp as being fulfilled in that which I experience. In naming this "table," I grasp it as fulfilling or manifesting a certain meaning which is just as much there for my thought as its color is there for my sense of sight; in calling the datum which is there for my sense of sight "color" or "red," or "mahogany," I am not simply perceiving this visual particular, I am aware of a generalized meaning present through the particular.

To name what I perceive is to do more than perceive. This grasping or conceiving in a con-cept (*con-ceptum*) grasps *something*; it doesn't grasp nothing. To use a fairly neutral term, we may call what it grasps a meaning. This is what Socrates and Plato originally meant by an "eidos": the meaning manifested in

Conceptual Knowledge

and through a particular sensory instance. We do not have to follow them into the metaphysical superstructure which they erected on the basis of this simple recognition; what is important epistemologically is to realize what is meant by saying that this meaning is really "there," that it is in a true sense a datum.

Man, after all, does not create meanings "ex nihilo." In understanding, he still turns to what is already there. When he names things, he seeks to capture in speech aspects of reality which are there before speech. Speech lives off experienced reality: it is essentially referential. This means that thought *discovers,* and does not create or invent what is real. This is essentially what Plato's doctrine on the "eidos" amounts to: just as the eye does not create colors, but finds them, so the mind does not create meaning, but discovers it. Then, whatever characterizes our concepts, our graspings of reality, must be in some sense real: for our concept just *is* this seizure of the real, and it would be contradictory to have a seizure of the real which did not seize it. Therefore, the meaning-value which is apprehended through the concept is actually present in that which is apprehended. In naming and knowing this as "red," "blue," "water," "table," "mountain," "air," "tree," I am aware of what-is.

Now the interesting thing is that the meaning apprehended is a meaning which is apprehended as transcending the sensory instances in which it is found. In knowing this thing present to the senses in its particularized immediacy as a "tree," I grasp a meaning which is not limited to this particularized immediacy. This meaning which I find here I could find elsewhere; I call other things "trees." Therefore, the *meaning* which I discover in the sensory particular transcends the sensory particular. It is realizable in other sensory particulars. "Red" refers not only to this particular color-item now impinging on my vision, but to myriad other possible color-items which could so impinge. As I look out the window, I observe the manifold leaves on the tree, and I see that they are all "green"; then this meaning "green" which I find in the manifold particular instances is not restricted to any of these instances. There is something really and objectively similar in all these leaves, and that is the meaning "green" which they manifest.

We are now in possession of a twofold insight: the meaning apprehended in the concept is objectively real, and yet it is real in a way which transcends sensory particulars. It is not itself real as a sense particular is real. For this reason it is called a "universal." This simply signifies that the meaning grasped through the concept is not a sense-particular: it is a one-in-many, a unitary meaning capable of being multiplied in many instances. As multiplied (that is, in so far as there exist instances of this meaning) it is found in each instance: each leaf really manifests the meaning "green."

At this point, the spontaneous "materialism" which afflicts us all may rebel. We protest that we cannot discover this "universal eidos" of red, or the "universal meaning" tree anywhere; all we ever seem to discover are the particular instances. The so-called concept seems to be simply a notion which we build up in our thought, but which has no application to extra-mental reality; the latter seems to be composed entirely of particulars. Some have disclaimed the very existence of "universal concepts"; others, while admitting that they exist for thought deny that there is really any universal aspect in *things*. Now while there is no denying that a certain incredulity on this score seems to be both natural and healthy, there is also no denying that if anything can be quite cogently shown in philosophy, it is the existence, nature, and objective reference of universal ideas. Many Thomistic philosophers are of the opinion that Thomism is fundamentally based on the value of abstract ideas; if so, it is based on a rather firm foundation. But let it be noted that the stress on the value of concepts is not a peculiar possession of any one philosophical system. The insight originates with Socrates and Plato, is adopted and adapted by Aristotle, and passes over into the mainsteam of the *philosophia perennis*. What divides adherents of this doctrine is often not epistemological at all, but the metaphysical or psychological aspects of the doctrine. It would seem that the epistemological issue comes down to this: are our universal ideas one way of making contact with the non-self? Or conversely, is a genuine feature of reality revealed to us through concepts? Stress will be put in the following discussion on this way of asking the question, and differences between Aristotelianism, Platonism, and other systems minimized.

NOMINALISM

One way of cavilling at the objectivity of ideas may be given short shrift, the claim that they do not even exist. In spite of the fact that some splendid minds have talked as if they held this belief, nothing is easier than to show its falsity. For what is given beyond peradventure of doubt is the fact that we use language, and that we use it in a certain way. We *name* things. And names do not name particulars. Our names "desk," "man," "triangle," "door," "building," "tree," are called in grammar "common nouns," meaning that they are applicable to whole classes of things. But of course the word is not itself the idea or concept; it is the utterance of an inward mental act of conceiving, but is not identical with that act. This is easily shown by the fact that many different words (as mere vocables) could express the same meaning: what I now express by the word "dog" could just as well be expressed by the word "glip" which is right now meaningless. We have only to consider that the meaning which in English is expressed by the word "man" is as a matter of fact expressed by quite different words: in French by "homme," in German by "das Mann," in Latin by "vir," in Italian by "uomo," in Greek by "anthropos" and so forth. Here the *sounds* vary, but the idea remains the same, proving a distinction between the two. We reach the realization, then, that ideas exist, and that they are not identical with words.

We may add that the *nature* of an idea is revealed in the way in which it is used. If they are used as signifiers of a common quality found in many subjects, they can be called "common" or "universal." For the time being, it is not even necessary to go very far into the nature of ideas. We need only the recognition that ideas exist, and that they function in a certain way (as signifying a quality which can be found in many). This alone is sufficient to substantiate the claim that we actually do conceive universal meaning: we do use ideas, and the way we use them demonstrates their universal character.

An ingenious way to bring out the impossibility of carrying out a denial of the role of ideas is simply to make the attempt to eliminate them and conceive of experience without reference to them. This is what Plato did in his dialog *Theaetetus,* and the results are shattering to the pure sense empiricist. If we take the latter with complete seriousness and consistency, the self-defeating character of his belief becomes graphically evident.

Let us suppose that there exists in human consciousness *nothing* besides sensory experience—no ideas, no universal aspects, nothing that is not present in the way a datum is present for the senses. What is left of experience? This amounts to asking what *is* experience for the senses as such (eliminating all the elements which as a matter of fact are contributed by the concepts which the empiricist also wants to reduce to sense data). What the senses experience is just a complex of diverse and transitory particulars; every sense datum precisely as sensed is unique in time, space, and quality. The senser as such is immersed in this stream of immediacy.

Perhaps we might be able to think of him as gleaning a certain order out of this sequence through habit and association, as animals do. But one thing he would not be able to do: he would not be able to *speak* about his experience, for speaking entails a certain transcending of the stream of immediate particulars. It entails first the deliberate "distancing" of one's own experience in order to communicate it; and secondly, as we have seen, it entails the use of language to do this objectifying. Words, by isolating the common elements of our sensorily fleeting experience, render

Conceptual Knowledge

it stable and communicable. This, however, means that they lay bare its universal aspects. Words are the utterance of the universal, and it is impossible to express by their means the fact that there is no universal. Animals really are pure empiricists, but because they are, they cannot tell us that they are.

Conversely, the fact that we do think about our experience at once demonstrates that there is more to that experience than sensory particulars. It also goes a long way towards rejecting the nominalist claim that ideas are nothing but words. We have clearly seen the difficulty of maintaining this, but at the same time we must not gloss over the mysterious and intimate union in human thought of language and idea; to say that the two are not identical is not to pass on to some over-facile disjunction between them.

But the nominalist contention that the idea is a mere "flatus vocis" and that there is *nothing more* in consciousness than words and the particular experiences which they *verbally* bind together is quite untenable. It is only held because one is able to forget that if he really meant it, it would render all thought arbitrary. Unless there were real resemblances apart from words, then my words could connect things *whimsically* and without a criterion outside themselves. It cannot be that when I call all the leaves on the tree "green," the *only* truth is that I am experiencing a host of sensory particulars and lumping them together by means of a word. There must be a real objective resemblance among these particulars, or else there is no reason why I should lump these particulars rather than others, or why I shouldn't include "roses" as an instance of "green."

The temptation to nominalism arises when one asks himself "Where is this idea which is supposed to be present as a universal in my consciousness?" and then begins to search about for it. He makes a kind of inventory of the items which are open to inspection in his experience. He can easily catalog colors, sounds, pains, and words—but he fails to find anything corresponding to an "idea" and decides at last that it must be nothing but the words themselves. This procedure is perfectly natural to man but also perfectly fallacious, for it consists in "looking" for ideas. They turn out to be undiscoverable because invisible.

The fallacy, however, is that this kind of "looking" guarantees failure from the beginning. We are asking the questions which his hearers mistakenly asked Plato: "Where is the eidos 'man'?" "How big is the eidos 'man'?" "What color hair does the eidos 'man' have?" "Is this ideal 'man' thin or fat?" etc. The implication, of course, is that there exists no idea "man" but only individual men.

These questions, which seem so persuasive at first, are really pointless. They are equivalent to asking about and searching for an idea as if it were not an idea but a sensory item. An idea is no-"where"; the only thing that can be some-where is a particular sensory item. An idea is *not* an individual (that is the thing we continually fail to grasp) and hence it does not exist as does an individual. To take inventory of our experience and look for the idea "man," "table," "blue," is like looking for the number "three" in a haystack. An idea is real in the manner of an idea. What manner is that? The manner revealed to us in our use of language.

If we want to look for ideas, we must look for them in the region in which they are real: the region of thought. To "find" an idea and to be sure that it exists is simply to turn to thought and to discover the constituents which make it to be what we know it to be. One of these constituents is the apprehension of meanings—ideas. Then ideas exist in the mode of thought, and it is futile to look for them in any other manner. The temptation to this futility seems to hold a permanent fascination for the human mind, but it must nevertheless be resisted.

CONCEPTUALISM

A position somewhat more plausible than the nominalist's is the stand of the conceptualist. He agrees that ideas exist and he also agrees that their reality must be searched for in thought. So much

Conceptual Knowledge   161

does he agree with this that he cannot see that they have any status at all *except* for thought. An idea, he acknowledges, is a universal datum. But the only way a universal datum can exist is for thought. Outside of thought, all reality is that of individuals. The conceptualist therefore dichotomizes experience into existing particulars on the one hand and universal thought-contents on the other. He denies that the universal character of ideas has a real reference. Our thought seems to him to transmute into a universal datum what in itself is through and through individuated. Thus, each leaf which I perceive in the tree exists with its own shade of green, each individuated from every other: that is what is real outside of my thought. When I form the idea "green," I have a universal notion, but in the thing itself there is nothing corresponding to this datum, but only the individual sense-particular.

It is a little difficult to deal with conceptualism without seeming to concede either too much or too little value to it. There is obviously a sense in which the conceptualist is "right," and traditional philosophy could be construed often enough as emphasizing his point: that only individuals exist. In a way this is the great point which Aristotle and St. Thomas thought they were making against Plato. Thought-data do not exist as they do for thought except—for thought. This is why the Aristotelian-Thomist-Scholastic tradition repudiates Plato's notion of the "Eidea" (Forms) as eternally real apart from their individual embodiments. Universals precisely as universal are not extramental.

Nevertheless, there is also a redoubtable obstacle to the conceptualist position. Even though the datum as *explicitly* universal has reality only as present to a thought-process (for example, the universal idea "man" has existence only for thought and not outside of thought), the fact remains that there are objective similarities among individuals. Each individual instance of man really does resemble each other instance in exhibiting the common meaning. Each patch of red deserves to be called "red," so that the universal meaning "red" really is manifested identically through its instances. This objective similarity, it is easy to overlook, also implies that each individual instance really does embody a meaning; we only recognize that different instances embody the same meaning, if we antecedently recognize that each instance does in fact embody a meaning.[1]

The meaning which we conceive as an explicit universal in our thought has *some* status outside our thought, for there are objective similarities among individuals; objective similarities among individuals cannot be founded on what makes them individual; therefore, objective similarity is a sure sign of a real foundation for universality. A sure sign of it, we repeat, but not its first confirmation. For the first sign of the objectivity of meaning is the recognition of any one instance as embodying a meaning. As soon as, upon seeing even one patch of red, I cognize it as embodying a specific color-value, I grasp that color-value as multipliable and therefore universal; so that I do not have to know many actual instances of a meaning to know that *as* meaning it can be multiplied.

Where, then, do matters stand? The facts are these. Particular instances really do yield meanings to my thought. In fact, individually different instances yield identical meanings.[2] There is no gainsaying this; it is not inference, but simple description of experience. Then there is no gainsaying that the meaning which I conceive as a universal thought-content has *some* application beyond thought. This is the absolute minimum which is guaranteed, and it is enough to overturn conceptualism and to vindicate *some* sort of realism. The fact is that particular instances can be and are dealt with by thought and serve the purposes of thought. If thought makes use of universals, and if particular instances lend

---

[1] In other words, we do not arrive at universal ideas by classifying instances which manifest meanings, for we must *first* recognize that each does manifest a meaning before we can recognize them as separable into classes; and this prior recognition already entails the conception of a universal. Therefore, the recognition of universals precedes classification and does not derive from it.

[2] Different instances given to preception yield the idea "red," or "loud," or "man," or "house," or "table," etc.

themselves to this use, then this is enough to show that these particular instances are in some way referred to by my universal ideas. The claim that universal ideas really do refer to reality is proven by the fact that they really *do* refer to reality. We successfully use ideas. Therefore they can be successfully used. There is no appeal from that. But if ideas are successfully used, if we know that by means of them we really can refer in a non-arbitrary way to particular instances, then obviously there must be real objectivity in the universal data.

That is the most unexceptionable way to express the viewpoint of "moderate realism," that my ideas have a "foundation in reality." It is, however, not at all necessary to make a choice between what is usually called "extreme realism" and this "moderate realism." Extreme realism is ascribed to a theory like Plato's which held that universals as such existed extramentally; these were his Forms ("Eidea," or Absolute Ideas), eternal realities, universal meanings subsisting in themselves independent of individual things. The reasoning that we have gone through so far does not automatically validate this Platonic realism. It shows only that the universal character of ideas (their meaning-character) has a status beyond our individual thought, that particular instances provide a foundation for these ideas. Whether we can go farther is not immediately clear.

Nor does it appear that the main epistemological question lies in the direction of reaching a decision between Plato and Aristotle. The epistemological question is always: to what extent does my knowing reach the non-self? To what extent does it have application beyond my individual self? It is sufficient for the moment to make plain that the universal-datum has an undoubted objective reference, without going further.

MEANINGS AND INSTANCES

It is in the attempt to go further that we tend to get bogged down in a quagmire of metaphysical and psychological difficulties.

We insist upon asking what is the relation between this universal meaning and its individual embodiments; how the idea can be one and many at the same time; how the individuation of the universal meaning takes place. The essential thing to cling to is that we do use ideas in the described manner and that this implies that things are already such as to serve the purposes of thought: that therefore there is a real sense in which the particular does not have its being entirely aside from the meaning, that it is a "carrier" of meaning. Sometimes the last point is stated by saying that the universal exists "in" the individual, and then we are in hot water again.³ For, having used this language, we begin poking about in the individual instances in an effort to turn up the universal meaning which is "in" it, and naturally we don't succeed. We continue to have on our hands meanings (universals) and instances (individuals) and no matter how we scour the latter to find the former, we fail. To seek the meaning "red" in this patch here present to my vision, or to seek the meaning "man" in this figure now ambling towards me is inevitably to revive the conceptualist suspicion that after all, an individual is nothing but an individual. What could an individual be but an individual? "In" this individual man will be found bones, blood, and muscles, but no universal meaning "man." And so with every instance.

But it must be plain that we are proceeding fallaciously here. A universal is not "in" the particular in any way that could allow us to find it by proceeding on these lines. It is not concealed in the particular in some way. The point is rather that the particular as particular is already, if viewed in the proper way, the manifestation of the universal. A comparison may help to make this clear, and to obviate the tendency to view the matter in a naively mate-

---

³ Sometimes this is even said to be the great contribution of Aristotle, that whereas Plato said that the Forms existed "apart" from individuals, Aristotle said that they only existed "in" individuals. The inappropriateness and vacuity of this language is quite complete, since ideas obviously exist neither "in" nor "out" of sensory instances.

Conceptual Knowledge 165

rialistic manner—as if we were searching for the ore of universality contained in the dross of particularity.

Let us ask what happens when a carpenter sets about making a table. He begins with a certain ideal model of this table which he already has in his mind, and which is there before the physical product. After he finishes operating upon his materials—wood, nails, varnish—his idea is now embodied in the physical product. There now exists a physical table. What is the relation between this physical table and the idea in the carpenter's mind which brought it into being? Evidently we can say that the table manifests his idea and embodies it. Does this mean that the idea is "in" the table? We would hesitate before putting it this way, since it seems to imply that if we carefully took the table apart we might find the idea. If we did speak that way, we might begin to puzzle our heads over how the mental idea could be "in" the physical table. And possibly to wonder how, if it cannot, the table could really manifest the idea. But if we stick to what is indisputable, we skirt such false problems. The table really does manifest the carpenter's idea.

Furthermore, if we meditate more closely and adopt the point of view of an observer who comes along and beholds the finished table, we can easily appreciate how this observer could recognize the physical object as manifesting a certain meaning. He could further recognize that this meaning which the particular instance manifested was not exhausted by this particular instance, but rather could be repeatedly embodied in many other particular instances (the carpenter could keep making tables corresponding to the idea which served as the model for this one). Then this observer in recognizing this physical particular as a "table" has simultaneously recognized that the meaning "table" here embodied transcends its individual embodiment—that it is a *universal* in respect to its embodiments, a unitary meaning which is not exhausted by its manifestations but is indefinitely multipliable. He recognizes, in other words, that the particular *manifests* the universal and he recognizes that the universal is just as real as the particular which manifests it. Does he also feel that the universal is "in" the particular, and begin to have a maze of problems about how the carpenter's idea can be "in" the physical table? Not unless he is fond of paradoxes.

In largely the same way, it is paradoxical to raise questions about how our universal ideas can really be "in" physical things. It is enough that we recognize particular instances as *manifesting* meanings to realize that some meanings have objective reference. We say that this is an instance of "water," "rock," "man," "red," "loud," "sweet," "animal," and so forth; and in doing so we simply recognize that the individual instance yields a datum for thought, and that therefore thought's way of conceiving it is founded upon reality. We don't simply discover particulars; we discover meaningful particulars. Our thought then deliberately turns away from the particularization to the meaningful character of which it is a particularization; but it must already be meaningful if we are to discover it as such, and therefore our thought-contents are grounded in the meaningful particular.[4]

Some may still insist on raising the issue of how a *universal* can be said to be embodied in a particular. An attempt may be made to make this understandable, but before doing so it should be reiterated that the previous comparison is the standard of reference. We might just as well ask how the idea of table can be embodied in a particular table—but the fact is, it *is* so embodied, and we should hold on to that fact. An explanation designed to make the "how" more comprehensible may be legitimate but must always remain secondary.

This problem happens to have been the primary, if not the exclusive, way in which the epistemological problem presented

---

[4] This would remain true whether we take a Platonic or Aristotelian view of the status of meaning. Even if the meaning is only *potentially* there, and can be activated variously by us, it still remains true that its potentiality for being thought characterizes the particular independently of our actually thinking it.

itself to the thought of St. Thomas, and an answer to it could be fairly easily couched in Scholastic terms. If the content of our thought is to be objective, it must exist in reality—but how can a universal exist in a particular? The suggestion is that the thought-content or essence as *absolutely* considered is neither universal nor individual.[5] As conceived by thought, it is a universal; as existing in things, it is individual. Considered absolutely in itself— considered, that is, apart from its real or mental status—it is neither. The essence absolutely taken prescinds from either order of existence.

The doctrine of the "two *esse's*" is a technical capsulization of this view. It is said that the essence may have two modes of existence: in one case, as individualized in the physical thing, in the other as grasped intentionally by thought. Since the essence is in itself neutral in respect to either of these acts of existing (although of course it must exist in either one way or the other if it is to be at all) there is no contradiction in saying that the same meaning which is present to my thought as a universal, is present extra-mentally as an individual. The explicit universality of the essence is conferred on it by thought, and the conceptualist is right here, that outside of thought there are no explicit universals; but the same datum which is thought as universal exists also in a singular manner. It is thus deemed possible to presume a thoroughgoing realism since there is an identity of essence (and therefore of meaning-content) within a duality of existence.

As to how we come to generate these ideas, we entirely bypass this question. Many texts include large doses of psychology in their justification of conceptual objectivity, but this cannot be proper. We cannot justify the objectivity of concepts in terms of a highly theoretical doctrine of abstraction, for that would be to justify the more evident by an appeal to the less evident. Since the whole doctrine of abstraction, which is elaborated to explain the

[5] For a clear exposition of the Thomistic view on this, see P. Coffey, *Epistemology* (New York: Longmans, Green and Co.), 1917, vol. I, p. 269ss.

manner in which universals are drawn out of sense experience, bears upon supposed processes carried on by the mind which are wholly non-conscious and wholly unavailable for direct awareness, it must retain a hypothetical character. How can it seriously be contended that an appeal to the ghostly mechanics of the electrolytic action of an agent intellect, *species, signa quo*, and so forth help to make the objective reference of concepts more comprehensible? To justify the evident by means of the hypothetical is not a useful undertaking. What we *know* is that phantasms are particular and concepts universal and that nevertheless concepts do refer to phantasms. The theory of abstraction is in the main a detailed statement of this: it is a careful enumeration of the conditions of the cognitive situation, but it leaves us none the wiser as to "how" ideas came to be, which may, in any case, be an unanswerable question.

JUDGMENT

The position is often held that it is only with the judgment that we reach existence, the order of ideas being at one remove from actual existence. Concepts like "grass," "green," "wicked," "cold," "poison," and so forth do not attach the mind to an existing state of affairs, but represent ways in which it could be so attached. When we advance to the judgment "This grass is green," "This man is wicked," "It is cold out," "Poisons are dangerous," we insert these meanings into an existential context. The judgment affirms, "Thus it is." Until this affirmation is made, the mind has not reached existence in a proper sense.

Now, no one can question that the judgment represents a cognitive addition to the idea, and yet some qualifications must be made. There should be no inference that ideas by themselves are merely "free-floating" meanings, detached from all existential setting. On the contrary, the reason that the idea as such does not reach existence is that it is fully immersed in existence. The idea is a

Conceptual Knowledge 169

mental reference: as reference it refers to a world of actuality. At the stage of idea, it might even be claimed that the mind has not yet withdrawn from reality. It must *learn* that not all ideas are equally referential, or referential in the same way. And it would seem that in this disengagement, the judgment has a hand. So that the judgment is not only what reaches existence, but some sort of judgment is involved in the recognition that every idea does not equally reach existence. In other words, the cognitional preeminence of the judgment is not just that it reaches existence, but that it is the instrument for the emergence of existence as such, whether reached or un-reached. In a way it is also the judgment which reaches essence, since the distinction of essence and existence only emerges in the judgment.

This is not said to countermand the importance of the judgment, but only to emphasize the existential foundation common to all thought. Once the fissure between essence and existence has emerged in the judgment, it is the judgment which re-attaches the concept to existence. The judgment is thus involved in the disengagement of meaning from the immediate, as well as being involved in discriminating the various ways in which meanings can be re-inserted ("man," "centaur," "blindness," "larger," "$\sqrt{-1}$," "justice," are not re-inserted in identical ways).

What the judgment basically does, therefore, is not to examine the relation between ideas as disengaged meanings, but to seize a present object in terms of these ideas. It applies the idea to the singular which confronts it in the existential present. "This man is wicked," is not a comparison of the ideas "man" and "wicked" but a seizure of the singular through an idea, an affirmation that "Thus it is" with a singular object now present to me. Sometimes the affirmation may be a bare existential, such as "This man exists," or "Scorpions are real," but even when existence is not the issue it is at least a concomitant theme. Admittedly this is a basic statement, applying most obviously to one particular sort of judgment and skipping somewhat lightly past such judgments as

"It is better to suffer than do injustice," "Circles are round," "The square root of 9 is 3," "Gravity is a universal factor," and a host of others. Some excuse may be given by appealing to the primary position of the singular existential judgments; unless we made these, there would be no way of making or justifying the existential reference of the others.

In this connection, the problem is often raised about how the intellect can know singulars. In order to affirm a meaning of a singular, it would have to know the singular, and since it knows through concepts (which are universals) there appears to be a puzzle about how it can achieve this feat. The familiar answer is that it knows the singular by a conversion to the sensory phantasm. We may take this to mean: sheer immediacy is contained in the senses, and the singular is always given immediately. True enough, the singular which the mind is usually after is not the singular of the sensory data (the singular "man" or "dog" is not the same as that of "red" or "furry") but its presence is experienced *through* the sensory data. The words "this" or "that" derive their application not from concepts, it might be said, but from the sheer here-and-nowness of sense experience.

This view is acceptable up to a point, but not comprehensive. There are many reasons to think that if it is meant to rule out non-sensory intuition, it begs the question. Obviously, if by "intellect," I mean the faculty of conceptualization, then the intellect cannot know singulars. This, however, is a tautology: it simply states that the faculty by which I know in a non-singular way (universals) is the faculty by which I know in a non-singular way. This decides nothing about how I *do* know in a singular way. It seems correct enough to say that the senses play a conspicuous role in my knowledge of singulars without thereby precluding that the singular may be present to me in a non-sensory way as well. Subjective and intersubjective experience, in their specifically non-sensory aspects, may in fact be a more important source of immediacy than the senses themselves.

CONCEPTS AS CREATIVE APPREHENSIONS

Up to this point we have attempted to clarify and vindicate the existence and objective reference of concepts. The traditional formula that they have a "foundation in reality" sufficiently indicates the extent of this claim to objectivity. The question which now naturally presents itself is that of the adequacy and exactitude of conceptual knowledge. This question is particularly imposed because of the doctrine of the two *esse's* which may seem to imply the total adequacy of concept to reality. In addition, the familiar contention among Scholastic philosophers that we have a "knowledge of essences" reinforces this possible belief that through concepts we know things exactly as they are in themselves.

Various ways of speaking lend credence to this attitude: the habitual claim that the senses give us superficial knowledge while through the intellect we penetrate to the nature of things; the insistence upon defining our terms, as if the correct definition captured the essence of the object defined; the standard metaphysical view that "essence," is the source of intelligibility and definition while "existence" is hyper-conceptual and indefinable. Consequent upon this latently rationalist attitude, there has often been a tendency to regard the ideal of knowledge as a set of interlocking, objectified, and perfectly transmittable definitions, in which our knowledge would perfectly capture experience. There are not lacking places in St. Thomas himself where he seems to speak as if the definition seized the essence of the object without remainder; so that to "know the essence" of a thing was equivalent to defining it, and conversely to "define" it was to know its essence.

Notwithstanding all this, the truth seems to lie in the other direction.[6] Granted that the essence may be the ground of intel-

---

[6] On a certain ambiguity in this in St. Thomas's thought, see Pierre Rousselot, *The Intellectualism of St. Thomas,* trans. by James O'Mahoney, O.F.M. Cap. (New York: Sheed and Ward), 1935, p. 101ss.

ligibility, granted that it may be what we aim at by means of our definitions, this is a far cry from holding that our definition *contains* the essence. This question is a many-sided one, and various clarifications are in order. What may be said in a preliminary way is that the referential character of the concept does not *ipso facto* establish its exact coincidence with the essence of things. It does, however, provide one solid reason for saying that we do know essences. If to know an "essence" means to know things "as they are," our thought surely knows essences, since it is aware of itself as a pure reference to things. In making such judgments as "This table is brown," "It is windy today," "The game was postponed on account of rain," my judgment is aware of itself as a completely self-effacing reference to the reality about which I judge, which makes no difference whatever to the object in-tended. This much is clear.

Some of the difficulty that arises when we try to go further stems from thinking of "knowing" too much by analogy with seeing. This analogy is both spontaneous and useful, but it has its built-in limits. If knowing is like seeing, I could begin to feel that if I "know" an essence, I ought to be able to enumerate its features as I could the features of an object I was "looking at." The trouble is that we do not find that the traits of essence are as available for listing as this image might suggest. If we regard a possible enumeration of features as a requirement of knowing essences, we may well hesitate to think that we know essences. Another frequent manner of conceiving our knowledge of essence, as the grasping of the "content" of the known thing, can also confuse matters. For we might think that if we lay hold of a "content," we ought to be able to unpack it and inspect it—and this we often find ourselves unable to do. But knowing is not seeing and it is not grasping contents; knowing is just—knowing.

To realize that both these images are faulty is to make some start in understanding how the claim to know essences does not entail the claim of a perfect equation between thought and reality. It will then not sound so peculiar to say that I can know what

Conceptual Knowledge

things are without being able to unfold and display their explicit content. Surely I know the essence of red, stone, man, dog, water, justice, sky; just as surely I cannot define them if called upon to do so. The paradox of this claim is reduced if we cease to think of knowing in terms of clearly defined viewing, and simply take it on its own unique terms. Our "knowing" admits of depths. If we must use metaphors (and we probably must) perhaps we might think of our knowledge of the essence of a thing as exhibiting progressive stages of saturation. This is still an image, and has its own limitations, but it has at least the merit of avoiding any either/or connotation. The essence is not something I either know or do not know, but an intelligible concentrate which may be present in weaker or stronger manner.

Now if our knowledge of essences consists in the progressive precipitation of meaning in experience, it clearly cannot be understood in terms of definition. To be aware of the essence of a thing is not to be able to define it. The view that this is what "knowing essences" consists of rests on the conception of an essence as a "content" which our definition can enclose. Perhaps only with artifacts could there be such a perfect equation between definition and essence. An artifact really is exhaustively known in our definition of it, for its only meaning is the meaning we confer on it. There is no antecedent reality in an artifact at all: *what* it is is exhaustively available to our thought, since our thought is the *measure* of its reality. A watch, a table, a hammer, just are what they are for human thought. But the reality of natural things is not measured by our thought, and their "essence" is not accessible to us in the same manner. What is water, tree-ness, justice, a man, a stone, color, a cow? Their meaning transcends our thought to the exact extent that their being transcends it. Our thought does not measure their reality but seeks to measure itself by them. Yet we can still be said to "know" their reality, since this effort of thought to measure itself by these objects is already a knowledge of itself as *open* to them: it is the first precipitate of meaning in experience. This "intelligible solution" of thought may become more and more saturated with meaning, but it is from the beginning knowledge of "essences." We may therefore speak of essences as being "given" from the beginning, but in a manner which allows for an indefinite purification.

Thomistic philosophy has always held that complex essences are reached by a great effort, built up by a process which includes judgment and runs the whole gamut of reasoning. Sometimes an opposite impression is given when there is glib talk of tree-ness or animality, or when class concepts like dog, cat, mountain, are offered as examples of how the intellect "knows" what the senses cannot. Yet it should always be kept in mind that these concepts are simply meanings which the intellect has been able to precipitate out of experience at a given stage in the process of thought. They are the means by which thought restores itself to an experience now rendered more responsive to its needs. Through these ideas we may be truly said to "know essences," since our judgment, in using them, experiences itself as the active assimilation of the real.

But experience is on-going, and these ideas are the creative instruments by which thought restores itself to an on-going experience. Through these concepts thought spans the flux of experience while re-plunging into experience. These concepts are not ways of fleeing from time into a secure realm of static abstractions, but ways by which thought re-enters time, but re-enters it thoughtfully. What else does St. Thomas mean by the oft-repeated refrain that in order to know, the intellect must return to the phantasms?[7] We would do better to think of this as a return to experience, however, rather than as a return to "phantasms," for St. Thomas's phrase suggests a devaluation of experience to the level of sense experience, which may be quite unsound. What is emphasized is that the meaning of an idea is not something which can be grasped in abstraction from experience. It is the paradox of human thought

---

[7] *Summa Theologiae*, I, qu. 84, a. 7.

that it both surmounts time and yet occurs in time and with reference to time.

It is this ambivalent situation which gives rise to the ambivalence of the claim of thought to "know essences." As a living referent to experience, thought is continually aware of itself as this knowledge of essences. Under one aspect this knowledge can be regarded as a stabilizing movement by which thought frees itself from time;[8] under another it is a creative means by which thought restores itself to time. Now the first aspect of this process can be separated from the second, and thought can come to rest in a detached and objectified structure which it regards as a terminus rather than an instrument. It can then begin to regard its knowledge of this objectified structure as a "knowledge of essences" and then when it defends its grasp of essences, it is speaking not of an openness to experience but a closed preoccupation with this simulacrum.

This way of "knowing essences" is a temptation, not a goal. It really represents the temptation of human thought to refuse its own conditions and to reify one side of a total process. This is what rationalism does. It is also what the human condition itself makes us liable to. For man, to think is to communicate; to communicate is to use language; to use language is to objectify. What inevitably happens is that our thought, coming to itself in an objectively established language and culture, often tends to stop with the objectification rather than using it to return to experience. Examples of this could be endlessly multiplied. Take a man who proceeds habitually on a vaguely acquired cultural conviction that thought is a matter of brain-processes and is ultimately reducible to cortical reflexes. In so far as he comes to rest in these bits of "knowledge" and ceases to measure them against experience, his thought is spurious. The danger of this seems to be inherent in language itself which, while an objectification of the spirit, threat-

[8] Since the universal meaning it discerns is not a particularized and transitory item.

ens to screen the spirit from its own experience. How many men dwell unreflectively in such concepts as people's democracy, liberalism, high standard of living, capitalist warmongers, our way of life? Once philosophers were content to conceive nature in terms of substantial forms, natural motion, appetites, and four elements. All categories in which thought simply comes to rest detach it from experience, the very experience which the categories were devised to understand. The genuine meaning which concepts have they have in so far as they are beams cast in the direction of experience. To *know* their meaning is, as St. Thomas suggests, to turn to the experiences which they illuminate. In so far as it genuinely uses concepts, thought grasps itself as referential.

The interesting point is that human thought grasps itself as referential *and* inadequate. Could we even say that it is referential *as* inadequate?[9] That is, in knowing itself as imperfect, as seeking fulfilment, thought grasps its reference to what surpasses itself. Shall we then say that we can know the essences of things only inadequately? But this quickly tends to be reduced to the banality that we know essences "partially," which in turn suggests that there are a few or many pieces missing from our knowledge. The implication is that if thought progressed far enough in the direction of supplying the missing pieces (which it is assumed are of the same order as the pieces which are present), it would eventually attain complete and adequate knowledge. Yet this is erroneous.

Thought is not inadequate because it is partial. It is inadequate because it is nonoriginative. The only knowledge that would be adequate is the knowledge that *makes* a thing. Thus, our knowledge of an artifact is perfect in so far as the artifact is something that owes its being to that knowledge. We know what a table is, because we make a table to be what it is. Now it is obvious that

[9] This seems to be in the thought of Maréchal, *op. cit.*, when he grounds the objectivity of knowledge in the "dynamism" of the intellect, by which it is related, as pursuit, to a transcendent reality; in Maréchal's view, objectivity does not derive from sense, but from the partial fulfilment by sense reality of the ultimate exigence which is the intellect's mainspring. See *Le point de départ de la métaphysique*, Cahier V, pp. 231–232, 261–262.

Conceptual Knowledge 177

in respect to the realities of our experience, we do not make them *in toto*. In so far as their being is not originated by us, they will always transcend the power of our thought to know. Our thought is always after-thought. As such it is a *mode* of knowing which is *essentially* inadequate. No amount of supplying "missing pieces" will ever fill in this inadequacy, for the necessity of proceeding in the manner of "supplying pieces" is already an inadequacy. The significant contrast, then, is not between knowing something partially and knowing it completely, but between knowing something originatively and knowing it derivatively.

No matter how much I know "about" water, a stone, a bird, I know them inadequately. Only if I created them would I know them adequately, for then my knowledge would be the measure of their being. Really, in so far as I know things at all, I know them by calling them into the originality which is my thought. We do not originate the beings of experience, but when we think, we do the next best thing: we address them in their originality and hail them into the original process of thought. It is right to speak of experience as a "given" from which thought sets out. But experience is not given as a possession, as an inert item which we can envelop. It is given as an *offering*. Thought is aware of itself as a response to an appeal. Our concept is a substitute for the originative knowledge which would know things in creating them. It is itself a creative act, and not a "copy" of something already there in sense.[10]

It is surely wrong even to talk of thought "and" experience, as if the two were juxtaposed in some way. An experience in which thought played no part is just as unthinkable as thought in which experience played no part. Thought does not come to experience from the outside. Thought, as question, is there from the beginning; concepts are the crystallizations of questioning thought in experience. As such, their meaning is dialectical. That is, it is the product of a reciprocal exchange with experience. The concept

[10] For a vivid version of this, see Rousselot, *op. cit.*, p. 98 ss.

lights up experience, but experience in turn illuminates the concept. The analogy here is with the idea of the artist, which makes the artistic process possible, but which only comes to birth in that process. It is the *work* which reveals the artistic idea—even though it is the artistic idea which is the source of the work. Just so, it is experience which reveals the meaning of concepts, even though it is the concept which makes experience possible.

Try to think of the meaning of stone, man, justice, color, liberty, tiger, purity, apart from their experiential reference, and this statement will become clear. Unless we conceived meanings we would not have the experience we have; but having the experience reflects back upon and alters the very concepts which are its own foundation. Unless the artist had his creative idea, he could not proceed to the experience of painting his picture; but as he applies the pigments to the canvas, the unfolding picture alters the very idea which is bringing it to birth. Because man conceives of "freedom" and "democracy" he constructs a society on the basis of these ideas; but then the developing society manifests to him what he really means by freedom and democracy. In its own way, every concept is a creative instrument which both transmutes experience and is transmuted by it.

The virtue of thought is that it is able to carry forward much of the meaning it has brought to birth in experience. It is only this carrying forward which allows progress to be made at all. This is where objectification acquires positive value, since this is what permits deductions, interrelations, systematizations. But at no point may the objectification be taken as anything but a principle of elucidation. Knowledge may enrich itself by commerce among concepts, but the whole order of concepts must turn back to the canvas of experience or risk total academicism. This is what Bergson was driving at in his distinction between *pensée pensée* and *pensée pensante*: inert, accomplished thought and thought as the ceaseless interchange with experience.

8 *THOUGHT AND EXPERIENCE: I*

ON "KNOWING ESSENCES"

What effect do the remarks of the previous chapter have on the question of whether we can know "essences" or "natures?" The ease with which this question is raised conceals the vastness of the difficulty in answering it. For we could not genuinely answer it except in terms of a review of the tremendous range of meaning in "essence," a variety too often skipped over. The "essence" means the what-ness of a reality, its "such-being." This "whatness" we try to grasp in concepts. But let us ask ourselves about the status of this "whatness" when we think about: the spirit of the times, Western culture, French provincial furniture, man, desk, triangle, the middle class, red, sweet, justice, society, virtue, person, cow, beauty, up, down, larger than, cause, substance, $\sqrt{-1}$, mystery stories, atoms, the second law of thermodynamics, and so forth. What does it mean to say that we know the "essence" of these things?

Obviously the meaning of essence undergoes a significant alteration as it is used in each case. It is legitimate to try to reduce this bewildering variety to basic "types," but it is a task of the first magnitude. It is by no means clear that to distinguish in a routine way between the essence of substance and the essence of accident does justice to the situation. Like all divisions, the division of reality into substance and accident conceals as much as it reveals. We are still at arm's length from understanding what sort of knowledge is contained in our conception of the "spirit of the times," "society," or "beauty," if we are content to classify the realities thus known as either substantial or accidental. Suffice it for this to be pointed out, without attempting the monumental task of exploring this question at length.

Our discussion will be confined to the more familiar and straightforward question of what it means to know the essence of substantial individuals. This question includes several presuppositions. It presupposes first that there are individual unities of a basic kind, "substances." For our purposes, we may take substance to mean a being existing as a complete and unitary principle of action, a "nature" of a certain kind. We experience ourselves, most people would feel, as such fundamental natures: not superficial aspects of some more fundamental entity, but autonomous centers of activity. When we observe the rest of reality, we seem to find examples of other such fundamental unities at least analogous to ourselves: dogs and cats seem to be individual unities of a fundamental kind; so do rosebushes and oak-trees; chemistry discovers, even at the inanimate level, a whole range of molecules and elements which seem to provide examples of "natures," basic sources of activity.

Now the question of whether we can know the "essence" of such things presupposes also that they are, *as* fundamental unities, determinate in kind. It is not only a metaphysical principle but a simple fact of observation that "action follows being." Not just anything does just anything. Characteristic activities belong to different types of being; that is principally why we speak of different types of being—because we presume a fundamentally diverse substantial nature to underlie fundamentally diverse activity. Rosebushes don't practice asceticism; monkeys don't write operas; acorns don't develop into cats. There are in nature, prior to any human intervention (and providing the indispensable condition for the possibility of any effective human intervention), fundamental determinations in the entities we encounter which assure a non-arbitrary character to their activity. These fundamental determinations in the individual unity *as* unity we call the "essence" of the being. So much is presupposed even in order to raise the question of whether we can know the essence of substances. Disregarding the difficulties which could be raised, let us proceed on the assumption of the validity of these presuppositions. We will ask only whether the claim that we can "know" essences entails the claim that our knowledge grasps the fundamental determination which makes this being to be what it is: is there a perfect equation between our cognition and the fundamental determination in the being which characterizes it prior to all cognition?

It is apparent almost at once that we must draw back from the claim that there is such an equation. We have seen already that it is an essential characteristic of conceptual knowledge that it is derivative; as such it is never the measure of the reality of what it knows. If to know a thing through and through is to make it, not to make it is not to know it through and through. This is apparent whether we feel that the things of experience are "made" at all.[1] It is even more apparent if we do believe that they are in fact made—created by God. On such a belief, then the only idea which adequately knows this plant, this dog, this man, this atom, is the divine idea which measures it in its origin. The "essence" of these beings is equivalent to the fundamental ontologico-intelligible determination as conceived in the divine mind. This is why Josef Pieper will assert[2] that far from St. Thomas claiming that we can know essences by means of definitions, he holds that we cannot know essences at all. In this sense of essence, only creative knowledge can know the essence of things.

Sometimes the recognition of this is confined to our grasp of the thing *qua* individual: we cannot know, it is allowed, what differentiates John from James or Rover from Fido, but only the universal "essence" of man or dog. But this is not enough. On the meaning of essence now in question, we cannot even know the generic or specific essence. The gap here is not between knowledge

---

[1] If they are not made, they are not known at all, by anyone.
[2] Josef Pieper, *The Silence of St. Thomas*, trans. by John Murray, S.J., and Daniel O'Connor (New York: Pantheon), 1957, pp. 50–67.

of individuals and knowledge of universals (in Aristotle's manner). It is between knowledge as derivative and knowledge as originative: in so far as the essence of man, dog, rosebush, amoeba, means the fundamental determination of these things in their origin, our knowledge does not coincide even with the generic essence. The "essence" in this sense is hidden in the abyss of the divine knowledge, and it would be rash to claim that we can plumb that abyss.

There is still much left, however, to the belief that we can know the essence of substantial beings. To know their essence means first of all to know them according to the category of essence. Thus, what is the difference between merely perceiving a cow, and "knowing" it as a cow? Do I know the essence "cowness?" Well, at least, I know this perceptible datum as a *"being* which looks like this." Manifested in the sensory experience, I grasp a certain fundamental structure; I seize this sensory appearance as the manifestation of a mode of being which exhibits a unity for my thought. Then I understand that the appearance and activity which my senses perceive in this case is not a haphazard one, but that it possesses a certain necessity. My penetration of this necessary structure may admit of many degrees. At first encounter, I may simply subsume these perceived data under the heading of a "thing"—but doing only so much, I still can claim to know the "essence." Even if I don't know the name of what I am looking at, it is still "something which looks like this." It is, then, the notion of thing or being which provides the basis for our knowledge of individual substances.

We can hardly claim to know the essence of horse, water, rabbit, sodium, rosebush, amoeba, in the sense that we can plumb it to its depths or that we can define it. In their depth, these things are the manifestations of a divine idea; in the essence as conceived in that idea, the full richness of actual and potential being of these things is meted out to them by this idea. No definition could possibly enclose this meaning. This meaning is a source of their reality; definition is never a source of meaning. Nevertheless, the claim to know the essence of these things is not empty. We will not think it is unless we conceive of knowledge of essence in either/or terms. In "knowing" a horse or cow, we think a perceptual appearance in its unitary ground. Thought is always at the origin: on God's side, creatively, on our side re-creatively.[3] Now, that experience can be thus dealt with by our thought is sufficient sign that we know the essences of things. Our knowledge is an original construction by which our thought assimilates itself to the ground of an ongoing reality. For our purposes, we discover, in that processive reality, structures, articulations, connections, necessities, repetitions: we discover them—therefore they are there. Then to "know" the essence of water, man, dog, horse, amoeba, stone, and so forth is to call forth the ground of unity in these perceptually encountered entities.

In so far as we reach out to this ground of perceptual unity, we know essences: we know what things are. A distinction between what we might call the "ontological essence" and the "gnoseological essence" would help here.[4] Let us say that in the being, prior to all human knowledge, there is present the determinate source of its activity and its potentiality, patent only to the creative knowledge whose thought founds its existence. In respect to its manifest activity, essence is the super-actual source of activity. This "ontological essence" is unreachable by human thought. But our knowledge projects itself towards this ultimate ground by its work of transforming the merely sensory appearance into a form answerable to the needs of thought. This intelligible transformation can go further and further, but at every stage we do know "essences," since the gnoseological essence we form is our original creative expression of an experience which is grounded in the ontological

[3] See Rousselot, *op. cit.*, pp. 98–122.
[4] Georges van Riet, *Problèmes d'épistemologie* (Louvain: Publications Universitaires de Louvain), 1960, p. 163, approximates this distinction. In effect it is present in Maritain's distinction, *op. cit.*, pp. 91–99, between "thing" and "object," the thing being the trans-objective subject existing in itself, and the object the thing's cognitional presence to the mind of the knower.

essence. We do not know God's idea of horse, nor can we define a horse. But in a sense we know the essence of horse, for our idea is a transcendence of sense experience towards the ground of the unity discernible in that experience.

Some may feel dissatisfied with this explanation, for it seems to leave our knowledge of essences in a fluid state, whereas often the insight into essences is thought to be the basis for the stability and permanence proper to knowledge. But we must tread carefully here. We may first distinguish two things: our knowledge of generic structures as precipitated out of the experience of individuals, and our knowledge of the individuals which we feel to embody those structures. Take the process by which we "know" a rosebush. First of all we may simply notice it as "a thing that looks like this," a "this-something." Then we may find out that its name is rosebush. From here we can go on either to enumerate the detailed features which are constant concomitants of this perceptual structure (its leaf pattern, petal arrangement, cell composition, etc.) as scientific knowledge does; or we can grasp it philosophically as an instance of what is meant by "plant life." In this case we see it as a special perceptual manifestation of "immanent activity at the physiological level." The meaning contained in this notion is a pellucid one, perfectly distinguishable from other meanings: in so far as we can apply this meaning to the rosebush, we *know,* in a permanent and unchanging manner, certain things about it: it is living, it is self-perfective, it is a natural unity of heterogeneous parts. Whatever *positive* meaning is embodied in the gnoseological essence thus conceived I know as permanently applicable to the individual which embodies this essence.

The only remaining issue is: 1) Does any given instance really embody this intelligibility? 2) Does any given instance embody *only* this intelligibility? The first question, in spite of various obstacles, we may take to be successfully answerable. But what about the second question? Even if I am sure that I am dealing with an individual which is really a rosebush, how can I be sure that there is not more meaning in it than this? If it is a rosebush, then I cannot say it is inert or a mere aggregate: if it manifests the meaning I conceive when I conceive "rosebush," then obviously it has that meaning, and anything I can say on the basis of this meaning will apply permanently and stably to it. Yet how do I know that in its ultimate ontological essence it does not embody *more* than this meaning? Perhaps potentially this individual which manifests merely vegetative life to me is also a conscious being, even though it does not manifest this potentiality as yet. After all, if I placed an amoeba and a human embryo at the unicellular stage side by side, all I could say about them both, in so far as I knew them according to the actuality they presently manifested, would be that they were physiological forms of life. Yet one of these, the human embryo, has the potentiality of becoming much more than this, of developing into an actually conscious and even thinking individual. When I observe the two microscopic cases, I know that they are *at least* physiologically alive; but I do not know that they are *at most* physiologically alive. For the physiological individual may (and in one case does) bear within it the potentiality for something more.

If I formed my gnoseological essence of man at the single-cell stage, I would completely overlook the wealth of the ontological essence. Why could not the same possibility be present in my "knowing" of plants, animals, or inanimate beings? Why could they not carry ontologically more meaning than they reveal? The answer to this seems to be that there is no way I can be sure that they do not carry such meaning.[5] To a large extent, the tendency to assume that reality lives up to the boundary lines drawn by my thought is a product of a tendency to see essences from the side of *classification*. If I draw my lines carefully enough, I can be sure that the genera into which I classify things do not overlap. But in order to know that individuals which are carriers of these genera do not overlap, I must assume that reality stops within

[5] The relevance of this to the process of evolution is too obvious to need stressing.

my boundary lines. The trouble is that the classifying tendency, right from its inception in Aristotle, is often preoccupied with *artifacts,* where hard and fast lines can be drawn. "Chairs" and "tables" are eternally different; what is one is not the other, nor will a chair ever become a table. But that is because an artifact is wholly formed to the measure of our concepts. Classification is comfortably at home here. Those natural existents, however, which have their measure outside of us, cannot be trusted to confine themselves to our generic concepts. In regard to natural beings, classification is at best an outline of the present and not a precept for the future.

Perhaps there is a great deal more in the individual rosebush, dog, atom, or amoeba than I can comprehend. Normally, I proceed on the assumption that if a being does not manifest a certain perfection, it does not possess it even potentially—but this is not an absolute necessity. What occurs is that I detect certain intelligible facets in the activity of beings: sometimes an event only gives me the meaning "motion," sometimes it gives me "self-motion," sometimes "consciousness," sometimes "thought." It is apparent to me that between these *meanings* there is an irreducible intelligible difference. The difference between "life" and "matter," or between "vegetative life" and "conscious life" is just as irreducible as that between red and green. I have all manner of stable and unchanging knowledge on the basis of these differences, and in respect to any individual beings which strictly and exclusively embody these meanings.

But there is the catch. How do I know that any individual embodies, in its ontological essence, *only* these meanings?[6] How

---

[6] A point along similar lines is made by Nicolai Hartmann, *New Ways of Ontology,* trans. by Reinhard Kuhn (Chicago: Regnery), 1953, pp. 110–112. Hartmann holds for a hierarchical gradation in being, but distinguishes between a stratification of categories and a stratification of individuals exhibiting these categories. The categories themselves (inanimate, organic, psychic, and spirit), are discrete, but this does not rule out a genetic continuity; the categories do not shade off into each other, but the actual individuals or structures carrying the categories may.

do I know, for example, that the rosebush is not potentially conscious? It is hard to avoid the answer that I cannot know this. Still this does not mean that I do not know its essence. My knowledge is a grasp of the actuality manifested in this individual; in so far as it really does manifest this actuality, I really do know *what* it is. Maybe it contains more actuality (and more potentiality) than I know, but it does contain what I know. Therefore it is possible to know all kinds of stable and permanent propositions concerning entities which are themselves processive and changing.

DEWEY, PRAGMATISM, AND TRUTH

We should examine in this context one of the most interesting and influential modern contributions to the question of human knowledge, that of pragmatism. Often the pragmatic doctrine is summed up in the formula that "truth is what works." A judgment is true if, in acting upon it, I achieve results which are useful and beneficial; it is false if, when I act upon it, disadvantage ensues. If any proposition makes no difference whatsoever to activity, then there is little sense in talking about it as either true or false, in the pragmatist's estimation. William James put this belief in a typically vivid manner when he said that the truth of a proposition is in its "cash value." What difference do my judgments make in human experience?—that is the pragmatic criterion. For many this has appeared to be a complete depreciation of the grandeur of truth; no longer is truth measured by the mind's openness to a reality beyond the individual, but it is viewed through the spectacles of a crass and vulgar utilitarianism. Let us look at the form the theory assumes in the hands of its most systematic exponent, John Dewey, to see whether these fears are really justified.

Dewey approaches his philosophical position from a socio-historical direction.[7] He asks: why has traditional philosophy

[7] See John Dewey, *The Quest for Certainty; a Study of the Relation of Knowledge and Action* (New York: Minton, Balch and Co.), 1929.

tended to dissociate knowledge from action, and to elevate the former at the expense of the latter? Contemplation (*theoria*) was viewed by Plato and Aristotle as the supreme good of man, man's participation in the ineffable life of the gods, and action was looked down upon as extraneous to the true life of the soul. Why was this so? The answer, Dewey suggests, is that philosophy came into being as a regularization of the quest for security which preoccupied primitive man. At the mercy of a capricious and cruel nature, primitive man first sought relief from the perpetual risk of action in magic and the propitiation of the holy. But no efforts to banish risk are completely availing within the sphere of action itself, which is always parlous and unpredictable. Therefore man now retreats to the realm of thought, where, at least, he feels that he can find relief from the ceaseless perils of life. Even action can afford an awareness of the difference between the recurring and the unlooked for, but when philosophy comes on the scene, it erects this disparity between the ordinary and the extraordinary into a difference between two *realms*. It decides that theory reaches the immutable, the antecedently real, true Being; while action is sunk in process, contingency, non-being.[8] The thought which seeks genuine knowledge should turn to the contemplation of this superior realm of stable being and leave behind the swirling confusion of temporal process. If it perseveres, it will discover norms for knowing and coercive rules for conduct which are "antecedently real"—real prior to all human thought—and its true good will consist in conforming itself to these transcendent standards.

The quest for certainty is then simply one side of a quest for security, which, as Dewey paints it, appears distinctly pusillanimous. What he suggests is that the whole procedure is mistaken and has prevented man from making contact with the wealth of his own experience. A new era must begin. Action must be al-

[8] Dewey is thinking of such views as Parmenides' declaration that change was an illusion and that true Being was immutable; following him, Plato distinguished between the "really real" domain of immutable forms and the inferior reality of temporal experience.

lowed to evolve its own standards and not forced "to conform to what is fixed in the antecedent structures of things."⁹ Our ideas are not privileged glimpses into transcendent standards; they are facets of our *action*. They are conceptions of the possible consequences of our operations. Where thought begins is where man begins—with reality as immediately experienced. This primary experience of reality is not itself cognitional; it gives us *materials* for cognition. Through our activity we transform the unruly plethora of directly experienced reality into the carrier of human values. It is only then that we can be said to know it. Ideas are the instruments by which we effect this transformation.

Often Dewey gives a quasi-biological cast to this position. Man's ways of knowing are the instruments he has developed in the course of an evolutionary process and their worth derives from their efficiency in furthering his adaptation to the environment. Ideas are working hypotheses, or anticipatory plans for projected action.[10] Inasmuch as these anticipatory plans are fruitful and render experience responsive to our needs, they are true. But their being "true" does not signify that they are glimpses into "essences" which are concealed somewhere behind experience; it signifies that they are instruments for the successful transformation of experience. Therefore the criterion for the truth of an idea is not some antecedently real essence to which our concept conforms; it is the value of the *consequences* to which this idea leads or would lead in experience. Knowledge and action are not, then, directed to different realms of reality. They are directed to the only realm there is—reality as actually experienced—and knowledge is only a kind of anticipatory doing.

For a long while, many Scholastic philosophers, as well as many other philosophers who defended the traditional concept of truth, have been repelled by the pragmatic approach and have exercised themselves in calling attention to its defects. The obvious aspect of relativism inherent in the theory makes their distaste easy to

[9] *Op. cit.*, p. 72.
[10] *Ibid.*, p. 167.

understand. There is reason to think, however, that this attitude is now passing, and that traditional philosophy will henceforth view Dewey's theory in a more favorable way, recognizing it as, in some ways, both a confirmation of and advance upon its own views of the nature of the concept. What Dewey is saying is not too dissimilar to what Thomism stresses against rationalism: that the meaning of concepts is not present to us except in an interplay with experience. It is surely only the thinker at the lowest rung of the ladder who envisions philosophy as a set of ideas which have yielded up their meaning without remainder and need only to be conscientiously "handed on." Tradition is not transmission; one can only "hand on" an idea as an idea, not as an inert thing. Much of the difficulty with Dewey arose because of vocabulary differences and differences in intent. If we take the trouble to listen to what he is saying, it will often be so obvious (discounting the sociological-political-religious bias evident in his approach) that one may well wonder how it could be questioned.

Is it not true that our idea of "what" things are is often, if not exclusively, a conception of the consequences of the possible ways of acting with or upon them? What does my idea of water, wood, grass, horse, amount to? In one sense, it is based on an appearance, what the thing "looks like." Beyond this, what else do I mean by, for example, "water?"[11] It is something which will give me a cool, wet feeling if I plunge my hand into it; if I light a fire under it, it will give off steam; if I push it, it will move rapidly away from my hand and yet continually surround it; if I drink it, it will refresh me; if I bathe in it, it will cleanse me; if I subject it to electrolysis, I may break it down into elements. Every one of these statements is a statement in respect to action. To "know" water, then, is to anticipate the consequences of a certain series of actions from and upon an appearance-unity. There is surely no particular difficulty with this. A similar point could be made in regard to our knowledge of artifacts: what a watch or a chair is is

---

[11] *Ibid.*, p. 158.

primarily conceived in terms of what it does. It seems justified to say that most of our knowledge of the essences of natural entities is likewise founded upon our action upon them and their interaction with us. We certainly do not conceive the "essence" of water or stone by reading it off some transcendent standard above the flux of time.

Of course, it may be properly objected against Dewey that nobody ever really said we did do this. He has stacked the cards against traditional philosophy by presenting a near-caricature of its position. In spite of this, he has done something valuable, for the distinction between essential knowledge and sense perception has historically lent itself to this caricature. It is much too easy for one who thinks that he knows essences to cease to test his conceptual coinage against the hard floor of experience; he may tend to treat his ideas as finished, as closed. The great virtue of people like James and Dewey is to bring us back to the *un*-finished and open character of thought. Human thought is not a timeless edifice, but the reflective apprehension of a meaning present in temporal experience. The meaning which is present for this thought always remains compatible with novelty.

It must be admitted that Dewey cannot be absolved from a share in the blame for the disfavor in which his thought has long been held by traditional philosophers. The cavalier manner in which he handles the nature of truth, the failure to clarify important issues in this regard, are not to his credit. It is often said, with textual basis in Dewey himself, that pragmatism has offered us a radically new conception of truth. Actually this is not altogether accurate. The older notion of truth continues to be operative in pragmatism. Pragmatism is probably better understood as a theory of meaning than a theory of truth; better still, it is a theory about the *discovery* of truth.

Dewey is pressing for the fact that the meanings of our thought are in perpetual dialectical interplay with experience and action and capable of an indefinite enrichment from that source. Our knowledge is said to reach "truth" when it gives rise to fruitful consequences. But obviously this view presupposes in multiple ways the traditional meaning for knowledge. First, it retains the pure notion of *awareness:* no more than anyone else is Dewey able to swallow up the irreducible act of awareness in action. Knowledge cannot entirely be reduced to the consequences of action, for there is an inexpungible necessity that we be *aware* of the consequences of action, and this meaning for knowing (awareness) remains *sui generis*. Secondly, there is the point that many have raised: we must be able to know that we have reached consequences which are fruitful. This would seem to entail the recognition of at least some types of consequences as fruitful in themselves; otherwise the process of reference to further consequences would proceed endlessly and knowledge would be by definition impossible. What I mean by calling my judgments true cannot simply be that they work out, because I must know it as true that they work out. Thirdly, while my knowledge of what I *mean* by water, e.g., may be largely in terms of the consequences of projected or possible actions, that this meaning really applies to an object remains true independently of any activity.

The confusion arises because Dewey fails to distinguish between truth and our knowledge of the truth. Granted that in many cases we could not *know* whether a proposition was true or false without testing its consequences, the fact remains that what I mean by calling it true or false is that my judgment conforms to the way things are. That my judgment does conform, I may know only after I test it, but its truth is not *conferred* by the test, but only disclosed. This is extremely obvious, and yet it is relevant to Dewey's other main point, that knowing does not consist in conforming to an antecedent standard but in consequent utility. What is unmistakably antecedent to my knowledge is the structure of reality which will determine the eventual fruitful or non-fruitful character of my idea. My knowledge does not create the conditions of its own fruitfulness. This is the antecedent recognition which the pragmatic theory of truth must make.

Thought and Experience: I

The superiority of the Western view of reality over the tribal view was conclusively demonstrated, says Vere Childe, when British bullets penetrated the supposedly infallible magic armor of their tribal opponents.[12] Yes, but the fact that the truth of the Western view was thus vindicated only means that its truth came to be *known* through being tested; but that reality will vindicate one view and repudiate the other is due to the antecedent structure of the real itself. The truth of my idea may be measured by its consequences, but the consequences are measured against the antecedent nature of reality. This realization is inevitable, unless we were to maintain the literally insane view that human thought creates *ex nihilo* the nature of the real. Dewey is really far from denying it; it is only that his attention is fixed elsewhere and he speaks in neglect of it. There are many occasions where he makes it plain that our thought must take account of antecedently real conditions. But this means that there is a structure in the real independent of all thought on our part. In his own words, nature is "potentially intelligible,"[13] and he is joined in this acknowledgment by many who espouse a pragmatic or sociological view of truth. But this admission is enough to make it plain that the pragmatic theory must be inserted into a larger framework in order to make its own point. To recognize the potential intelligibility of nature is to recognize that our knowledge is measured by a meaning which transcends it: our actualization of the meaning latent in nature cannot proceed arbitrarily. Clearly then, Dewey does not and cannot deny that our knowledge must conform to an anteced-

[12] Childe, *op. cit.*, p. 113.

[13] Dewey, *op. cit.*, p. 215. *Cf.* Vere Childe's remark that the assumption of all inquiry is that reality has a pattern (*op. cit.*, p. 63); similarly C. I. Lewis, *Mind and the World Order*, p. 343, declares that the requirement for the possibility of knowledge is that the world be "orderly," that it be susceptible to organized knowledge. See, too, the further statements of Dewey, pp. 148, 164, 167, which grant some standing to pre-existing conditions. The alternative to such acknowledgments is actually chaos. But it is not seen clearly enough that even a minimal acknowledgment of this kind concedes the most important point to the traditional theory of truth.

ent realm of meaning. He is really concerned with the manner in which we bring this potential meaning to light; his decision is that for man action is an instrument of knowledge. Our knowledge of nature is principally a product of our ability to act upon nature.

Even so, some might take exception to this approach, since it confines our knowledge to nature itself and seems to preclude any transcendent use of concepts. If our knowledge is principally of the consequences of action, the full range of intelligibility seems to be limited to the realm of action, and Dewey is quite consistent in the "naturalism" which rules out metaphysics. Could we allow full scope to his approach and still admit metaphysics into the realm of knowledge? Does Dewey's approach admit of being completed in the direction of metaphysics? There does not seem any compelling reason to deny the possibility. All that is required is that we see human knowledge as the rising towards an absolute out of an experiential ambience. What Dewey leaves unexplained (what no genetic or naturalistic theory can explain) is the original contribution of thought by which man is impelled to *think* experience at all. This original impulsion is *already* a participation in an absolute, and renders all naturalism inadequate. Surely it is right to say that thought only comes to recognize its own participation in the absolute through a continuing dialog with experience— but what it reads out of experience is not just experience, but experience as held fast in the questionability of being. The more I search, the more I am able to become aware of reality as inexhaustibly searchable. Then there is no contradiction in viewing thought's orientation to time as simultaneously an orientation to the absolute—for its *way* of being oriented to time is a way only possible for a being oriented to the absolute. Human thought is not oriented to the absolute by means of the brittle clarity of concepts but by means of their unclarity. For our thought, the sign of depth is darkness. A thought oriented to experience is nearer to the presence of this darkness and mystery than a thought preoccupied with glossy conceptual security.

The fact that Dewey often selected science as the example of the interplay of knowledge and action has led to the erroneous impression that he depreciates other sources of cognition. The fact is that he is to be counted among those who stress the abstract character of the scientific method; he expressly declares that scientific "objects" do not have any privileged status. They are ways in which we enrich the ordinary objects of experience with meaning, but "the final thing is appreciation and use of things of direct experience."[14] Nor does Dewey mean by "experience" what a sensist like Hume would mean by it, a series of sense impressions. He is talking about the fullness of life-experience, which is a variegated qualitative panorama. Not only does he deny the right of the scientist to construct reality solely in the image of the primary qualities and to consign the secondary qualities to limbo,[15] but he frequently defends the irreducible status of the whole qualitative face of lived experience:

Empirically, things are poignant, tragic, beautiful, humorous, settled, disturbed, comfortable, annoying, barren, harsh, consoling, splendid, fearful; are such immediately and in their own right and behalf.[16]

Science is *one* highly selective way of thinking about experience, but there are open to man many kinds of knowledge—that of the historian, the poet, the artist, and so forth. These are independently cognitional and do not have to justify themselves to the canons of science. Once we abjure the "spectator" attitude of the scientist, and realize that all knowledge is tributary to the lived participation in experience, we will no longer see any need for a slavish subservience to the world-view of science.

If Dewey's insights are to be incorporated into traditional philosophy, they must be supplied with a metaphysical foundation.

[14] *Ibid.*, pp. 221–222.
[15] *Ibid.*, pp. 104, 120–121, 131.
[16] John Dewey, *Experience and Nature* (New York: Dover Publications), 1958, p. 96.

But once they are supplied with such foundation, the incorporation would not appear to be very difficult.[17] No traditional philosopher, however he may sometimes talk, really feels that he can "read off" essences in the manner that Dewey abhors. Our knowledge of essence is a product of a continual traffic with experience. Does Dewey preclude a resulting knowledge of "natures" or "essences?" He himself may neglect it, but his philosophy, like all thought, presumes the antecedent structure of the real. Our knowledge of "human nature" or "animal nature" would then be the gnoseological deposit which experience has left in thought. But on the basis of this deposit of actual intelligibility, we may claim to say various permanently true things about man. For example, we may know him as a "person" and know that certain behavior towards him is forever incompatible with his worth as a person. We don't "read off" the essence of person, but we do awake progressively to it in the confrontation with experience. Having awakened to it, we are then in the presence of meaning which is not ephemeral but enduring. Nothing that Dewey says can eliminate the possibility of this; much that he says is enlightening in showing us how this awakening is to be pursued. Finally, much of what he says is a salutary warning against a premature belief that it has been consummated; we are still in the process of finding out what man is, just as we are still in the process of finding out what reality as a whole is.

Obviously, many of the questions raised by Dewey's approach come up in the field of ethics, in which traditional philosophy has relied on the "natural law" approach. If the "natures" of things are as elusive as Dewey indicates, small room would seem to be left to settle ethical questions by measuring human actions against

---

[17] For a sympathetic discussion of Dewey by representatives of traditional philosophy, see *John Dewey: His Thought and Influence,* edit. by John Blewett, S.J. (New York: Fordham University Press), 1960, and Robert J. Roth, S.J., *John Dewey and Self-Realization* (Englewood Cliffs, N.J.: Prentice-Hall), 1962.

the "nature" of man. But even here the disparity between Dewey and Thomistic philosophy is more apparent than real. No natural law advocate with any sophistication applies this method in a pseudo-deductive fashion, but always proceeds circumstantially and historically; conversely, no Deweyite can really ignore "essences," since this is the presumed criterion to which experience converges. Neither Thomist nor Deweyite would think it desirable that man act in an inhuman way. Dewey stresses the role of experience in deciding what is the properly human conduct; Thomism stresses the imperium of man's nature in enforcing an unconditional sanction to this demand for genuinely human action.

SOCIAL AND HISTORICAL DIMENSIONS

The contemporary mind finds it natural to pose speculation about the relation of thought and experience in terms of the social and historical character of thought. It was Hegel who first emphasized the omni-historical character of concrete reality, and the 19th century learned its lesson well, as the ideology of Marx and the biology of Darwin show. As a result, we cannot today conceive of any existent in isolation from its historical dimension, and knowledge is no exception. Epistemology may consider the historical dimension of knowledge in two ways: first, as a difficulty in the way of the claim that we reach objective truth, secondly, as a contribution towards the understanding of the meaning of objectivity.

It is the first question which has usually preoccupied epistemologists. How can a thought which is circumscribed in time and culture mount above time to a stable and independent order of truth? At the very least we must wonder about this, and more than one will be inclined to view "objectivity" and "historicity" as mutually exclusive; a thought constituted by social and historical processes is, in this opinion, *essentially* doomed to relativism. For the way things appear to it from its social and historical perspective is not necessarily the way they will appear to a thought in a different social and historical perspective; what is "true" today is not necessarily true tomorrow, or the next day, or for all men.

Now two points may be quickly made: it is quite evident that human thought is socially and historically conditioned; it is by no means evident that this leads to relativism. After all, in this case what is historical is *thought:* not dress, custom, or conduct, but *thought*. What makes thought historical is not the same thing that makes it thought. The task for the philosophy of knowledge is to do justice both to the historical character of thought and to its cognitional character. That it can have both is plain from the outset, for the power of thought to recognize its own social and historical limitations is, in a sense, already evidence for its transcendence of those limitations.

It is only from the standpoint of a hyper-scrupulous rationalism that the historical character of thought should appear as a scandal and a threat. For one who regards his ideas as mental properties whose content can be publicly displayed, the notion of a "development of truth" is very trying. He feels that one either "has" or "does not have" these ideas, either possesses or does not possess the truth. Yet, if an idea really is a creative apprehension, then it is not something one "has" at all, any more than the artist "has" his creative idea. To acknowledge this is not to surrender the domain of truth, but to occupy it more effectively. The unity of knowledge is not destroyed by its being subject to growth and development, any more than the unity of the individual self is destroyed by the development of the individual consciousness.

The meaning of "development" can probably most easily be brought out by reference to the development of individual consciousness. Development is not a process of the *addition* of items to an originally meager supply. It is the simultaneous transformation and preservation of previous states. The adult's consciousness is not related to his childhood consciousness simply by way of addition or replacement; it is at once continuous with and beyond his childhood self. Nothing is preserved in consciousness except by being transformed. It is transformation which *provides* continuity. In a somewhat similar way, the history of philosophical ideas should be conceived neither as an addition of intact items of knowledge nor as a rivalry between competing items. Part of the trouble is that we instinctively think of "knowledge" rather than of *knowing*. No knowledge is separable from the minds in which it comes to birth. Philosophical categories are not things literally "handed down" through the generations. They exist only in so far as the process of thought exists; what really traverses time is the process of thinking. A conversation between minds is not the transferring of objective thought-items back and forth; it is a mutual turning of minds to each other and to the process in which alone minds really exist. "Objectivity" is generated by the existence of this process; the very idea of objectivity rests on the notion of a datum to which many minds can mutually refer themselves, and it therefore presupposes the living dialog between minds. The possibility of communication (commun-ication) is a testimony to such a common reference. Then the historical character of thought cannot militate against objectivity, since it is one component of the conception of objectivity.

But could not one retort that what objectivity presupposes is that an identical datum is there for a multiplicity of minds, and that if the sociologists of knowledge are correct, this cannot be so? It is one of their favorite themes, usually directed specifically against positivism, that the notion of a "pure fact" is a myth.[18] A "social *a priori*" provides the frame of reference within which every empirical datum is seen; all human knowledge is ineradicably "perspectival" and to achieve an objectivity unaffected by the social perspective is a hopeless ambition. It is quite apparent that

---

[18] Karl Mannheim, *Essays on the Sociology of Knowledge,* edit. by Paul Kecskemeti (New York: Oxford U. Press), 1952, pp. 150ss; Werner Stark, *The Sociology of Knowledge* (Glencoe, Ill.: The Free Press), 1958, p. 126; Lewis, *op. cit.,* p. 121ss.; Childe, *op. cit.,* p. 54.

this difficulty is one manifestation of the larger puzzle about how a thought which arises out of a non-cognitional background can be truly objective. With good reason, then, Karl Mannheim, one of the pioneers in the field, defined the sociology of knowledge as the analysis of the "relationship between knowledge and existence."[19] Instead of attending to such non-cognitional intrusions as diet, physiology, temperament, neurosis, economics, or other possible factors, the sociologist concentrates on the social determinants of thought. But the problem is the same: how can a thought which is *essentially* perspectival reach an absolute?

That this is not impossible is insisted upon often enough by those sociologists of knowledge who protest that they are not defending relativism.[20] Any opinion which held that our thought was totally determined by social influences would destroy its own value as knowledge; sociological relativism of this type is as self-refuting as any total relativism. Describing the social-historical dimension of a proposition does not settle its truth or falsity. What has to be decided is this: can the notion of truth or falsity really apply to perspectival thought? We might begin to draw the teeth out of what strikes too many as a grave difficulty merely by asking a counter-question: why not? Just examine the supposition which is the foundation for the objection. It apparently rests on the belief that objective knowledge is equivalent to absolute knowledge. Or that the absolute must either be revealed absolutely or not at all. Failing this, all other knowledge is robbed of value and consigned to a "subjectivist" or "relativist" status. What can be the justification for this very strange belief? Is it supposed to be a contradiction that an absolute be revealed perspectivally? To hold so would appear to be a flagrant *petitio principii*. C. I. Lewis

[19] Karl Mannheim, *Ideology and Utopia*, trans. by Louis Wirth and Edward Shils (New York: Harcourt, Brace), 1952, p. 237.

[20] See Paul Kecskemeti, in the introduction to Mannheim's *Essays on the Sociology of Knowledge,* pp. 28–29. Werner Stark adds a strong disclaimer of relativism, p. 152ss.; and of course Scheler was strongly anti-relativistic. Even Mannheim, who is accused of relativism by Stark, tries to escape its clutches, *op. cit.,* p. 171.

points out in a somewhat different connection,²¹ the fact that A presents different perspectives to x, y and z is no argument against the existence of A but rather an argument for it. A similar thought prompts Werner Stark to adopt the device: "To the absolute through the relative."²² He means this in the manner of Max Scheler, from whose writings the contemporary sociology of knowledge may be said to spring; for Scheler, the perspectival manifestation of "essences" like "man," "justice," or "good" were obscure revelations of an eternal *eidos* (an ideal archetype) which could be descried through them.²³ But a similar statement could be made in respect to the Absolute which is the ground of all existence, even if we frame this merely hypothetically. If there is an Absolute Source of existence, it can obviously not be revealed *absolutely* to finite existents; yet it is nonsense to think that this would logically preclude all approach of the finite to the Absolute. What it does mean is that every revelation is at the same time a concealment.

The possibility that man's perspectival knowledge can reach insights with enduring value sounds presumptuous largely because it is too often discussed in generalities without reference to the many simple instances where the possibility is evidently actualized. Once our consciousness has awakened sufficiently, we are able to understand very well the truth that "Kindness is better than cruelty," "Hitler's slaughter of the Jews was a monstrous crime," or the falsity of "Slavery is preferable to freedom," "Conceit is a moral virtue," or "Children ought to despise their parents." To say that we know these truths is not even to say that we have a clear idea of "kindness" or "slavery"—the "exact" meaning of terms like this is a will o' the wisp. Yet, we nevertheless know that the truths enunciated in these propositions in some sense

---

²¹ Lewis, *op. cit.*, p. 178ss. Lewis's thought in this work, however, has strong elements of relativism.

²² Stark, *op. cit.*, p. 196.

²³ See Stark's summary of Scheler's work, *Die Wissenformen und die Gesellschaft* (1926), *op. cit.*, p. 328ss.

transcend time. "Kindness" is only perspectivally revealed to me—but on the basis of this revelation I know that no future social perspective will warrant anyone to judge truly that cruelty is better than kindness. It does no good to argue that many issues are much more obscure than this, for the existence of obscure cases must be understood from the vantage point of non-obscure cases, and not vice versa. Nor can the lack of a consensus be conclusive. What we are trying to vindicate is the *possibility* of enduring insight arising out of perspectival knowledge, and there is no call to be optimistic about its frequency and certainly no call to assume that this insight will have the support of a social consensus. The basic theoretical issue is sometimes confused with the practical one of how we can decide between divergent perspectives, which is quite a different question. Since no human agent, individual or political, transcends the perspectival condition, it is the part of political wisdom to refrain from imposing any perspective by coercion—but that is quite a different thing from the admission that one perspective is as good as another. We know very well from our own individual consciousness that at some moments our vision is clearer than others; we would not say about ourselves that all our opinions are equally enlightening, nor should we say it about humanity in general.

The more ontologically rich are the categories, the more they will be subject to development. It is difficult to credit that notions like "substance," "thing," "knowledge," "matter," "good," "I," "person," "God," "necessity," "freedom," "love," have some univocal packet of meaning which is transferred through the ages. Take a concept like "substance," which begins with Aristotle and continues through St. Thomas, Descartes, Spinoza, Hegel, and the moderns. When the modern Thomist uses the word does he mean the same thing as Aristotle? The answer seems to be "yes and no." And this does not signify that he means the same thing *plus* a few more things. The successive transformations undergone by the word do not allow us to identify some univocal core of meaning. To cite only one example: the distinction between essence and existence, which Aristotle did not make, is not merely *added* to the notion of substance which he had, but it completely transforms this notion. Likewise, all the philosophical categories have histories. Their continuity gives us a kind of one-many relation through time; they are analogically, rather than univocally, similar.

Only the abstract is non-historical. Philosophy is, or should be, an effort to think the concrete. That is why it cannot attempt to surmount the conditions of temporality by seeking out categories which seem to be exempt from history, as do mathematics and logic. It is true that any mind at any socio-historical perspective would have to agree on the validity of an inference like: If A, then B; but A; then B. But such truths are purely *formal* and do not tell anything about the character of existence. If metaphysics views its categories as intelligible in the same manner, it has really taken refuge in formalism and forsworn the concrete. That is why a metaphysics which conceives itself in this way has such a hollow ring to it.

Let us now consider the second aspect of the sociology of knowledge, its positive contribution. For the impression must not be left that the social and historical dimensions of knowledge are simply a difficulty to be somehow "handled" by one who wants to continue to maintain the objective value of our knowledge. This would be to miss the very real contribution made by the modern historical mode of thought to our appreciation of what objectivity *is*. Here we may advert to the remarks made in connection with Kant's view that we can only be properly said to know *things* and that only phenomenal consciousness (a combination of formal category and sense intuition) apprehends *things*. To this we may add, with Dewey and the pragmatists, that *action* is also involved in the conception of a "thing."[24] There appears to be, at a mini-

[24] See esp. Lewis, *op. cit.*, p. 142.

mum, a genuine psychological justification for saying that our knowledge feels truncated unless it is dealing with "things" and that a thing is a triplex of concept, sense, and action. That is why Kant withheld the label of "knowledge" from metaphysical concepts, since they did not bear upon things in this sense.

Now with this in mind we may confer a very positive cognitional relevance on the social and historical dimensions of human existence. For if metaphysical categories like "being," "soul," "God," "immortality," "freedom," "love," "person," and so forth are to afford us the same assurance as phenomenal knowledge, they must be *filled in* with some kind of content—they must begin to bear upon something approximating a "thing." Now obviously this content cannot come from the side of sense intuition as such, which cannot exhibit these notions. It *might* come, however, from action of a superior kind. And here is where the social and historical dimensions become extremely relevant. For it is through his higher activity as a social and historical being that man gives a visible manifestation to the meaning creatively apprehended in these philosophical concepts. His grasp of himself as a trans-phenomenal being is weakened and rendered cognitionally unstable unless he can read it back out of his existence. Therefore, the historical process by which he creates an authentic human existence for himself is integral to the cognitive grasp of the transcendent dimension of reality.

In line with the analogy we have used before: as the artist cannot affirm his creative idea except as he embodies it on canvas, so man cannot affirm the transcendent character of his own existence except as he embodies it in history and society. Or to revert to the comparison with individual consciousness: A man says "I" at five and at fifty. But his meaning for that word has radically developed and is inseparable from the life-process in which he has learned it; so, too, humanity recognizes itself as "man" throughout human history, but it must learn what it *means* to be man, and that meaning is inseparable from the historical process.²⁵ Can anyone seriously contest that we are in a better position today to understand what it means to be a person than was, say, a slave in pharaoh's Egypt? Man knows what it means to be a person by making himself a person.

We could say similar things about the other categories: we convince ourselves of immortality by bringing forth immortal works, of love by creating the climate in which it may flower, of freedom by producing a free society. Most audaciously, could we even say that in order to know God, we must *make* God? That is, we must make the reality of God in-stant in human existence. We must bring God forth from hiding and let Him appear as the ultimate meaning of human existence. Such a conviction seems to have animated the thought of Teilhard de Chardin.²⁶ His phenomenology of man is a phenomenology of man as a movement to the end of history. The intelligibility of the end falls across the present. Perhaps only at the Omega Point do we really know God truly, but we may speak less and less stammeringly as we move toward that point. And thus the historical growth which propels this movement is an integral part of our cognition.

In speaking thus, in trying to do justice to the relation of history and knowledge, we must beware of any vulgar optimism which reduces the whole discussion to the single word, "progress." "Progress" is a word to beware of in philosophy, for there is a sense in which philosophy is more a continual thinking at the origin than it is a progress. Certainly there is no guarantee that a thinker who appears later on the historical scene than another automatically stands at a better vantage-point for the vision of philosophical truth; as an example, nothing said above would commit us to the belief that Sidney Hook is a better philosophical guide than Plato. Things are not that simple. Just as there are

---

²⁵ Cf. Michael Polanyi, *The Study of Man* (Chicago: University of Chicago Press), 1959, pp. 82–83.

²⁶ See Pierre Teilhard de Chardin, *The Phenomenon of Man*, trans. by Bernard Wall (New York: Harper and Bros.), 1959.

moments of great purity and intensity in the consciousness of individuals by which the rest of their experience can be measured, so the great thinkers represent moments of great purity and intensity in the consciousness of humanity. What history does is to pool the experience of the past and to offer it as a fuller opportunity for philosophical penetration.

9 *THOUGHT AND EXPERIENCE: II*

INDUCTION

Induction is defined as reasoning from particular instances to a general conclusion. According to the number of such instances, induction is called complete or incomplete. Complete induction means reasoning from all existing instances to the generalization; incomplete induction means reasoning from less than all existing instances to the generalization. Complete induction deserves only the briefest notice, since it is "reasoning" only in the loosest sense of that word. If I check a certain block and observe successively that each single house on the block has a tree planted in front of it, I may generalize to the statement "All houses on this block have trees." By completely tabulating all instances of this generalization, I place the generalization beyond doubt and beyond dispute. The only thing is, I "reason" here in only the weakest sense, for all I am doing is stating succinctly what I already know. I have not advanced my knowledge, but only summed it up. Therefore, while this complete induction is unexceptionable, it is also uninteresting, since if our knowledge were confined to it, we would not progress at all.

Incomplete induction is much more important and also much more puzzling. For it seems to involve a process of passing from "some to all," a process against which formal logic has consistently warned us. (It is well known that the truth of an I or O proposition does not warrant an inference to the truth of an A or E proposition.) Yet, when we employ incomplete induction, we infer from an observation of either few or many instances (in any case, not all instances) that something is true of all instances of this class. We do this in an everyday manner when we state confidently such familiar facts as that "All men laugh," "All dogs bark," or "All unsupported objects fall to the ground." Nobody has ever observed *all* men, *all* dogs, or *all* unsupported objects; the observation is impossible in these and most cases—which is another reason why complete induction is relatively useless. But if we haven't observed all cases of a class, how do we know with certitude that they *must* exhibit a certain trait? Why couldn't there be non-barking dogs or unsupported objects which remain comfortably suspended in mid-air?

Yet physical science, and indeed all systematic knowledge, relies very heavily on incomplete induction. Medicine speaks of the properties of a malaria or typhus germ; biology of the normal structure of a human cell; chemistry prescribes the atomic structure of molecules and lists the weights of elements in a table. Yet nobody has observed or could observe *all* typhus germs, all cells, or all elements of a certain kind. How then, by observing only some, can we prescribe for what is true of all? How can we distinguish a valid induction from a hasty generalization? Nobody would, on fair consideration, grant much value to such pretended generalizations as "All Irish are drunkards," "All doctors are quacks," or "All politicians are cynical." We would counsel a person who made such statements that he was judging on the basis of a few instances and proceeding fallaciously. When, then, are we validly inducing and not generalizing hastily?

In one sense this question simply means: in what cases are we proceeding according to the proper and recognized canons of a certain field? Thus, the hasty generalizations cited above sin against the cardinal rule of all induction, which states that the existence of even a single *negative* instance destroys the universal character of the conclusion. Any pretended induction which violates this rule is immediately to be tossed out of court. That much is easy to see. To go further in establishing the correct procedures of induction in given areas requires prolonged consideration, and practitioners of the separate sciences and of the logic of discovery have devoted much time to it.

Mill's method of agreement and differences is one example of an attempt to lay down general criteria. Actually, though, this way of stating the question has largely to do with the procedures valid in a certain science and is principally to be settled by the practitioners of that science.

The philosophical question proper only begins where this one leaves off: after a valid scientific conclusion has been discriminated from an invalid one, what is the *status* of the knowledge thus acquired? Is it merely probable, is it certain, or what? For instance, let us say that a chemist can successfully tell the difference between the right and wrong way of determining the structure of a molecule and can write its formula. The philosophical issue is: having arrived at the scientifically correct conclusion, is the knowledge which is thus gained *absolutely* certain or is it simply highly probable? The philosophical question does not have to do with the rightness or wrongness of procedures within science, but with the question of the status of the knowledge which can be reached with this *sort* of procedure.

HUME'S OBJECTION

The best known attack ever mounted against the *necessity* of conclusions reached inductively was that made by David Hume in the course of his quarrel with the principle of causality.[1] Hume's point may be epitomized in this way: experience is always of particulars, and therefore it is always at one remove from any generalization that can be made about it. What is given to us is a stream of perceptual particulars. No doubt they are linked in certain customary sequences, but they are still given as particulars. When we try to raise ourselves to an entirely different level and

---

[1] *Hume Selections*, pp. 34–38. (From *A Treatise of Human Nature*).

decree as to how this sequence *must* appear, we have dealt ourselves an extra card. "Laws" of nature pretend to be valid for all cases, both observed and unobserved—but where do we find the *absolute* warrant for this? What makes us sure that the cases we have not observed must be like the cases we have observed? "All unsupported objects fall to the ground," "All hydrogen combines with oxygen to form water,"—are these really *certain* pronouncements or only satisfying probabilities?

Hume's point can be made especially striking by relating it to time. For every "law" of both common sense and science feels itself to be a pronouncement about the unobserved events of the past and future, as well as about spatially remote and unobservable events. But as such, according to Hume, it is proceeding on the assumption that the *future must resemble the present,* and this must remain forever an assumption. What makes us so confident that it must be true? Just because something has happened in a certain manner in the past is no guarantee that it will happen in that manner forever afterwards. Perhaps ten thousand years from now (or ten seconds from now) the law of gravity will no longer hold good. Our mind boggles at the possibility—but who can prove that it *can't* be? Or why shouldn't the behavior of bodies alter altogether, so that fire no longer burns paper, and hydrogen and oxygen no longer combine to give water? We cannot appeal to the past to prove what will happen in the future.

Nor can we even say that in the past the future always resembled the past, for that only repeats the issue. Just because the past future resembled the past past, how does that prove that the future future will resemble the future past? Always involved here, says Hume, is an *assumption*. No appeal to experience can ever justify the assumption, for every appeal to experience re-introduces the assumption. A pseudo-generalization, such as the appeal to the "uniformity of nature" will not help either, since this simply hallows as a fact the very principle whose validity is at stake. This is the question: how can experience ever provide the evidence for a pronouncement about what is in principle beyond experience (as the future is always in principle beyond any accumulation of experience)?

Many people at first find Hume's reasoning merely captious. But he has actually done thought a great service by placing the reality of the empirical in the sharpest relief. Every thinker who brings us to the extreme enlarges our vision, since philosophy is a matter of thinking at the extreme point. At the same time, it is true that not everyone would have this problem quite in Hume's manner. For his particular difficulty is heightened by his basic assumption in respect to the character of experience. He believes experience to consist in the awareness of a stream of particularized impressions given without intrinsic connection. If what is given is *mere* sequence, clearly no reason is discoverable why a past sequence should be repeated in the future. Something is missing from this picture, however, and it may be variously supplied.

In the language of Scholastic philosophy, what Hume's sensist theory of knowledge does not allow him to recognize is that we do not experience mere impressions or activities, we experience *beings acting*. In grasping the events of our experience as the activities of different kinds of being, we have passed beyond sequence to the foundation of the successive activity in the nature of the beings which are acting. Hume's sensism does not allow him to grant meaning to the notion of "nature" or "kind of being," but we need limit ourselves thus only if we arbitrarily adopt this beginning. Once allowed the realization that there are "things which" act, we have the notion of a determinate kind of being which underlies its manifestations as their permanent source and ground. What a being is, its determinate ontological structure (its "essence"), determines what it does. Therefore, we can give at least a hypothetical answer to the question of why the future should resemble the present. As long as there is this kind of nature in existence, it will act in a manner proportionate to its nature. Action is not arbitrary nor are the experiential sequences groundless: action is rooted in nature, and sequences of action in interacting natures. And so it is safe to assume that as long as there is the kind of "nature" we call hydrogen or oxygen, there will be the typical activity proper to this nature.

Putting things in this way opens up the possibility of a criterion for a valid induction. Whenever on the basis of observation of particular instances, we may discern that a certain feature or a certain way of acting belongs to the nature of which this particular is an instance, we may then induce that all instances possessing this nature will exhibit this feature or this mode of acting. For, if it is founded in the nature of this being, it will be shared by all who have the same nature. Thus, we may safely conclude by incomplete induction that "All men are risible" (even though we have not observed all men) since laughing is a property seen to be grounded in the combined animal and rational nature of man. We can say this, it is felt, of all possible past and future instances of this nature, since it is a property of such a nature. Such a statement could not be made about "white" or "short" or "strong" which are not necessarily connected with the essence "rational animal." Wherever we can glimpse the connection between property and nature in this way, we may feel secure in our induction.

Yes—but the trouble is that this simply tends to transpose the problem: how do we *know* that a certain feature or action belongs to the very nature of a thing? In the case of man we may seem to have a privileged example, but suppose we take the essence "tiger" or "swan." Is "All tigers have stripes" or "No swans are green" an example of a valid induction and does it give us absolute certainty? This amounts to asking whether "having stripes" is a necessary property of the nature of tiger. We might hesitate a long while before saying so—even though we may never have observed a non-striped tiger. Suppose an offspring were born to tiger parents which was completely non-striped. Most people would probably accord him the prerogative of tigerhood in spite of his deficiency. And couldn't there just possibly be "green swans?" Or would we draw the line at that?

What is, at any rate clear, is that we begin to get into a rather nebulous area once we pass beyond obvious examples drawn from man's "risibility" or "tool-making ability." The criterion is still the same (the necessary connection between feature and nature) but the opportunity to apply it is only slight. The trouble is that we have comparatively little insight into the "nature" of tigers, swans, horses, water, atoms, or the whole panorama of non-human entities, and so very little capacity to judge what does or does not comport with their nature. It therefore seems that even on the philosophical assumption that there *are* permanent natures, there is ample reason to believe that our inductive knowledge of them is extremely limited. In the case of the physical "laws" which are based on these natures, we must also stop short of claiming an unconditional necessity. Even if the universe is a system of permanent natures (which Hume overlooked) the most that this would unconditionally warrant is a certitude as to the existence of necessary laws, and not a certitude that our knowledge had formulated them in any particular instance. It would seem that reasoning which is inductive in the usual sense *and nothing more* is going to be confined to an approximate and probable conclusion.

AYER'S TAUTOLOGY VIEW

To many minds there is a comparatively easy way out of this puzzle about induction, that along the lines so lucidly expounded by the logical positivist, A. J. Ayer.[2] Ayer's position simply is that aside from definitions, all truths about experience are corrigible in principle and hence merely probable. Conversely, every truth which is not corrigible in principle is simply a definition and hence tautologous. Thus, suppose we are puzzling our heads over the question of whether gold has to be yellow. Ayer would simply say that this is a matter of the way we decide to use words. If we include as part of our meaning for "gold" the quality of "being yellow," it is the clearest thing in the world that "All gold is yellow." If we don't, if we content ourselves with defining gold

[2] Alfred Jules Ayer, *Language, Truth and Logic* (New York: Dover Publications), n.d., pp. 72, 94–95.

without any reference at all to its color (say by reference to its atomic weight and structure) and if we are willing to let this be what we mean by gold, then there is no reasoning at all which would ever sufficiently establish that whatever fulfills this definition *must* unconditionally also be yellow. Every time we discover that an instance of this definition is also yellow, we are really discovering something; but because we are, we cannot say that this connection *must* hold good in every future case. Our assertion is "corrigible"—future experience may show that something can have all the other properties of gold and yet not be yellow.

So with "green swans" or "non-striped tigers"—to ask whether these things are possible is just to ask whether you would be willing to call such things tigers or swans; and to ask this is just to ask how much you include in the definition of tiger or swan. Someone who roundly asserts that "No swans are green" is simply declaring that he will not acknowledge that any green thing is a swan. Or suppose a chemist came upon an element which gave all the other reactions of hydrogen and yet stubbornly refused to combine with oxygen into water. In all likelihood, he would at length decide that this element could not be hydrogen but some hitherto undiscovered element; which would only indicate that he *must* be able to say that "All hydrogen combines with oxygen to form water," because otherwise he will not recognize it as hydrogen.

But then *all* pretended inductive generalizations are really definitions. "All gold is yellow" would not be a statement about experience but a statement about how I have decided to use words. I include the property of being yellow as a defining characteristic of gold—and hence I can safely declare that all gold is yellow. If it isn't, it is not what I mean by gold. No experience can correct my statement since it is not a statement about experience. In a parallel way, if I were to invent a word "brable" to signify "tables which are brown," then the statement "All brables are brown" is unconditionally true, and no experience in the future can ever contradict it or make me rescind it. But it is true because it is a tautology: the predicate repeats what is already contained in the subject. According to Ayer we have a simple choice: to make statements which really do refer to experience—but which are then open to correction by future experience; or to seek the unconditionally valid—but then we are simply decreeing how we will use words, and not revealing anything about experience at all.[3]

The gist of Ayer's position is quite similar to that of Hume: we cannot make necessary statements about experience as such. Now in great part this is what philosophy aspires to do. It is not satisfied as some mathematicians might be, to think of itself as elaborating the implications of concepts; it wants to achieve necessary insights into *existence*. Ayer tells us that this is impossible. But if we look more closely, we find that the basis of the impossibility is that the evidence to warrant necessity is unavailable—and this in turn directs our attention to Ayer's narrow view of what is evidential. To speak about experience is, in his view, to speak about a sequence of sense data; what is "given" is this sequence and every meaningful statement must refer *to* this sequence or else be tautologous. This is the gist of his "principle of verifiability." He denies all role to what could in any way be called intellectual intuition. To surmount his view, then, it is only necessary to inquire whether he is entitled to restrict knowledge in this manner.

In answering this question, traditional philosophy instinctively thinks of the notions of being, unity, cause, substance, essence and so forth, which it regards as fundamentally intelligible and yet not in a manner acceptable to the verifiability principle. Nor does it regard these conceptions as purely formal in Kant's manner. It holds that there are data which are available to intellectual intuition which are not given to the senses—although they are given *through the senses*. Unless this is understood, the old Scholastic formula, "Nihil est in intellectu quod non prius fuerit in sensu" would be rather hard to distinguish from the verifiability principle.

[3] *Ibid.*, pp. 77, 95–96.

Ayer wants to reduce all meaning to what is available *for* the senses; but these meanings are not so available. Scholastic philosophy, in pressing for their non-tautologous necessity, is really holding that we can know more than is available in and for the senses. Thus the proposition "Every event requires a cause" is not a tautology, but a statement about experience which necessarily holds good. It is not precisely reached by "induction" in the usual sense; the universal meaning is not the result of an extrapolation of particular observations, but discovered with necessity in each particular instance.

Here it seems a definite concession must be made to the opinion of those like Ayer. Induction considered simply as enumeration will apparently *never* give necessity. That is, the intelligibility which consists in adding up particulars *and nothing more* is excluded from the domain of necessity. Where what appears to be enumerative induction leads to necessary conclusions, it will turn out that something more than this was involved. Thus, even in the example, "All men laugh," this is not a conclusion reached by the extrapolation of a merely enumerative induction. It is an *insight* into the relation between rationality and risibility, an insight for which enumeration might provide a favorable occasion, but which is theoretically possible on the basis of a single case.

What is usually called induction, then, is really an amalgam of enumeration and insight. Where the latter is not possible—where the meanings dealt with are too opaque ("swans," or "tigers," for example)—induction can never rise beyond probability. When we *can* rise beyond probability, then some role must be allowed for insight. That is, the particular must be capable of being the vehicle for a revelation which is at once existential and intelligible. Ayer would not admit this, but his reason for refusing to do so is the verifiability principle, which tends to beg the whole question: if we assume that this is the criterion for meaningful statements, then necessary statements about experience are, of course, eliminated. But why assume it?

Could we not go much further than the habitual reply of

Thought and Experience: II

Scholastic philosophy, which is usually confined to the metaphysical principles and certain large distinctions between inanimate things, plants, animals, and men? There would seem to be a whole range of meaning which we can know in a manner other than what Ayer suggests. His fundamental mistake is to equate knowing with *definition*. This approach inclines us too hastily to the belief that all definitions have the same status. I can define terms any way I like, and then whatever I go on to say on the basis of these definitions is irreproachable—but not informative about experience. We tend to forget that the possibility would still be open that some of our definitions reach unities which exist as such beyond our thought, even if others are merely verbal. We forget this because the approach from the side of definition turns us away from experienced reality towards the attempt to express it verbally. If we recognize that any definition is simply an attempt to envelop succinctly features which have been experientially encountered, we may think differently.

If we can *know* reality without being able to define it, then some experience may provide a foundation for necessary truth. It surely seems accurate to say that we can know by acquaintance whole swathes of experience long before we can define them (if we ever can). I know what it means, in a sense, to think, exist, will, hope, remember, live, rejoice, admire, disapprove, and so forth, entirely apart from any definition. And because I "know" these things, I know with necessity certain truths about these processes which are not tautologous. Thus I may be said to know that "Memory involves an identity through time" and I can discover by laborious penetration of my direct (but obscure) knowledge of remembering that "Memory is not to be equated with mechanical repetition," which is what Bergson did in one of the most acute philosophical reflections ever carried out. The first proposition I may know rather easily, the second only after profound thought; but in each case I know two things: there is an existential reality reached by my concept "memory," and the proposition I now enunciate is *necessarily* true about this reality.

This proposition is not a matter of definition and not a tautology. It is an insight that has been reached by bringing into sharp focus the intelligible components and consequences of a meaning usually present in an obscure manner.

I do not begin with a "definition" of memory and then see what it "contains." I begin with the experience of memory, and as I bring it into clearer focus, I have the insight that the experience I undergo in "remembering" is an intelligible constellation whose figure I can discern at least to some extent. Likewise, the basis for my apprehension of the truth of the proposition "Moral values are not reducible to self interest" or "One man should not utilize another as a mere thing" is not the fact that I perceive that the predicate is contained in the definition I have assigned to the subject. It is the fact that as my thought turns to the lived experiential encounter with man or moral value, it is able to lay bare the strata of meaning contained in these experiences. Our thought reaches necessary insight in experience and about experience. That this is possible, Ayer's theory notwithstanding, is attested only in the doing of it.

VON HILDEBRAND AND PHILOSOPHICAL INSIGHT

Probably no one has contributed more to our understanding of this point than has Dietrich von Hildebrand, in whose writings it is a main theme.[4] In keeping with the phenomenological school from which he derives, von Hildebrand stresses that all philosophical thought must gravitate around a "given" which is embedded in lived experience. This notion of a "given" should not be construed as a dogmatic club to silence discussion. The point is only that reflective thought takes its rise from a fuller experiential source and must be faithful to that source. The "given" is not necessarily what is plainly available to everybody. It may be a

[4] Dietrich von Hildebrand, *What is Philosophy?* (Milwaukee: Bruce), 1960, Chapters IV, VII.

matter of the greatest exertion to get back to original experience; there is reason to think that philosophical genius consists primarily in this rare ability. The fact remains that thought should be continually conscious of proceeding with reference to this experience. Von Hildebrand holds that our thought may discover in experience meanings which are indisputably there and indisputably real, and which are apprehended in a way that allows "eternally true" statements to be made on the basis of them. These "givens" are not grasped in conceptual definitions but lived encounters, and hence the insights founded upon them are unconditionally referential to reality. The examples suggested above might be supplemented by others such as these: "Moral values presuppose a person," "A promise founds an obligation," "Love entails a will for the good of the other," "It is better to suffer injustice than to do injustice," "Generosity is different from purity."

Certain realms afford us the opportunity for a fruitful penetration not open in others. It may be that my meaning for "atom," "electron," "swan," or "gold" is, beyond a certain point, largely a matter of construction. But my meaning for "person," "love," or "justice" is not a matter of construction but is founded upon direct experience. I do not really "induce" these things in the familiar sense. I grasp them in their singular manifestations, and I find that, having grasped them, they provide me with a depth I may continually explore. If I am to make necessary statements about "swan" or "gold" I must rise beyond their specific character to another level of abstraction, and grasp them as "being," or "substance," or "living"; but in the case of "person," or "love" or "justice" I can discover necessary truths about them in their own specific character.

Again, this does not mean that I can *define* them. The propositions mentioned above are not "analytical" in Kant's or Ayer's view: that is, it is not the case that the predicate is already contained in the content of the subject. These propositions are *revelations:* they are the unrolling of a rich scroll of meaning which I have actually discovered in experience. Von Hildebrand points out that the insight into the necessary reference of "moral values" to "persons" is really an insight. It is not part of the definition of moral value that it can exist only in persons. The fact that I psychologically encounter moral values in persons would not make the proposition tautologous; I discover aesthetic values in persons too, but they are also found in non-personal beings. My realization of the essential and necessary connection between moral value and person is a discovery of the meaningful character of a special dimension of being. This is an *experiential* discovery, since the meaning of "justice," "moral value" or "love" is not an arbitrary construction but the grasp of something really present as an intelligible unity in experience. These propositions are indubitably referential to a dimension of the real. But the interesting thing is that the reality to which they refer can yield up insights into its structure which are *neither* tautologous *nor* corrigible by future experience.

Remember here that the discussion centers on the lived encounter with these realities and not on our concepts of them. When we speak about "moral values," "justice," "generosity," or "purity" we are not speaking primarily about the *concepts* with which we deal with these experiences, but about the experiences themselves; just as when we speak of "red" or "green" we are speaking of the encountered reality of colors. "Generosity" and "purity" are as different as "red" and "green," even though their intelligible structure may be more complex. As our thought brings this intelligible structure into focus, it is able to enumerate truths about it in its unity which are just as eternally and necessarily true as the statement "Red is not green." The latter proposition is not a tautologous definition or a mere decision to use words in a certain way, but a statement about a non-verbal facet of reality. In like manner, the statement "generosity is not purity" is not a tautology but an insight into a non-verbal difference in experience. The additional factor is that "generosity," "purity," and similar givens are complex unities and that they are intelligible *as* complex. "Red" and "green" do not yield up meanings readily, due to their extreme simplicity; "red is not green" is about as far as we can go in this case. But the intelligible complexity of love, moral value, generosity, purity, and so forth, is an extremely fruitful one: it allows not only the simple recognition of irreducible unitary differences, but the further necessary insights provided by the progressive penetration of this unity in its complex character.

The fact that von Hildebrand speaks of these things as "givens" and stresses the "objectivity" of such "essences" and the "eternal" character of the truth they underwrite may cause needless confusion. As we have seen, the notion of a "given" should not be understood in a rationalistic manner. Their intelligibility is characterized by depth; they are invitations to explore further. Nor does the fact that they make "necessary insight" possible mean that once we delve them out of experience, we can disregard experience thereafter and merely peer into their timeless structure to comprehend them further. Sometimes von Hildebrand speaks as if this were the case, but actually to penetrate a given "essence" of this sort is not to turn away from experience but towards it. It is not unfaithful to von Hildebrand's position to say that the "given" is always not-yet-given, or not-quite-given. Surely it makes insights possible, and surely it underwrites "eternal truths" which we do not have to keep re-verifying and which are not subject to correction. But just as these insights are originally the products of a close focusing upon experience, so their retention is a product of a continuing adhesion to experience.

The meaning contained in the concepts of person, justice, or love is not an acquisition snatched out of experience and wrapped in mental cellophane; it is the intelligible epiphany of a certain mode of experience. To explore these "essences" I must continually rejoin in thought the experiences from which their meaning shines forth. This meaning is not "given" in the sense that I can unfold its explicit content from the beginning; it is given in the sense that it is only with reference to it that certain insights are possible. For example: even though the full meaning of "love" is never available to me, still such truths as that love entails benevolence, or that love is a value response, or that love is not reducibile to an instinctual urge, are eternally vouchsafed to me even in my limited penetration of this experience. Even so, this does not mean that once I "see" these truths, I retain them as permanent intellectual property; really to "see" them, I must continually re-see them—I must dwell thought-fully in the experiences in which their truth is manifest. The "given" is not a permanently acquired premise from which I deduce consequences; it is a meaning emergent and clung to in actual experience. As experiential it nevertheless generates unconditional certitude. In this way it differs from other experientially encountered meanings which do not warrant certitude.[5]

As has been pointed out, this view presupposes that there is more in experience than Ayer would acknowledge. It also implies that there is much more in experience than Scholastic philosophy is in the habit of adverting to. Too often the latter rests content with the "Nihil est . . ." formula and conceives experience in terms of it. A few words are in order here. If this formula were really taken literally, there would be nothing to distinguish Scholasticism from pure sense empiricism. Now and then some Scholastics themselves fall into the groove of speaking as if the "something more" in experience beyond the data given to sense are notions like cause, substance, necessity, and so forth. This gives a quasi-Kantian concept of experience which completely neglects the abundance of meaning which is *neither* sense datum *nor* a category of this sort. For one thing, the whole reality of personal existence is overlooked. Willing, rejoicing, loving, hoping, responding, admiring, envying and their *objects* are every bit as irreducibly given as are "sense phantasms." St. Thomas stresses that we have a direct knowledge of the soul through its activities; we know that it exists, even though we may know little of its "whatness." No doubt a notion of "soul" is a relatively late intellectual arrival, the

---

[5] Sometimes von Hildebrand speaks in a rather objectified manner of this "eidos" as imposing itself on me, as if it were an atemporal external thing, but this manner of speech is not integral to the doctrine.

product of various inferences; and yet not only the *that* but the *what* of willing, rejoicing, loving, and the rest, are immediate data of experience.

It would be perfectly vacuous to treat these experiences as abstractions. We surely have abstract concepts of these things, but the concepts are drawn from directly experienced singular instances. No one thinks of disclaiming our immediate encounter with instances of red, loud, or sweet, because our concepts of them are abstractions. Just so, the concept of justice, generosity, or love, is generated by an encounter with these realities in singular instances. Experience contains singular instances of love, hope, or justice, just as it does of red, sweet, or loud. The alternative to recognizing this would be to treat sense data as the only directly given reality, and then to treat the other data as somehow "abstracted" from the sense data. It sometimes is wrongly inferred that this is the meaning of another Scholastic formula: the proportionate object of the intellect is the essence of material things. In some ways this formula is even more misleading than the first. It seems to say that only material things are known directly, and that all of our knowledge of spiritual reality is indirect; but St. Thomas makes it quite clear that we know the acts of our own soul directly—and indeed, how else could we know them? It further seems to say that we know the essences of "material things" (such as, perhaps, the natures of stone, tree, or cow) better than the nature of a person. In one sense, of course, even this is true, since I can easily grasp the referent of these words, and I would never get mixed up if I were given the job of sorting out stones, trees, and cows. But beyond grasping their ostensive signification, I know very little about the essence of stone, tree, or cow. Contrariwise, I may have little superficial ostensive knowledge of love, justice, or a person, and I may have to win through to such knowledge quite laboriously; and yet what I can *know* of these realities far exceeds in depth what I can know about a stone, tree, or cow.

It is surely true that we ought not to take the Scholastic formula to mean that we know material things better than persons. It is, unfortunately, just as surely true that its wording facilitates this misinterpretation. Some of the difficulty would be avoided if we simply understood the formula to mean that the proportionate object of our thought is being as it is revealed through the senses. This is distinctly less exceptionable, though still unsatisfying. Actually the genuine residue of meaning in the formula seems to be little more than the insistence that my incarnate situation is the vehicle of my knowing and that it colors and conditions all my knowing. This is a fair enough statement, but it could be put in a manner less open to misinterpretation. It is not true to say that all our knowledge of spiritual reality is indirect, as the formula could be taken to imply. Nothing is closer to us than our interpersonal existence and this is a spiritual mode of existence. Of course, if one wants to emphasize that it is the spiritual mode of existence of an incarnate being, that is unobjectionable; we have no direct awareness of the mode of existence proper to disincarnate spirits. Yet then the statement that we know properly and proportionately the "essences of material things" widens to mean that we know *persons* best—which is rather far from its original implication. We now stipulate that a "person" is the essence of a material thing: a highly unilluminating manner of speaking.

The last interpretation is suggested by Thomistic philosophers who wish to preserve the experiential orientation of Thomism and yet bring it into alignment with the clear truth of experience. Thus de Finance proposes that what our intellect is primarily ordered to is not just the "essence of material things," but other *persons*.[6] It would seem just as legitimate a procedure to stop using the formula. Once we use it, we are stuck with it. For once having employed the formula we are impelled to try to squeeze all experiential data into this mold. The attitude inherent in it is what led Aristotle to try to understand man in terms of a "material thing," albeit a material thing of a special kind. It is a thankless task to try to understand how we can rightly represent a person, beauty,

[6] Joseph de Finance, S.J., "Being and Subjectivity," trans. by W. Norris Clarke, S.J., *Cross Currents,* VI 163–178; see p. 169.

Thought and Experience: II

justice, number, generosity, $\sqrt{-1}$, law, charm, history, ambition, and a million other realities as the "essence of a material thing." No doubt the one who holds this formula goes on to acknowledge that we can have an inadequate grasp of *all* being; but this acknowledgment is considerably qualified when we realize that he ordinarily means by this simply that we can grasp reality according to the very general principles made possible by the concept of being. The real point is, however, that we can have an immediate experiential contact with realities which are not sense data and not usefully understood from the side of sense data.

There is very little doubt that Thomistic philosophy implicitly recognizes this truth, but its habitual terminological dependence on a delineation of experience as "phantasms" on the one hand and generalized intellectual concepts on the other impairs this recognition. Historically there is no doubt that it has not exploited this recognition. If a constricting vocabulary or formulas with very limited usefulness stand in the way of a philosophical appreciation of experience, it would seem the course of wisdom to relinquish them and move on.

10 *EXISTENTIAL TRUTH*

ON THE NATURE OF EVIDENCE

We have already met the fairly standard definition of truth as the conformity between mind and reality. In this relationship of conformity, it is natural to think of reality as having the initiative. This is what the conception of "evidence" likewise suggests: reality imposes itself upon me, and in the presence of the evidence, I submit. In submitting, I confirm to what-is, and thus my judgment may be denominated true. There is not the slightest question that this way of conceiving things has a permanent validity, but the manner in which we spontaneously express it may be both highly questionable and highly misleading. Implied in it is what might be called a "billboard" theory of evidence. It is as if the mind stands off and reads evidence which is posted before it, and then the assent is inevitably forthcoming. The problem of error then becomes that of comprehending how anyone could fail to read evidence posted plainly on the billboard of reality.

There can be little doubt that there is operative in this conception of things another instance of our succumbing to the intellectual temptation which Bergson has called irrevocably to the attention of philosophers—the temptation of substituting a mental scheme or image for the reality which we are trying to comprehend. Our thought has an habitual reliance on the imagination, and the imagination is primarily a faculty of spatial representation. If we try to deal by means of spatial imagery with a reality which is essentially non-spatial, difficulty is bound to arise. That appears to be what happens in the case of the familiar conception of the relation between mind and evidence as outlined above. What is experientially given is some kind of distinction between thought and being, or thought's experience of itself as not *in toto* originative. As soon as we express this distinction, however, we fall into the conception of it as an *externalization* of thought and being. As soon as we think any duality, we represent it, and involved in this representation is the imagination. Now the only way in which the imagination can represent things as dual is to represent them as spatially outside one another. For a faculty of spatial representation, it is impossible that there be *two* things unless these two things are external one to the other. The duality of thought and being is then conceived as a quasi-spatial juxtaposition of one to the other.

All our language about mind and evidence tends subtly to reinforce this representation. We speak about the evidence "imposing" itself on us, conjuring up an obviously spatial image. Even the seemingly inevitable tendency to speak of "knowing" analogously to "seeing" leads to the same result. For in literal seeing, the seer is spatially other than what he sees: I am here and the seen object is there, outside me. Then if we "see" evidence (and who can help talking this way?) we spontaneously picture the relation between knower and evidence in a quasi-spatial manner: here is the mind, and there is the evidence. Again, we say that knowing is a confrontation of the mind with evidence. But "confronting" is also a spatial relation. Is it possible to escape this spatial way of speaking? If not, what then? Are we enjoined from speaking about the reality of knowledge altogether? No, but we are put under the necessity of being constantly aware of the limitations of our own ways of speaking. We will, no doubt, go right on using these involuntary images, but we will be aware of their hidden presence and try to surmount them. In fact, the very ability to recognize the incongruity between image and reality is in its own way a transcending of the image. We are in a much better position after we have realized that knowing cannot *literally* be likened to seeing and that therefore the problem of knowledge cannot literally be either posed or answered in terms of seeing than we would be if we had not adverted to this. And we are better off even though we may go right on using the image. Philosophical reflection often amounts to this going beyond a distorting imagery. What we find when we thus go beyond may be relatively less communicable than what preceded it, but it is nearer to the adequation of thought with reality.

This brief excursus on the nature of evidence should be useful as a preliminary to the present chapter, for it brings out what might be called the "unstable" structure of evidence. Paradoxically, it might be said that the status of evidence is not entirely evident. Modern existential thought can be interpreted as an attempt to exploit this realization in one important direction. It begins on grounds not unlike those explained above. For the juxtaposition of mind and evidence is conceived, in one familiar form, as the juxtaposition of subject and object. Knowledge, it is said, consists in a judgment which a subject makes about an object. Almost immediately (through this spatializing tendency) there arises in our mind the conception of a subject standing off and characterizing an object which is juxtaposed to his subjectivity and his thought. The implication in this (which often passes unnoticed, but which is all the more influential for being unnoticed) is that subjectivity is irrelevant to truth. If the object is juxtaposed to my thought, if the evidence is posted out there, then the only function of the subject is to be a pure viewer of this object. A pure viewer, however, is one in whom all the impediments to viewing have been removed and whose gaze is turned pellucidly to what he views. But the impediments to viewing are not from the side of the object, which simply offers itself to view. They are from the side of my subjectivity. Perfect knowledge would, then, consist in the reduction of the subject to a cipher: a perfectly transparent eye opening on a world of objective evidence.

Something like this is what Edmund Husserl, the founder of phenomenology, declared to be the ideal of knowledge. If awareness is other than its object, then pure awareness is purely other than its object; and phenomenology aimed at the delineation of these "essences" or evidential structures which offered themselves to the view of a subject which conscientiously *reduced* his own contribution to nullity and converted himself into a pure viewer, or what Husserl called a "transcendental subject."[1]

Actually, Husserl can be regarded as simply extrapolating and making explicit an attitude which is exceedingly common. Everyone is familiar with the shibboleth that if we want to get at truth, we must be "objective" in our inquiry; we must not let personal prejudice, passion, interest, or emotion sway our judgment, but see things as they really are. Apparently, then, the knower who sees things as they really are is the one who eliminates from his scrutiny every intruding element of subjectivity which could mar and distort his vision. On this basis, the knower who reaches "objectivity" is the characterless cipher-subject. It should not pass unnoticed how clearly this rather strange conclusion is linked to the conception of knowing as *viewing*. If knowledge cannot be adequately seen in terms of this analogy, then there is from the start something wrong with the reasoning which poses the question in terms of it.

There is no denying that this conception of things has a genuine basis in our knowledge. We do experience knowing as an unconditional desire to explain what is. I do not want to be trapped by wishful thinking; I want to know reality just as it is in itself, regardless of my own wishes. Furthermore, I recognize this desire as one of the things that is best and noblest in me, this desire to say "yea" come what may. Even if the truth hurts, even if it crushes me, I want to know it. I experience my judgment as this aspiration to leave its object untouched, to abdicate completely before what is affirmed. Unless my knowledge reaches the real exactly as it is in itself, unless the act of judging makes no difference whatsoever to what is judged, then it is not knowledge at all. Cognitively, I am this aspiration towards pure, transcendental subjectivity, this abnegation in the face of the evidence. There is

[1] See Edmund Husserl, *Ideas*, p. 14. It is interesting to observe that ultimately Husserl's subject manages to be not such a cipher after all, since it emerges as the constituter of the objective panorama which, as pure knower, it beholds.

not the slightest doubt of this. And yet. . . . And yet the question of truth also contains the question of the origin of evidence. I want to submit to what is there. But how comes it that there is anything there? Evidence is the way reality is present to my thought. But why is reality present in the way in which it is? Cognitively, my judgment is an assent to the given. But why is there anything given? This is a rather crucial sort of question, and it is the sort of question which the existentialist will ask. Even if I were to agree that my cognitional ideal would be to convert myself into a transcendental subject for whom there was a pure vision of reality as evidentially present, there would still remain the question of what subject carries out this conversion. As an existing human being, I may be a pursuit of the ideal of pure cognitional meaning, but I am not the achievement of it. The transcendental subject remains for me an ideal which propels my reflection; but my reflection is the work of an existing subject.[2]

Furthermore, this transcendental viewing would have to be conceived of as *purely passive*: a pure abnegation before what-is. The trouble is that for a purely passive consciousness there seems no reason to think that there would be anything present at all. The only reason that there is anything present to human consciousness is that, from another standpoint, I am *not* a pure viewer, but an acting, existing being. My reality as existent is the source for the given which is there for me as knower. First I exist, then I know. All cognitional consciousness, then, occurs against a pre-cognitional or extra-cognitional background. Therefore, even if, as knower, I want to affirm objective evidence (the way reality is present) my mode of existing has a hand in determining the way reality is present. Subjectivity cannot be considered irrelevant to truth, for subjectivity is not irrelevant to evidence. Thus, the central existentialist contention may be summed up in this way:

---

[2] It would seem that the transcendental subject must be considered as either: 1) Actually constitutive, and therefore supremely active, as a sort of absolute self. 2) Purely formal, a mere name for the structure of certain aspects present to consciousness, as with Kant, and perhaps, too, Husserl. 3) Purely ideal, the ultimate term of an ideally realized reflection.

man's ultimate verdict on reality is a function of his manner of existing as a human being, and hence of his subjectivity and freedom.

This thesis, while radical enough, is not as foreign to traditional thought as might at first appear. The Thomist, for one, has always held that the known is in the knower according to the manner of the knower, and he might incorporate the existentialist thesis into this framework. It has always been recognized that knowing is a total act, but the insight usually does not go much beyond recognizing the sensory-intellectual composition of knowledge. The existentialist may be taken to be extending the insight to mean that the knower's whole mode of existing is contributory to the way in which reality is present to him. Traditional philosophy comes closest to this view in its notion of "connatural knowledge," knowledge which involves an affinity of the knower to the thing known: thus, the good man's knowledge of what is right may proceed simply from his sensitivity to moral value, and yet be as dependable in its own way as the ethician's theoretical and conceptual evaluations. From yet another standpoint, the existentialist may be taken as treating with ultimate seriousness the metaphysical maxim that "agere sequitur esse" ("as a being is, so it acts"); for what he stresses is that "as a being is, so it knows." Knowledge, as the act of an existing subject, cannot occur in abstraction from the existence of that subject.[3]

KIERKEGAARD AND SUBJECTIVITY

We may first consider this insight in the presentation of it given by Soren Kierkegaard, in whom the modern existentialist temper first appears.[4] Kierkegaard's position is probably best orchestrated around the central theme of what it means to be an "existing

[3] A remark of Pierre Rousselot, *The Intellectualism of Saint Thomas*, p. 33, is very much to the point here: "So little is knowledge indivisible that it varies necessarily with the nature of the thinking subject."

[4] "Existentialism," it may be noted, is a new name for a fairly old philosophical attitude, going back to Pascal, St. Augustine, and, in many ways, to Socrates and Plato.

reason." The development of this theme by Kierkegaard resulted from his violent reaction to the rationalism of Hegel.[5] Hegel had conceived of reality as through and through rational: logic was the static form of rationality, and history its dynamic unfolding.

Time and history are, then, the outward manifestations of a rationality in which human thought also participates. The sign of rationality is system, since to understand is to see things as *articulated wholes*. Then, man's reason progresses towards explicit understanding in so far as it progresses towards a comprehensive conceptual system. Kierkegaard seems to have felt that Hegel regarded this conceptual adequacy as self-enforcing: that is, given the rationality of a system of concepts, the assent to its truth would be automatically forthcoming. Human reason was simply a phase or moment in the coming-to-explicit-rationality of the Absolute Idea and hence for man to form adequate concepts was the same thing as affirming their application to reality. That the Absolute exists and has entered into history were two truths which Hegel thought could be validated simply by exhibiting the fact that an adequately rational system incorporated them.

Against this optimism, Kierkegaard championed the view that conceptual adequacy would never be enough to enforce assent in man. Man is not just reason, he is *existing reason*.[6] His existence inserts a wedge between his thought and the Idea. His existence estranges him from reason; at least, it means he is not just reason. His existing through time is not just a stretching out of a timeless abstraction, it is an irreducibly unique dimension. One idea may "necessarily" imply another; two premises may "necessarily" imply a conclusion; but no ideas and no premises necessarily imply man's automatic assent. There is a gap between existence and reason. Reason cannot close this gap because reason is always the reason

[5] At least we may speak of the rationalism of Kierkegaard's Hegel, a version of the master which many Hegelians would not recognize.

[6] On this, see *A Kierkegaard Anthology,* edit. by Robert Bretall (Princeton: Princeton University Press), 1947, pp. 201–207. This passage is from *Concluding Unscientific Postscript*. All references to Kierkegaard will be to this convenient edition.

of an existing being. Man is not a syllogism, nor a moment in a self-articulating system. There can be a system of abstractions, but there is no system of existence. Man exists, and his existence places him in an extra-conceptual order where the validities of concepts are not decisive. Only abstractions are airtight, but abstractions do not apply to existence and to the thought which thinks existence. As an existent I am not the embodiment of an abstraction or of a reasoning process. Therefore, when I try to think existence, no conceptual process can be automatically validating for me.

Kierkegaard considered Socrates to be an exemplary representative of this insight, and the doctrine of reminiscence to be his expression of it.[7] For, stripped of its mythical accoutrements, what the doctrine of reminiscence signifies is that man both does and does not belong to the truth. He is existing reason. As reason, he participates in the truth; as existing, he is separated from the truth. If he were totally estranged from the truth, if he were in no sense already attached to it, he would not even be able to seek it; if he were totally coincident with it, he would have no need to seek it. Furthermore, when he does seek it, when he does strive to assimilate into his existence the intelligibility which he "remembers," he never succeeds in achieving a perfect coincidence with that intelligibility. His philosophical inquiry cannot be conceived as a search for self-validating arguments. We may, building upon Kierkegaard, illustrate this by means of Socrates' arguments for the immortality of the soul, as given in the *Phaedo*. Not even to Socrates do these arguments have the character of self-enforcing processes; there is always something left over, some gap between evidence and assent. But Socrates fills in this gap from the side of his own existence. He does not feel the "objective uncertainty" as a factor against the arguments. It is almost as if it were part of the evidence, an intimation of the abyss of existence which is the source for our hope of immortality. These arguments for the

[7] *Ibid.*, pp. 155–157. This passage is from *Philosophical Fragments. Cf.* also pp. 210–217 (*Concluding Unscientific Postscript*).

immortality of the soul are not processes which could be given to an abstract thinker, for the evidence upon which they rest is a function of the exigence or demand of the existing consciousness for whom they arise. Socrates' own hopeful confidence has a hand in constituting the evidence upon the basis of which he is able to say "yea" to these arguments.

Actually there is no argument for immortality which could be constructed in such a way that the subjectivity of the arguer would not be implicated. For this argument is spoken directly to the existing subject. His assent to the "immortality of the soul" is not detachable from the affirmation "Yea, *I* will live forever." The argument for immortality is a translation into cognitional terms of the experience of oneself as *spirit*. A man cannot affirm himself as spirit *abstractly,* but only as a free, singular subject. What Socrates attempts to do in these arguments is to bring before his eyes the rationale of his whole life, the rationale of his existence. Only for Socrates, or for one who lives as Socrates, do these proofs contain "evidence." Only because, as existent, his life is pervaded by a transcendent appeal, can he give cognitive expression to the evidence for immortality. One who lived his life otherwise would have no such "evidence" available to him. A man at Kierkegaard's so-called "aesthetic" stage of existence, whose life was dissipated into a series of transitory sensations, would not be able to see the evidence requisite for these arguments. For the element of depth which characterized Socrates' existence is a component of the evidence which was there for his knowledge. It is implicated in the "given" which reflection discovers. It therefore cuts across the simplistic dichotomy between subject and object in knowledge. This evidence may be an unqualified revelation of reality, but it is a revelation which is only there for an existing subject and not for a neutral observer.

Kierkegaard himself may be accused of slighting the truly *cognitional* character of this kind of revelation and of treating it too much like "faith" in the stricter sense. We will call it "existential truth," truth in which my own existence is involved.[8] Kierkegaard's definition is that "truth is an objective uncertainty held fast in an appropriation-process of the most passionate inwardness."[9] Truth is the objective, conceptual inadequacy taken up and sustained by the lived yea of my existence. It must be emphasized that this condition is not a *defect* of my knowledge which we somehow ought to aim to eliminate—as if it really would be better if this truth *could* be established in a more abstract way, and we should make a noble effort to manage it. The point is that this truth is spoken to existence and that there just is no way to establish it or even to express it abstractly.

The role of subjectivity is not an unfortunate factual state of affairs. It is essential. A certain kind of intelligibility is only available *through* subjectivity. To eliminate subjectivity would be to eliminate the intelligibility. We will soon provide more examples, but for the present we may adduce the meaning of spirit as one category of freedom and subjectivity, only meaningful in so far as it incorporates these.

Secondly, it should be quite clear that what Kierkegaard has in mind is applicable to a certain sort of truth only. Statements like "200,000 radios are sold in the U. S. every three weeks," "Columbus discovered America in 1492," "It is raining out," "Your shoelace is untied," surely do not have the same status. Kierkegaard naturally would make a distinction between this sort of merely factual truth and philosophical truth. Philosophical truth is not simply a characterization of some item within my experience, but a characterization of the meaning and value *of* my experience itself: it is the affirmation of the transcendent dimension of my existence, and as such it can only be made by the existence which experiences itself as thus transcendent.

Thirdly, it may strike us that the formula "Truth is subjectivity"

[8] Although he himself calls it "essential truth," a bit of nomenclature puzzling to modern ears.
[9] *Op. cit.*, p. 214. (*Concluding Unscientific Postscript*).

could be carried still further. If certain truths emerge by being incorporated into my existence, then it may not be amiss to say I *am* these truths. We may then distinguish in the fashion of Gabriel Marcel between truths which I have and truths which I am. It is to Marcel that we will next turn for a further explication of the notion of existential truth.

MARCEL: PROBLEM AND MYSTERY

Marcel's thought does not in any sense derive from Kierkegaard's, and therefore any similarities between them should not be put down to a genealogical relation; if anything, they serve to indicate that there is something authentic in the thought of each. Marcel's views are most profitably explored from the standpoint of his already classical distinction between a "problem" and a "mystery," a distinction peculiarly well suited to epistemological presentation.[10]

The differences between problem and mystery are manifold, but all have their root in Marcel's view of the type of datum to which each question is directed. A problem is an inquiry which is initiated in respect to an "object," in Marcel's semi-technical use of that term. Etymologically, an ob-ject is something which is thrown in front of me, something which I encounter as external to me and over against me. In an objective situation, I am here and the object is there, complete and open for inspection. For the reason that I meet the object as juxtaposed to myself and as not involving

---

[10] Grateful acknowledgment is made to Fordham University Press for permission to reprint the following several pages which comprise part of Chapter III of the author's *The Philosophy of Gabriel Marcel* (New York: Fordham University Press), 1962. For Marcel's scattered treatment of this subject, see *Being and Having*, trans. by Katherine Farrer (Boston: Beacon Press), 1951, p. 100ss., 117ss., 126ss.; *The Mystery of Being*, vol. I, p. 204ss.; and the entire text of the essay "On the Ontological Mystery," published in *The Philosophy of Existentialism* (New York: Citadel Press), 1961.

myself, I can envelop it in a clear and distinct idea which delineates its limits. With this clarity comes perfect transmittability, and with the transmittability the object begins to lead that public and independent life which is the privilege of the world of the "problematic." Marcel does not fail to notice the peculiar coincidence that the Greek roots of the word "problem" are perfectly correspondent to the Latin roots of "object": a pro-blema is something which is thrown in my path, something which is met along the way.

A problem, then, is an inquiry which is set on foot in respect to an object which the self apprehends in an exterior way. Such would be a problem in algebra, or the problem a mechanic faces in fixing an automobile. The engine and the man are two quite isolable entities; the engine is something complete and entire outside of him, which he may literally inspect from all sides. Not every object, naturally, presents a spatial externality of this sort, but the problematic datum is always *regarded* as juxtaposed, converted, as it were, into a possessed thing. Thus, the attempt to solve the equation $2x^2 - 3x = 2$ would be a problematic inquiry even though the elements are essentially mental rather than spatial. The point is that the data as presented do not include myself; in conceiving the numbers, I do not conceive myself: I retreat from them and regard them intently as posed in front of me. The area of the problematic covers a wide range of human knowledge. The mechanic and the mathematician may stand, perhaps, as types of the domination of nature which the problematic knowledge of science makes possible. Science embodies the ultimate achievement of problematic knowledge. From the theorists of cybernetics to the researcher pursuing the links between cigarette-smoking and cancer, science is uniformly the application of the mind to an *object* in Marcel's strict sense of this word. But it is not only science which fulfills the notion of a problem. A bored student doing a crossword puzzle in class, a reader frowning over a "whodunit," a clerk consulting an orderly office file, all are engaged in solving problems. In each case, the data of the questions are such that I can effectively divorce myself from them and concentrate upon them as manipulable external objects.

A mystery, on the other hand, is a question in which what is given cannot be regarded as detached from the self. There are data which in their very nature cannot be set over against myself, for the reason that as data they involve myself. If I ask "What is being?" can I regard being as an object which is thrown across my path? No, for being, as datum, includes me; in order to conceive being as a datum, I must conceive it as including me. I cannot get outside of being in order to ask questions about it in a purely external way. The attempt to isolate what is before me from what is in me breaks down completely here. Being, then, is not a problem at all, but a mystery. If I decide to treat it as a problem, to stand on all fours with it and approach it as just one more manipulatable object, I no longer have hold of my original question. A mystery is a question in which I am caught up. In the area of the problematic, the status of the questioner is completely prescinded from, and only the object is called into question. But if I ask "What is being?" the question recoils upon my own status as a questioner. Who am I who question being? *Am* I? At this point the "problem" of being impinges upon the intrinsic conditions of its own possibility and becomes the mystery of being. For the condition of a problematic research is that the subject wear the regalia of unquestionability, and it is only this privilege which qualifies him to render the object totally intelligible. But to question being is to question myself as questioner. That is, this "being" at which I would like to direct questions is not an object given to a non-obscure subject which may direct all its uncertainty outward; for here, in questioning the object I call myself into question.

Being is not an object I can inspect from all sides. If I were to have a clear and distinct notion of being, I would be completely an object for myself (since being envelops me, and in order to objectify being I would have to objectify myself). But I cannot objectify myself; I cannot observe myself from the outside. The question "What am I?" is another example of a mystery. I do not even know for sure what the question means—and here we can say that as a problem it encroaches upon its supposed data. In the case of a true problem, the elements are clearly given; so that I may use them to proceed to the unknown. In a problematic situation there are always traceable analogies of the splendidly lucid conditions of geometry, "given" and "to find." For instance, in a crossword puzzle: given, the dictionary meaning of valley; to find, a four-letter word which equivalently conveys it. Or, in the mechanical problem: given, the known functions of the various parts of the engine; to find, which has broken down. But in a mystery the given itself is not clear and distinct. Thus, the "I" which causes me to tremble when I call it into question contains no element exempt from the mystery which wraps the whole; there is in it no small segment framed within defined limits and exhaustively known, to serve as an opening wedge from which to launch an encircling ratiocination.

Therefore not every reality can be the target of a purely problematic inquiry. Wherever I deal with something which encompasses the self, I may never hope to keep contact with its authentic nature if I treat it as if it does not involve the self. The supreme example of this, of course, is the mystery of being. I am a mystery to myself in so far as I *am*; all things are mysterious in so far as they *are*. Only what is not being—or what is not encountered as being—is not mysterious. The only thought which does not run full tilt into mystery is deontologized thought, thought which, by immunizing itself against the opacity at its own center, succeeds in conferring the same kind of immunity upon its object. This operation is quite possible, even desirable, in vast areas of human knowledge.

But there are certain realities which in the nature of things are not amenable to this sealing-off process; because what they are involves the self in all its singularity, I cannot prescind from that singularity when I conceive them. We have seen that the question of being and the question of the self are examples of this, but we may mention others. My body in so far as it is *mine* cannot be adequately rendered in problematic categories; the body which the physiologist studies is an objective structure available for an observer, but the body as *mine* simply is not accessible in this manner. In fact, my *situation* as a whole is non-objectifiable and refuses to be reduced to a problem. I cannot pass judgment on the world as if I am a spectator; every judgment on the world as a whole is passed on *my* world since I qualify it through my participation. Again, suffering and evil only *are* what they are inasmuch as they involve me; looked at from the outside, evil seems the mere malfunctioning of a mechanism—that is to say, it is not seen as evil at all. So too with love and with knowledge. We will see at greater length in the next chapter that the co-presence of love cannot be regarded as the juxtaposition of two "objects." In effect, we have already seen in the refutation of scepticism that knowledge is a mystery: if I ask "what is knowledge?" I can in no sense get outside my own knowing in order to describe it in an exterior way. The act through which I would like to objectify knowledge in order to study it is already an act of knowledge. So it is, apparently, with most truly philosophical questions. They bear on non-objectifiable data, realities which it is forever impossible to externalize. Freedom, time, space, sensation all seem to fall under this classification.

The second characteristic of a problem derives immediately from the first. A problem admits of a *solution*. By use of the proper techniques, a "period" can be put to our inquiries. With diligence (expended at the proper hourly compensation) the mechanic will eventually put his finger on the defective part of the engine and declare confidently: "There is your trouble." In the algebraic problem, the inquirer may, by suitable manipulations, reach the ready conclusion that $x = 2$. At that point, the problem is finished, over and done with. Final results have been attained and further thought is unnecessary. The possibility of a solution is directly linked to the objectified nature of the datum; because the datum is isolable, it is subject to being circumscribed and dissected by one who has the necessary skill. Its solvability is not

Existential Truth

what makes it a problem; but because it is a problem, it is solvable. And because it is a problem, the notion of a "result" applies to it in the strictest sense. The notion of a "technique" is strictly correlative to this kind of definitive result, and that is why the problematic can provide the arena for the "expert," the man who "knows-how," who has mastery of a style of techniques fitted to wrest results from objects which he has at his mental disposal.

But the notion of a "result" cannot be applied in this sense to the region of mystery. Here it is not possible to reach the point where I can say "That is done with," the point at which further thought is unnecessary. There is no Q.E.D. in a mystery. What is being? What is freedom? What is the self? These questions ceaselessly renew themselves. They are not susceptible of a solution in a sense univocal with that of a problem. On the contrary, there is the prevailing impression of an inexhaustible profundity, of depths which no amount of thought can ever fathom. The best that we can do is to locate ourselves within the mystery, but this can hardly be said to constitute a solution.

The third characteristic of a problem is based upon the fact that an object is conceived of as indifferent to me; it is simply there "for anyone." Because this is so, it follows that the self as conscious of an object is just anyone—an anonymous impersonal mind for which any other mind might just as well be substituted. The object is what is thrown in front of a purely logico-sensory subject. As a logico-sensory subject I am perfectly "interchangeable" with anyone else: I share the neutrality of the object itself. But since the mystery involves my singular self, then I cannot prescind from that self in pursuing it. The datum about which I raise the question includes my singularity, and hence the process by which I explore the datum includes my singularity.

TRANSCENDENCE AND "PROOF"

Now the repercussions of Marcel's distinction are manifold, but its significance for epistemology can be appreciated by concentrating on its consequences for the notion of "evidence." We have seen that as this notion is usually presented it presumes some kind of dichotomy between subject and object. If, however, there is a kind of evidence which transcends this dichotomy, which is in fact only available in so far as this dichotomy is transcended, the consequences are drastic indeed. No longer can we visualize the knower as an autonomous subject "in the face of" or merely evaluating evidence. The knower of mystery is not a spectator but a participator: *some* evidence is only available to the participant and not to the neutral observer. As existing subject, I am essentially being-by-participation. I am founded by this participation, and I have no priority to the participation in terms of which I can require it to present its credentials. The participation is the foundation for my subjectivity; my knowledge is posterior to participation. Therefore, there is no way in which my knowledge can evaluate the participation in a purely exterior way, since it is not available for inspection in this way. If evidence is the ground of cognition, still participation is the ground of evidence.

In the region of mystery what my thought does is to try to recover and express a participation which is there prior to thought. The thought which attempts this expression must do so by returning to the participation itself. This means that we are not dealing with a "proof" in the ordinary connotation of that word. It means that the sort of "proof" which is typical in the area of problem cannot be transferred to the region of mystery and so cannot be regarded as the norm for all reasoning. In a problem we can demonstrate; in a mystery we can only "monstrate." A typical example of this has already been cited in the case of Socrates' arguments for the immortality of the soul. To "prove" the immortality of the soul does not consist in demonstrating that a certain property belongs to one class of "object"—it consists in showing or "monstrating" that a certain mode of existing opens beyond the phenomenal. That this is true can only be comprehended by a knower who inhabits this mode of existing.

An even more obvious example is the question of the existence of God. The traditional attempts to prove the existence of God do not sufficiently distinguish proofs in this area from proofs in the area of problem. A realm of inquiry in which despair is possible is a realm in which the last word does not belong to argumentation. I cannot raise questions about the existence of God as if God were an "object," for He is supremely non-objectifiable. He is not out there, external to me, juxtaposed to my existence. If my thought poses the question of God as if God were another "something" about whose existence my curiosity has been aroused, it has already guaranteed its own futility. Nor can I raise this question as a mere spectator or an anonymous subject. It is not a matter of mere curiosity for me whether God exists or not. It is a matter of concern. If it isn't, then obviously I am not even raising the question at all. I cannot engage in theodicy in the mood of the geometer or grammarian, for then I am not engaging in theodicy at all. The question of the existence of God is raised only in function of an *exigence* which is felt by the subject.[11] No one who does not feel this exigence can be a metaphysician.

What about the "proof" for the existence of God? What the proof does is to raise to the level of self-recognition an intelligibility which is already contained in the exigence. For the exigence is a form of participation. Man's longing for God is not epistemologically irrelevant, but uniquely and irreducibly evidential. Nor should we only visualize this as the stipulation that the evidence is "there" independent of this exigence, but that we require the exigence in order to see it. This puts the exigence on the side of a prerequisite "subjective disposition," while preserving the "objective" evidence intact—thus reintroducing the schema of a dichotomy between subject and object which is the basic difficulty. The point is rather that the exigence is in no sense *external* to the evidence. The evidence for the existence of God is there only for an apprehending self and the mode of existing of this self is a component of this evidence.

---

[11] On the ontological exigence, see Gabriel Marcel, *The Mystery of Being*, vol. II, trans. by René Hague, pp. 33–51; and on the question of a "proof" for the existence of God, see *Being and Having*, pp. 121, 124–125.

Sometimes the impression is given that we argue syllogistically to the existence of God; but obviously the notion of being cannot function in the same way in a syllogism as can a limited concept: Thomistically stated, it is a transcendental idea (it includes everything, and every difference between every thing) and hence spans the distinction between subject and predicate, and is present in all terms of the syllogism. But not only that, the genuine notion of being also spans the dichotomy between subject and object. Hence its meaning is not available in a purely objectified way. If I want to know what I mean by being, I cannot prescind from my own subjectivity, for then I have a pseudo-notion, "being as object." On the basis of this pseudo-notion, no argument for the existence of God is possible. Only a genuine notion of being will provide the approach to this proof. And such a genuine notion must *include* my own existence.

It would be perfectly possible for me to fulfil all the requirements of a phenomenal community of knowing subjects without encountering the evidence for an authentic notion of being. As a member of such a community, I require merely orderly sense perception and the apparatus of logical thought; I could not claim "rationality" in the ordinary sense without this endowment. But logical thought *as such* does not provide me with the genuine notion of being. Logical thought is the mode by which a subject characterizes an object. But being is not an object. That is why it is easy enough for a knower who is "rational" in the ordinary sense to fail to give meaning to the arguments for or assertions of God's existence. Ordinary "rationality" is a social property. It does not of itself reveal to us the trans-temporal abyss contained in the notion of being. Rather the opposite. One who is accustomed to have his attention turned in the direction of the phenomenal serviceability of thought will treat as simply vacuous any thought which cannot justify itself in these terms. The real then becomes identified with the publicly verifiable. This is what happens in the case of the logical positivists, for whom any question of a "truth" which surpasses the phenomenal and verifiable is simply meaningless. The existence of God (among other things) surely cannot be verified in this manner, and hence the assertion of God's existence becomes meaningless.

Now how do we rise to the affirmation that there *is* such a thing as truth beyond the verifiable? It must be by contact with the potentially infinite intelligibility contained in the notion of being. This intelligibility, however, is available only as including me in my unique singularity. A notion of being which *leaves out* subjectivity will, as de Finance has pointed out,[12] deteriorate into a pure Kantian form, an empty concept, which could never serve as a point of departure for an argument for God.

When Marcel and others say, in a deliberately inflammatory way, that "theodicy is atheism,"[13] they mean that by not differentiating its mode of approach from ordinary scientific knowledge, philosophy may treat God as a "something" alongside of other somethings, a special kind of object for thought. That is the basis for the oft-quoted remark: "When we speak about God, it is not about God that we speak." To speak *about* someone is to refer to him as absent, a "third person," an "it." But God is not an absent third. He is absolute presence, or, as Marcel says, Absolute Thou.[14] Whatever is true of the infinite being, it clearly could not be correct to represent Him as *outside* the finite. The plenitude of being *includes* me. Therefore, the thought which seeks the infinite cannot approach it as it approaches things which *are* "somethings" alongside of other things. And the knower who affirms the infinite cannot be an anonymous epistemological subject, but a unique singular self. What Marcel calls the "ontological exigence," the yearning for the plenitude of being, is the ultimate face which participation presents to my thought. My "proof" of God is my translation of this experience into language. This insight as to the cognitive import of the exigence for being is, of course, fundamentally Augustinian and

[12] *Op. cit.*, p. 167–168.
[13] *Metaphysical Journal*, p. 64.
[14] *Du refus à l'invocation*, p. 53.

Pascalian in character. We have only to recall Augustine's cry "Show me one who longs, and he will understand what I mean," and the revelatory use which Pascal made of man's experience of himself as an "infinite lack." It even goes back to Plato, for whom the philosopher's quest was an élan to the absolute, an upward rising of the whole self, in which his need and poverty were the dynamic principles of discovery.

FREE CERTITUDE

For some, the approach of Kierkegaard and Marcel will seem to be the substitution of an arbitrary emotionalism for intelligibility, a kind of usurpation by wishful thinking of the proper place of reason. On the surface it may sound like this, and we must always be on our guard against reducing it to this in fact. However, what is involved is precisely the question of the *criterion* for intelligibility. Marcel does not regard mystery as confused or unintelligible. It is hyper-intelligible. Participation is a *source* of meaning; mystery is the light which issues from participation. We have so far spoken mostly of the mystery of being, but this may be particularized further. What of such experiences as love, hope, admiration, despair, fidelity? Are they cognitive revelations? The logical positivist, and many others, would treat these as merely psychologically significant and dismiss their role as revelation of reality. But to do so presupposes that they have a norm exterior to the experiences by which to measure the meaning of the experiences—and this can be denied. Hope reveals something of the ultimate nature of man—but only to the hoper, or to one whose thought inhabits the realm of the hoper. The truth here discovered is a truth which a certain kind of thought will refuse to acknowledge. Yet the issue always comes back to whether this refusal can be justified without begging the question.

The objection may be raised that if mystery is not demonstrable that the "knowledge" here gathered may be only an illu-

Existential Truth

sion. Marcel's answer is that the metaproblematic is given as indubitable—but only to the participant.[15] There is no point in asking it to justify itself by standards other than its own. Actually any such process would turn out to be regressive, since the standards would in turn require justification *ad infinitum*. If Marcel asserts that nothing but hope can be the source of the cognitive justification for hoping, he is not taking such an extraordinary position as might appear. All intelligibility is its own justification; he is only asserting that the sources of intelligibility are more widespread than we usually realize. It should be added that the "knowledge" which is generated in the return of thought to these experiences is not a securely possessed and transmittable theorem of some kind: it is never something I have at my disposal. It is something that I *am* rather than something that I have. The cognitive value of love or hope is sustained by a creative re-attachment of myself to these experiences. Since it does not bear on an external datum, it shares the elusive character of my own existence.

Finally we must note that since the unique, singular subject is involved in the recognition of mystery, then freedom is involved. This is an extraordinary point. The singular self is a free self. If some evidence is only revealed to me as a singular being, then some evidence is only there for my freedom. Often the "evidence" is thought to be something which imposes itself on me whether I like it or not. It is as if I am hit over the head by the evidence and have no choice but to submit. But if Kierkegaard and Marcel are right, there is one sort of evidence which is a *function* of my freedom. This is not meant in an arbitrary sense, of course. Marcel tells us that in certain areas the subject is neither autonomous nor heteronomous; this division is simplistic.[16] The evidence is indubitably there—but it is there as *appeal*.[17] It is sustained as there by my response.

---

[15] *Being and Having*, p. 114.
[16] *Ibid.*, pp. 173–174.
[17] *Du refus à l'invocation*, pp. 87–88.

To designate this state of affairs, we may employ the somewhat startling term "free certitude." Startling, because certitude is often thought to be necessitated or else not really certitude. But this may easily be a consequence of the spatial schema which we usually frame for ourselves. What Marcel holds is that the intelligible evidence contained in the experiences of hope or joy is truly there, but not there for an impersonal observer, a merely logico-sensory subject, but only for a singular self. Then it is only there for freedom. It is indubitably there—for one who responds. Shall we call this "knowledge?" Why not, if knowledge is the openness of thought to reality? Why not, if there is no other way for this type of evidence to be present?

A question which immediately ensues is as to the range of this kind of "certitude," since Marcel's own explorations by no means exhaust the wealth of revelations possible in the area of mystery. The full examination of the answer to this question is quite beyond the scope of this book, but the area most clearly indicated is in moral and aesthetic experience, which will be briefly dealt with.

What Marcel's conception of mystery as "knowledge" comes down to is that there is that in human experience in virtue of which man can affirm himself as trans-phenomenal. Man is not only a being-in-a-situation, but a being-beyond-a-situation. In fact the great philosophical questions can be brought back to this one question: how does man affirm himself as a being-beyond-his-situation? Marcel's central point (and it is not unlike that of other existentialists) is that this affirmation cannot be made by a mere subject-in-general. The transcendent value of human experience cannot present itself to a mere logico-sensory subject. Thus, the issues of God, freedom, and immortality, and all the other questions they bring in their train, cannot be raised or settled by an impersonal knower. Reality as evidential presents a different countenance to this kind of knower than to a knower who thinks out of the ontological exigence. This exigence, therefore, functions as a kind of "blinded intuition" of plenitude which is a source of illumination and therefore a source of evidence.[18] This intuition is not an object of vision but a principle of vision.

For the sake of explanation, we may liken it to the "creative intuition" of the artist. The artist's idea is not something which exists ready-made and pre-dates its embodiment. It comes to be in the artistic process. This is a strange and paradoxical truth, but a truth nonetheless. When the poet or artist sits down to write or paint, he does not already have in his possession a completed idea which he then simply transfers to paper. He does not first invent his idea and then embody it: he invents it by embodying it. Yet the strange thing is that his obscure intuition actually *guides* the process in which it comes into full being.

The poet may not already know his idea prior to writing, but as he goes along he eliminates passages which do not adequately express this idea. Thus, he is judging his work relentlessly in the light of an idea which does not even exist until the work reveals it to him. The creative idea is not like a recipe or blueprint which is mechanically followed: it comes to be in the work itself. It is like a light shed on the work from which it is then read back. Just so, thinks Marcel, man has a creative intuition of being (of plenitude, of the transcendent dimensions of his own existence): this is not an object of vision, but a hidden light which is shed upon experience and then read back out of experience. Experience is the revelation of man, but it is also the revelation of the transcendent to which human existence opens.

Again, however, if we ask which subject can *affirm* this dimension, the answer must be the subject which belongs to the creative intuition. The transcendent is present to human experience precisely as appeal. Just so, the artistic idea is present to the artist's consciousness as an appeal by which he is haunted: he can only affirm the existence of the appeal freely, in so far as he responds to it. He could not, as pure sensory consciousness or impersonal intellectual knower, assure himself that his consciousness con-

---

[18] On the "blinded intuition," see *Being and Having*, p. 118, *Mystery of Being*, vol. I, p. 13.

tained this appeal: the only subject who can affirm the appeal is the one which responds to it. This realm of subjectivity is *called forth* by the appeal and does not exist in separation from it. Here, too, participation founds subjectivity: the subjectivity of the artist is not an autonomous ego, but exists only in the appeal and response of the aesthetic process. Just so, the only thought which can affirm a transcendent dimension in man's existence is one which participates in that transcendence.

11 *INTERSUBJECTIVE KNOWLEDGE*

"OTHER MINDS"

The epistemological problem of the existence of other selves is both easier and harder to solve than is the more general problem of the existence of "objects" other than ourselves. It is at once apparent that our conviction that there are other selves asserts considerably more than does the mere conviction of an objective world in general. For in asserting that other selves exist, we are not merely asserting that objects exist, but that other *subjects* exist. When speaking of objects we do not at first experience in any urgent way the need to conceive the "inside" of these objects; an object is, so to speak, all "outside." This is especially true in the case of an inanimate thing like a stone or a mountain; we do not proceed by conceiving these things as there "for themselves" in the way a conscious subject is.[1] But the assertion that other selves exist does immediately entail the belief that there is more to certain entities than the corporeal front which they present to perception. This being sitting across from me on the subway train is not only a rather complicated kind of bodily object; he is also, I am sure, a subject. Maybe I am only observing his "outside," his bodily behavior, but I am sure that there is an "inside," a conscious experience similar to my own.

On reflection, however, the justification for this assurance may

[1] This is not to say that eventually a problem of this kind will not arise in respect to objects, since in some analogous way they too must be conceived as "subjects."

strike us as hard to come by. For is not subjectivity just what is most private, most intimate, most non-communicable of all things? Surely I know that I exist as a subject, for I am in a privileged position with respect to my own experience: I *am* my own "inside." But this "inside" of mine, my interior consciousness, is, one would think, available for me alone. No one is present to my consciousness in the way that I am. No one can read my mind—my consciousness is that which is concealed from the probing scrutiny of others. My body is observable by others, but not my mental processes. In the same way, one might think that if there really are other subjects, still their subjectivity is just as concealed from me as my subjectivity is from them. Then how can I be sure that there are other selves if I do not directly observe them? Can I possibly *directly* experience any subjectivity besides my own? We would be inclined to say no. But then, whence do I derive the assurance of the existence of such subjectivities? From one standpoint this problem is manifestly more perplexing than the problem of other "objects," since it adds a completely new dimension to my claim to make contact with what is other than myself.

Yet from another standpoint it is easier to get at than the more general problem. Even though I may be perplexed as to how I can be certain that other selves exist, I do not seem to experience much difficulty with the *meaning* of the assertion that they do. That is, I have a perfectly good notion of what it means to exist as a self, and I experience no great barrier in conceiving what it would *mean* for other selves to exist. This is in sharp contrast to the difficulty I feel when I try to imagine the independent existence of a cloud, a leaf, a stone, an atom, or a lump of earth. I may be convinced that these things do exist independently, but I am very confused as to what it "feels" like to exist in this way. There is no such obstacle in grasping the meaning of the existence of other selves, for the mode of existence here asserted is the mode of existence which I myself actually experience. We stand, then, in a peculiarly ambiguous condition of assurance and uncertainty in respect to this question.

The question is not a particularly old one in the history of philosophy, and it may first be dealt with in the form of the "problem of other minds," which was first posed by John Stuart Mill and which has become what might be called the traditional form of this question. Let it be noted that the problem of "other minds" is significantly, though subtly, different from the problem of "other selves." A mind is conceived specifically as the interior psychic concomitant of a bodily process. If my retina is stimulated by a light-wave, I may perceive the color red; or if the tympanum of my ear is set vibrating by a sound-stimulus, I may hear a shrill noise. Any witness may observe the stimuli and my outward reactions, and a physiologist may even observe and measure my neural and cortical reactions; but no witness may observe my conscious perception of red or shrill. That is available to me alone. What is true in the case of sensations is apparently even more true in the case of emotions or thoughts: I may be "observed" in a fit of pique or a brown state, but this observation is restricted to my grimaces and bodily postures, and does not extend to an awareness of what I am feeling and thinking.

This line of reflection led Mill to his problem of why, if it is true that we cannot directly observe the interior life of consciousness of another, we ever can be said to "know" that other minds really exist. His answer is the "analogy" argument, which was once standard but has lately lost favor.[2] The circumstances of the situation are this: Only outward behavior is available for observation, and it must therefore be that outward behavior gives us the

[2] For criticism of the analogy argument, see Max Scheler, *The Nature of Sympathy,* trans. by Peter Heath, intro. by Werner Stark (New Haven: Yale University Press), 1954, p. 239ss.; John Wisdom, *Other Minds* (Oxford: Blackwell), 1952, p. 68ss., p. 194ss.; Louis Arnauld Reid, *Ways of Knowledge and Experience* (London: Allen & Unwin), 1961, p. 237ss.; W. Wylie Spencer, *Our Knowledge of Other Minds* (New Haven: Yale University Press), 1930, p. 55ss.

basis for our inference in respect to the inner concomitant. This is possible because in one instance, our own life, we have a privileged access to the inner concomitant. We then proceed by this reasoning: In my own case I realize that certain bodily processes are accompanied by inner conscious processes (unified under the term "mind") and therefore I decide that when I observe these bodily processes in others, I may infer that they are accompanied by mental processes not directly observable by me. My certainty that others exist is a product of an analogical inference which sets out from my own existence and its known connection with my bodily actions.[3]

Now in spite of an initial plausibility, this view is open to various objections which rather conclusively refute it, and which have more or less led to its abandonment. Of these objections, we will mention only two. First of all, there is what might be called the "mirror argument," which has been very frequently employed against it.[4] What Mill has contended is that I argue to the consciousness of others by supplying a missing link in a chain of analogy which begins with my own behavior, a patent fallacy. In order for me to argue that behind the bared teeth and squinting eyes which I now observe in this face confronting me there is a feeling of kindness and good humor, I would, on Mill's terms, have had to observe my own inner feelings as united to similar outward conduct: I would have had to observe myself smiling. But that, of course, I do not do. I don't know how I look when I smile, or am angry, or embarrassed, or sad. In my own case, I have the inner feeling but not the outer view. If I wanted to have the outer view of myself in the grip of these emotions, I would have to observe my facial and bodily contortions in a mirror—hardly a standard procedure. Therefore I do not comprehend that certain bodily behavior is the sign of another mind by comparing it to my own bodily

[3] John Stuart Mill, *An Examination of Sir William Hamilton's Philosophy*, Chapt. XII.
[4] See Scheler, *op. cit.*, p. 240; Reid, *op. cit.*, p. 238; Spencer, *op. cit.*, p. 67.

behavior, for the simple reason that this is a comparison I could not possibly make, never having observed my own behavior.

Secondly, it can be shown that if I did proceed by analogical inference in this way, such an inference could never give me the *other*. Mill suggests that I *derive* my knowledge of the other by this means, but this is impossible. Unless I already had an awareness of the other, then the best I could do by means of an analogy would be to argue that behind a certain bodily facade was *my own* consciousness. That is, beginning with this proportion: this sort of bodily behavior is accompanied by my consciousness, then whenever I met this sort of bodily behavior, I would infer that it is accompanied by my consciousness. For the analogy to be strict, there would have to be some middle term that could serve as a sign of the presence of another; but if *behavior* is the middle term, then I only know what behavior signifies in the case when both the sign and the signified are present—my own conscious experience. Therefore, behavior signifies my consciousness, and it could only validate an inference to *my* consciousness. Nor could we claim that we must distinguish between *my* behavior and the *other's* behavior, for that is just what is in question: the behavior is supposed to be the basis for my awareness of another self, and I cannot begin by assuming that I already know it to be the behavior of another self.

This reasoning seems to be sufficient to deprive the argument from analogy of any claim to explain the origin of our knowledge of other selves. This is not to say that analogical inference in a broad sense may not be frequently used in interpreting others' conduct, but it cannot explain our awareness of the other as such, since it already presumes this awareness. We note already that the approach to the problem of other selves taken by this argument presumes that this knowledge is not primary, that it is the product of some sort of inference. There is no need to take much cognizance of this belief in its most aggravated form, the contention that the only things directly given to consciousness are bundles of discrete sense data, and that everything else is a matter of construction or interpretation. This view itself is an assumption, and a very shaky one. It will help to begin with the confidence that much more can be given to direct experience than the sense-datum theorist or the phenomenalist will admit.

Actually, anyone beginning with the phenomenalist viewpoint has a literally impossible task in reaching another self. On the phenomenalist's assumption, only transitory and discrete sense-data are available to consciousness. Given this assumption, even the *meaning* of the assertion that other selves exist becomes doubtful. If, on the phenomenalist's basis, an "object" is simply a logical construction out of a set of sense data, then so is a subject. What it would mean to reach another self as a logical construct is very hard to imagine. Not only would this construct be indistinguishable from the object-construct, but it would have independent reality only in the meaningless Pickwickian sense of all phenomenalist "objects."

Yet, even if we start with the expectation that much more can be directly given to us in experience than impoverished sense data, there is still a very special difficulty in wondering how another mind can be directly given. Here we may consult the exhaustive and entertaining presentation of the problem which was made by John Wisdom.[5] Wisdom's difficulty comes down to this: Once we have made the plausible distinction between the inside and the outside of experience (mind and body), how can we ever be sure that any outside is the sign of any inside? That is, if we distinguish between any emotional state and its bodily expression, and say that the second is observable while the first is not, how, given this split, can the second ever be taken as a sure sign of the presence of the first? For example, I might hold as an obvious fact that the pain which I *feel* is not to be identified with the gnashing teeth, rolling eyes, and clenched fists which manifest this pain outwardly. What I mean by saying that I am in pain is my excruciating, non-outward feeling. So with gaiety, delight, sorrow, disappointment,

---

[5] Wisdom, *op. cit.*, p. 84.

anxiety, or any psychic state—we may distinguish the mental state from the bodily manifestation.

Then, says Wisdom, what possible guarantee do I have that this bodily state in another corresponds in him to a mental state such as it would correspond to in me? I *assume* it does, but do I know that it does? Since I don't observe his emotional state, it always seems at least logically conceivable that it is very different from what it would be in me, given similar bodily manifestations. Here I see someone rolling his eyes, clenching his fists and screaming, and I say he is in pain. But how do I know that this is not the way in which he expresses delight? I don't observe his felt pain, I only infer it. Similarly, a mother playing with her baby may observe what she takes to be all the outward signs of joy: laughter, waving arms, gurgling. Yet can she be logically certain that these particular gesticulations are not the manner in which this particular being expresses his grief? Isn't it conceivable that the mother is inflicting the tortures of the damned upon her baby and that he is expressing it in this unfortunate manner which misleads his doting parent? Obviously, this sort of question here bears on the accuracy with which we can read the inner life of the other and not on the question of how we can know that there *is* another there. Yet it could be easily generalized, for we might think of the misreading being extended without limit, so that we could misread as conscious responses what were only the responses of an automaton.

The bizarre character of such reflection inevitably forces the suspicion that there must be something fundamentally wrong with posing the problem of other selves quite in this way. No doubt the mind-body distinction is valid, and no doubt there is an irreducible difference between mental and physical processes. Yet to treat the body as a kind of facade behind which the existence and nature of mind has to be verified seems to get things off on the wrong foot. We might try to recover a certain balance even within this framework by suggesting a "king and three sages" type of inference to other minds. Perhaps, one might hold, we do not infer immediately to the inside of others, but go through our own. That is, I can infer that the other understands *my* inner life. This could happen somewhat as follows: Suppose I am in a position where someone is causing me pain, let us say a dentist drilling my teeth. Eyes tearing and blinking, knuckles white, face contorted, I finally complain that it hurts. I may reason as follows: if he understands by the word "pain" what I understand by it, he will do what I would do if I understood what he meant by the word "pain" and he told me that I was hurting him. The dentist stops drilling. I then infer that he and I mean the same thing by the word pain. If he thought that by "pain" or "hurting" I meant pleasure or delight, he would smile cheerfully and keep blasting away. The fact that he doesn't indicates that the word "pain" signifies a reality about which he and I feel the same. The example, of course, could be extended to take in not only pain but pleasure, joy, sorrow, and so forth. What happens is not that I infer how another feels, but that I infer how he would act if he knows how I feel.[6]

Suppose, while still remaining within this general assumption of an "indirect" knowledge of others, we try to situate the problem of "other minds" against a wider background. The child certainly becomes aware of the existence of others before he makes the distinction between mind and body: he knows himself as a member of a class of which there are other members. Subsequently, one may suggest, he realizes that he has a "mind" and he wonders whether his natural belief that the other members of the class likewise do is well founded. How might he assure himself of this?[7] One route to this assurance might be the *responsive* character

[6] The example given here includes language, whose crucial importance is clear. But it might be proved without bringing in language at all. If I merely wish the dentist would stop, yet refrain from saying anything, while my physical symptoms are identical, and if he actually does stop, I infer that he understands *my* physical symptoms. He does what I would wish him to do if he understood my inner life. Does this prove that I can read *his* inner life? At least it shows a certain mutuality between us which, I might assume, could just as well run from my side to his.

[7] The ensuing remarks owe much to the discussion of Spencer, *op. cit.,* pp. 20–48, who makes many interesting and instructive points on this issue.

which distinguishes the behavior of certain objects of my experience from others. The child crying for the rattle he has just hurled from him elicits no response from the bars of his play-pen or from the carpet, but a human being nearby may retrieve it for him. There is thus built up the realization of a close connivance between this behavior and his wishes. His reaching out finds response in one case and not in another. There is a reciprocity which is missing elsewhere. Some might insist that these responses are still physical, that the other is doing what I would do with my own body if I could—and that hence this approach does not give us another mind. The fact that this is a true response of the other and not an extension of my own will is brought forcibly home in the instances where the response is of rivalry or resistance.

Further, there are cases where the response called for and elicited is not just another physical act; sometimes I require collaboration in a fully conscious process, and then the response becomes evidence for a fully conscious respondent. Some activities call into play our full nature as human beings, and those who are able to respond and co-operate in such acts evince thereby the presence of other minds. It is the other who actually calls us forth into full self-consciousness. The parents playing with the child are not opaque "others" to an already conscious individual; they are instruments by which the individual is brought to consciousness. *Their* response is implicated in *his* consciousness. As this consciousness expands, it expands in reciprocity with the other: in friendship, in common endeavors, in shared enthusiasms, the other responds to me in my entirety as a human entity, and therefore his entirety is present in his response. We now approach the realization that it is not quite right to think of the "mind" of the other as concealed behind a bodily facade. If our self comes-to-consciousness, then the respondents in this process of coming-to-consciousness are already present as minds. Mind, then, is at the boundary of the self and the other: it is a revelation of the other as well as the self. The primary manifestation of this, of course, is language, which is a perfectly "open" reality. Human consciousness finds itself in language. Then in finding itself it does not find only itself.

The objection may be raised that this awareness of others as respondents does not explain our rich and detailed awareness of *individual* selves, since it is rather indiscriminate and generalized. The point is valid enough, but the question may also be asked how we know our own selves as individual and unique beings. It is too easily assumed that the meaning of "I" is clear, but the meaning of "thou" is obscure. The truth may rather be that the profound meaning of "I" is equally hidden, that here, too, the revelation is a reciprocal one. Perhaps I only become "I" in the encounter with "thou" and perhaps apart from that encounter the only referent I have for "I" is a tatterdemalion succession of psychic states. Many modern philosophers have come to believe that this is the case. If something of the sort is true, then the problem is not of "other minds" or even of "other selves" but just the problem of "persons." Not even "other persons," for if these philosophers are right, the category of person already includes a reference to the other, and for one who knows himself as a person, there cannot be a problem of other persons.

DIRECT KNOWLEDGE OF THE OTHER

Before following up the suggestion contained in the preceding sentence, it will be interesting to inspect some views which make the transition to it easier. The primary drawback to the approaches outlined above is that they regard our awareness of "other minds" as indirect. Even where an attempt is made to avoid the errors of the "analogy" explanation, the assumption continues to be that the reality of other minds is not an immediate datum but is known through an inference of some sort. Now one way of undercutting this whole difficulty is obviously to make the opposite assumption—to assume that the other is given directly and does not have to be argued to at all. This alternative may strike us as outlandish if we are accustomed to conceiving experience in terms of "sense perception." But in equating experience with "sense experience" we tend to forget that we could be led rather quickly to a *reductio ad absurdum*. For if only what is given immediately "to" the senses is a primary datum, then the only primary data are the discrete and multiple snippets of color, sound, scent, and so forth. On this view, not only must we say that we don't perceive other selves directly, but also that we don't even perceive tables, chairs, or trees directly: we don't perceive "things" at all. With this, the epistemological bark is once again stranded in the backwaters of phenomenalism. Actually the plight of phenomenalism is extremely grave, for if the only hard datum is the discrete sensory immediate, then it becomes extremely difficult to see how the entire *past* does not disappear from the catalog of the immediately known, and with it the continuing personal identity of the knower. Once the circle is broken and the suspicion dawns that direct perception may include much more than "sense data" it will not seem such an implausible claim that we may know other selves directly.

One philosopher who pressed this claim was Max Scheler.[8] Scheler's thesis was that *expression* was a primary datum and that as such it was the direct revelation of the other self. It is nonsense to say that we infer the existence of the other analogically, for the child who recognizes and responds to the warmth and friendliness of his mother's face is completely incapable of such an inference. Rather, the warmth and kindliness are expressive phenomena, just as much directly given as the color of the mother's hair or the size of her face. What we perceive are not "bodies" or "minds" but integral wholes: our distinction between the "body" and the "self" of the other post-dates this primary perception. Once we break out of the bonds of an empiricism which is essentially unfaithful to experience, we will see that our primary experience is that of configurational unities. Therefore, there is no problem of how I infer the reality of a mind behind a bodily facade, since I only arrive at calling this thing a "body" by

[8] *Op. cit.*, p. 239.

subtracting something from the original experience. By adopting a certain attitude, I can see the bared teeth and squinting eyes as purely a physiological facade; but from a different posture, I see a smile. I cannot "compose" the smile out of "purely physiological" features, for the smile is not accessible from the mental stance in which I am able to identify something as a "purely physiological feature."[9] Neither can I break it down into physiological elements. The smile is an original phenomenon of expressiveness.

Scheler goes even further. His contention is that, far from it being "self-evident" that I cannot experience another's experience, it is perfectly natural for me to do so.[10] The apparent impossibility of it is assumed because I think too exclusively with reference to another's bodily states when thinking of his "experience."[11] It is true that I cannot feel his pain or experience his sensation of seeing or hearing. As part of the bodily complex, these are tied to the purely private nature of the bodily complex. But the situation changes in regard to the higher spiritual states, the emotions proper. There is no reason why I cannot experience another's grief or joy. I do not "argue" to these or infer their presence behind a corporeal facade. In some cases we may even speak, says Scheler, of *one* emotion shared by two selves. A father and mother standing together by the body of their dead child have their grief in common. There are not here simply two consciousnesses, but two consciousnesses sharing one identical sorrow. They experience it as "our sorrow."[12] In the face of such experiences, the problem of "other minds" loses all standing.

Similarly, Scheler adduces the nature of *sympathy* as a patent example of reaching the experience of the other. Sympathy is somewhat different from the parents' shared grief, for I may sympathize with another's grief without actually feeling that grief myself. My sympathy in another's grief (or joy) cannot be

[9] *Ibid.*, pp. 261–262.
[10] *Ibid.*, pp. 244–247.
[11] *Ibid.*, p. 254.
[12] *Ibid.*, pp. 12–13.

regarded as an original revelation of the existence of the other, for the act of sympathy already presupposes knowledge of the reality of that with which I am in sympathy.[13] But sympathy is an irreducibly given experience and its existence is a standing rebuttal to those who declare that the experience undergone by another is sealed off to me. Sympathy exists precisely because of the accessibility of the emotion of the other for me; consequently, it is a testimony to that accessibility. My commiseration with another's grief or rejoicing in his joy is consequent upon the transparence of his emotional consciousness for my own.[14]

Another philosopher who reaches the other directly and without any sort of inference is Jean-Paul Sartre. His views are fashioned in a metaphysical context peculiar to himself, but possess a value by no means restricted to that context. Where Scheler concentrates upon our experience of sympathy, Sartre finds the presence of the other most piercingly revealed in the experience of *shame*. It is not too much to say that for him our experience of shame *is* the experience of the other. Actually Sartre begins his analysis by regarding consciousness as a hyper-isolated knower. Proceeding by a strict act/object analysis of consciousness, he arrives at his now famous distinction between the *en-soi* and the *pour-soi,* into which we may follow him just far enough for our present purposes.[15] Consciousness breaks down into awareness *(pour-soi)* and object of awareness *(en-soi).* The primary fact about awareness is that it is *not* its object. The primary fact about the object is that it excludes whatever is introduced by awareness. We then begin with a dichotomy between two different modes of being: being as awareness and being as the object of awareness. The first Sartre calls being-for-itself *(pour-soi)* and the second

[13] *Ibid.,* p. 8.
[14] To make this viewpoint stand up, Scheler must show that sympathy actually does have this intentional reference to the other and that it is not reducible to elements which do not require this interpretation. This he does on pp. 37-50.
[15] Jean-Paul Sartre, *Being and Nothingness,* pp. lxiv-lxix, 21-24, 73-79, *passim.*

being-in-itself *(en-soi)*. All negation is introduced into reality by consciousness: consciousness *is not* its object; its pure being-for-itself and not-being-its-object is the source of all negation. The in-itself which is purely *other* than consciousness escapes all negations and is conceived by Sartre as a massive self-identity, a kind of solid block of being.

All this is mentioned in order to lead up to the revelation of the other, as Sartre conceives it. Consciousness, the for-itself, exists as a kind of pure spontaneity which faces the inert passivity of the in-itself like a god in splendid isolation. All the world is a stage and it is the solitary player. In fact, as the solitary actor (the in-itself is inert), it confers the character of being a stage upon the in-itself. It *makes* a world wherein it can act. This is what Sartre calls the "project" of consciousness, by which it constitutes the arena in which it disports. But now, in a typically flamboyant manner, Sartre introduces the jarring presence of the other. The other's presence announces itself as my shame.[16] Suppose, says Sartre, I am engaged in some reprehensible activity, say kneeling down and looking through a keyhole. In this situation, the for-itself is a pure spontaneous looking-at an object; at this moment it projects its world in an absolutely autonomous way. Its frivolity is like the extreme of a fiat which constitutes its world and its own freedom. Suddenly, while I am in this ridiculous posture, I hear footsteps round the corner and look up to see two contemptuous eyes peering down at me. At once, my world collapses. Now I am not viewer but viewed. I feel myself looked at, and my autonomy and spontaneity ooze away. I am no longer a for-itself, but *for-another*. I feel the muscles in my jaws tighten, my mouth dry up, my body become a ludicrous and unwieldy bulk—I feel myself congealing to the rigidity of the in-itself. The other is the gorgon's head which turns me to stone.

Shorn of all specifically Sartrean trimmings, this is still a powerful example of what would be meant by the direct experience

[16] *Ibid.*, pp. 221–222, 259–263.

of the other. This is no inference, no argument by analogy. The other is there as directly as my shame. His presence is so directly felt that it causes my own to shrivel. Far from having to *argue* to his existence from my own, I would give anything to be freed from this utterly obtrusive presence, so that I might gather up the pieces of my own shattered existence.[17]

With these two examples as beginnings, it will occur to many that this approach could be broadened to include various other instances. What sympathy and shame do is to distill into a very pure form a quality which is widely, though more weakly, present in experience. We need only think of such states as admiration, loyalty, expectation, or anxiety; or such conditions as loneliness or boredom, which are testimonies in reverse to the reality of the other. Much could be done to show that these experiences are phenomenologically unintelligible except in relation to another self. Loneliness is an especially clear example of this. The experience of loneliness is built upon the experience of the other, but the experience of the other as now absent. Reference to the other is to such a degree an ontological dimension of the self that in the complete absence of all others, my being is still turned towards the absent. There is no possibility of explaining this inferentially or of reducing it to different terms. This consideration was in Scheler's mind when he declared that an imaginary Robinson Crusoe who had never in all his life perceived any beings of his own kind would still be said to know the thou and possess the notion of community.[18] Scheler's position is that the knowledge of the nature of community and the existence of the thou in general is an *a priori* factor, given as an irreducible background to any encounter with individual persons—given, one might say, as a

[17] We need not follow Sartre into the consequences which he drew from such cases. He became so obsessed with the "look" as the revelation of the other that in his thought, human relations become a mutual "staring-down" process, the "other" is consistently regarded as either a threat or an opportunity for appropriation, and the whole positive side of intersubjectivity is largely lost.

[18] *Op. cit.*, pp. 234–235.

structural component of the human person. The sphere of the thou is just as essentially and irreducibly a sphere of the fundamental being of man as is the sphere of the "external world." Seen in this light, the human person *is* a reference to a thou, and his coming to self-consciousness is mediated by this reference and impossible without it.

I AND THOU

The most promising area of escape from the problem of "other selves" seems to lie in the direction of suppressing the assumption upon which it rests. This is the assumption that the intelligibility contained in the "I" is anterior to that contained in the "thou." If this is not so, if on the contrary the meaning of "I" is a function of the "thou," then it is clearly inconsistent for the I to raise the question of the existence of the thou. Among the philosophers who press for this solution, the most prominent name in the last century was that of Josiah Royce. According to Royce, the self was through and through a *social* entity: whatever meaningful content I have for the word "I," I build up out of an original experience of relationship.

I am not first self-conscious and then secondarily conscious of my fellow. On the contrary, I am conscious of myself, on the whole, as in relation to some real or ideal fellow, and apart from my consciousness of my fellow, I have only secondary and derived states and habits of self-consciousness.[19]

And again:

Speaking in psychological terms, one can say that our finite self-consciousness is no primitive possession at all but is the hard-earned

---

[19] Josiah Royce, *Studies of Good and Evil* (New York: Appleton), 1898, p. 201. See also *The World and the Individual*, Second Series (New York: Macmillan), 1900, pp. 245–277.

outcome of the contact between the being capable of becoming rational and the rationally disposed world in which he slowly learns to move.[20]

The individual does not first know himself as a rational conscious being and then search about to discover whether, behind external appearances, there are other beings like him. Rather, his gradually developing explicit consciousness of himself as a rational, conscious being is an interpretive awareness of himself as a focal point in a social whole. Rational consciousness is essentially social; all philosophical questions are raised by rational consciousness, and it is therefore barren to raise as a rational issue the existence of other selves. In this outlook, Royce is true to and inspired by the earlier idealism of Hegel, from whom the whole conception of the social nature of consciousness ultimately seems to derive. But his idealism finds echoes in quite different sorts of thinkers, such as the somewhat behavioristically oriented American philosopher, G. H. Mead, who was long preoccupied with this issue and sums up his feelings in the declaration that "It is impossible to conceive of a self arising outside of social experience."[21]

Martin Buber and Gabriel Marcel speak a different idiom from that of Royce, but the conception of the self as social is the cornerstone of their thought. Much of the point of this thought will be missed unless it is understood that they do not treat the self as an already realized entity which remains identical throughout the gamut of its experiences. The self is essentially a creative category: it is something which exists and is achieved in the order of freedom. Marcel and Buber locate the full potentiation of the self in its encounter with the thou, and it is in their discovery and exploration of the unique nature of this encounter that their contribution to the discussion consists. Others have emphasized the social

[20] *Ibid.*, p. 207.
[21] George H. Mead, *Mind, Self and Society*, edit. by Charles W. Morris (Chicago: University of Chicago Press), 1934, p. 140. See the interesting comparative study of Mead and Buber done by Paul E. Pfuetze, *The Social Self* (New York: Bookman Associates), 1954.

character of the self in more general terms, but Marcel and Buber put their stress upon the singular character of the thou.[22] Whatever the "I" is, it is as unique; whatever establishes the "I" in its uniqueness establishes it in its authentic being. Whatever questions are posed about the other are either posed by a generalized "I" (say, an epistemological subject-in-general, or a social self) or by the "I" in all its uniqueness. Many have had a tendency to approach the problem of "other selves" from the side of a merely generalized "I." Marcel and Buber drive towards the unique and unrepeatable "I" and attack the problem in terms of it. But what they discover is that the unique and unrepeatable "I" only knows itself as such in the face of a "thou." Apart from my relation to the "thou," I am not aware of myself as a unique self at all—I am a mere bundle of sensations, series of experiences, or logical thinking subject. Here is a paradoxical discovery: the unique is a category of communion. If I want to say "I" in the most intense and fully realized way, I must say "thou." The unique dimension of existence represented by the "I" only emerges to consciousness in so far as there is an encounter with a "thou."

This means that my full experience of selfhood does not have priority over others, but is a co-emergent of communion. If anything, it is the other who has priority: the thou gives me to myself. What Marcel and Buber have discovered is the thou as an original dimension of existence. They make a fundamental distinction between an "I-it" relation and an "I-thou" relation. They make this as an ontological distinction, and not merely a psychological one: that is, we cannot represent things as though there is one identical "I" variously related to others, but existing in the same ontological manner through the various relations. Rather the "I" is a relational category, and its status in being varies with its

---

[22] A convenient place to meet Buber's thought on this is *I and Thou*, trans. by Ronald Smith (New York: Scribner's), 1958, esp. p. 3ss. This "I-thou" theme is scattered through Marcel's whole work, but special reference may be made to *The Mystery of Being*, vol. I, p. 176ss, *Metaphysical Journal*, p. 219ss, and *Du refus à l'invocation*, pp. 50–52.

relation: the "I" of the "I-it" relation is ontologically different from the "I" of the "I-thou" relation.[23]

Certainly we may see what is meant by saying that an "I" which was reflexively conscious of itself in an "I-it" relation would not be conscious at the same ontological level as the "I" which was reflexively conscious in the "I-thou" relation. What this amounts to, then, is that the thou introduces us to a new dimension of being. In my relation with another person, being is revealed to me in a manner in which it is not revealed in any relation with a non-personal reality. "Things" or "objects" are not there for me in the way in which a thou is there. They are always to a certain extent "absent"—truncated, alien presences. Only in a personal encounter do I undergo the full experience of presence; and this is a twofold assertion: only in a personal encounter am I really present to myself, through the presence of a thou. Self-presence and the presence of a thou are two sides of one coming-to-presence which is the creative achievement of human communion.

This must not be taken to mean that wherever I am as a matter of fact dealing with a human person, I actually do encounter a thou. The tragedy of the human condition is exactly that the experience of the thou is so fugitive and tenuous. Clearly the "presence" spoken of here does not refer to simply physical presence. The table or chair is "with" me in that sense. Other human beings who are occupying the same region of space with me do not automatically become "thou's": my fellow workers in the office, the people sitting across from me on the subway, or standing shoulder to shoulder in the elevator, even those with whom I am ostensibly "talking" can be mere "absent thirds." The genuine experience of the thou is a relatively rare and privileged one. That is why Marcel will concentrate on such experiences as love, hope, or fidelity, which are thematically centered on the thou in the fullness of his presence. It is in experiences like these that the full ontological originality of the thou can be appreciated.

[23] Buber, *op. cit.*, p. 3, 12.

For the thou to whom I am related in love cannot be grasped in the manner of a thing "about which" I speak. He is precisely incommensurate with all descriptive language. Love does not bear on a "content" or a characterizable object. The beloved being is not a repository of certain predicates in which I can summarize the foundation for my affection.[24] Love bears on an uncharacterizable presence. It opens me to the mystery of the singular. Precisely in so far as a being is beloved, he is beyond all inventory which I could take of him to explain why he is beloved. Objects can be characterized; objects can be given predicates; in fact an "object" (in the sense of Buber and Marcel) just is the presumed structure upon which I can hang my set of predicates. But that which I characterize, that to which I assign predicates, is always that "about which" I am speaking: it is spoken of in the third person. A "thou" is not that about which I speak, but the one to whom I speak: it is addressable only in the second-person. Presence, second-personness, cannot be approached from the side of objectified structure. It therefore represents an original revelation of being, a revelation which is inaccessible by any other route.

This last remark will help in answering a question which is bound to come up at this point: in what sense can the experience of the thou be called "knowledge?" It may be thought that I have added very little to my store of expressible information through the experience of love or fidelity, and there may be the renewed suspicion that these are only psychologically interesting states of an individual subject. Now it may be allowed at the outset that if knowledge is identified with "information," this objection is well taken. For all information bears on "objects," and a thou is not an object but a presence. All information, too, is conceived as transmittable through the ordinary channels of language to any properly equipped observer: but the truth of the thou is not transmittable to an observer at all, but to the "I" which is co-present with it, and which is a participant, not an observer.

[24] *Ibid.*, p. 17.

Nevertheless there is a defense for continuing to use the word "knowledge" here. First of all, "knowledge" can be extended to take in the *ground* of a propositional statement, and in this sense any original source of evidence is freighted with cognitional value. Here, the I-thou experience clearly qualifies: the *only* way to know another person in his singularity is to *love* him, and hence love is cognitional. But further, to the extent that this experience can be *expressed* at all, its expression can be said to acquire the status of knowledge in so far as it is an instrument by which thought regains the experience and recognizes the revelation inherent in it. Not transmittability, but *expressibility* may be taken as the hallmark of knowledge. With this proviso, it is not hard to assign various cognitional aspects to the I-thou relation.

As has been seen, it is a revelation of a new dimension of being, inaccessible in any other way. The "thou" is ontologically unique and cannot be reduced either to an object or to a projection of the self. The uncharacterizable presence which I discover in love, hope, or fidelity, reveals something to me which cannot be revealed to sense perception, logical thought, or objectified knowledge. To the extent that I succeed in expressing this unique dimension of being, I may be said to know what I could not otherwise know and therefore this expression is undoubtedly a sort of knowledge of being.

In what sense can it be viewed as knowledge of the *single* one?[25] That is, what do I know of the thou whom I love which I would not otherwise know? Here we must tread carefully. In one sense, I don't know anything more. That is, since the thou is not known as a characterizable object, I don't add to my aggregate of "facts" about him through love. The thou cannot be reached as a toting up of traits, and therefore reaching the thou does not increase my objective knowledge about him. Yet, this must be emended. For surely, let us say, a young man who loves a girl "knows" her in a way that others do not. Far from being blind, love is rather a

[25] *Ibid.,* pp. 62–63.

principle of knowledge. Still, he does not "know her better" in the sense that he has been impelled to study her personality more closely and observe features which others might just as well observe but don't bother to. He knows her in a manner that only one who loves her can know her. For her "being" or her "person" is not an already-realized objective reality viewed by him from a more advantageous perspective: it is a creative category. The boy's love is the creative invocation of her being: it is a participation in the mystery of her uniqueness. He does not simply see better traits which are already actually there: he calls forth perfections which are virtual in her—and virtual in the order of freedom.[26] Her beauty, her charm, her goodness are not for him the same traits available for others: they are assimilated into the mystery of her uniqueness and appeal to him as revelation of that mystery. His response is a hope, a summons. Naturally love is impelled to declare itself, for the declaration makes more in-stant the qualities which it perceives. Love desires to call forth perpetually the beauty which its privileged vision sees, to bring to birth what is already born. This is true not only of the love between man and woman, but equally and perhaps more plainly true of other sorts of love. Aristotle made the same point, albeit intermittently, in respect to friendship. Consider, too, the love of parent for child, where these features are thematic. The mother and father, in going out towards the person of their child, know themselves to be going out towards a being which is largely virtual and latent; they are enraptured by a singularity which they are conspiring to bring into being. Nothing could better illustrate the twofold character of love as both creation and response. My love calls forth the being of the other; but I love the other because I have found in him a being which I desire to call forth into the approval of my love.

Do I in this manner "know" his uniqueness? If this means, can I enumerate what makes him unique, the answer must be "no."

---

[26] This is so even if his love is unrequited or unproclaimed.

Intersubjective Knowledge

Enumeration cannot reach the unique; for enumeration adds up "properties," and properties are always multipliable. Objectified thought, or indeed conceptual thought, must fall short of the singular. But I reach his uniqueness in the only way it can be reached—in the same way that he reaches it. For this person does not know his own uniqueness "objectively." His way of being present to himself cannot be reduced to an aggregate of traits; he does not know himself as a "what," but as inexpressible presence. But what quickens this presence and unfolds its fullness is the encounter with a thou. Thus the unique "I" stands at the boundary of giving and receiving. Love knows the unique because it is a creator of the unique.

As a consequence, there is another way in which the "I-thou" relation is cognitional; it is an instrument for my self-knowledge. The encounter with the thou is not only a revelation of the thou, but a revelation of myself. As we have seen, the "I" of the "I-thou" relation is met only within this relation. In relation to the thou I know something about myself that I could not otherwise know. Obviously this does not mean that I can enumerate more attributes of myself. But the uncharacterizable presence of the thou is also a revelation of an abyss of existence within myself. The whole "I-thou" experience is, so to speak, bottomless. It occurs in a realm that is transcendent in relation to objectified knowledge. In so far as I belong to this experience, I belong to a realm of being which is specifically inexhaustible. That is why Marcel will say "To love a person is to say to him, 'Thou at least shalt not die.' "[27] This is not to be understood as some kind of objective information which I have come across; it is simply the translation into language of the experience of presence with which communion is flooded. It will do no good to say that nevertheless he *will* die since all things come to an end, for the prophetic affirmation of love is precisely a proclamation that the beloved

---

[27] *The Mystery of Being,* vol. II, p. 62.

as beloved is exempt from the penalties of thingness. The thou is not a thing. That is why the "I-thou" relation can provide the basis for a privileged kind of knowledge.

Only to the extent that I can affirm myself as spirit, as transphenomenal, can I be said to have "knowledge" of the "immortality of the soul" (which is a rather unsatisfactory objectified phrase). Then the experiences which enable me to grasp the unique meaning of non-thingified personal existence occupy a crucial position for this sort of knowledge. The traditional "proof" for the immortality of the soul (as simple and spiritual) proceeds as if we could have an objective grasp of the soul as a special sort of thing with attributes implying natural immortality. But once the soul is approached in the objectified mode of thought, we are in danger of coming to rest in an implication of concepts. At best we have proved that the soul is a repository or an efficient cause of universal ideas and that thus it is immaterial. But an "it" which is not material is a rather negative notion and rather vulnerable to the formalist reduction of Kant. The positive intelligibility of existing as a person, rather than a thing, is given in the experience of communion. Only a thought which clings to communion remains attached to the meaning which makes the affirmation of immortality possible. It is not an object called the soul which is immortal; it is "we" who are immortal. We, here together, bound in love, we grant and bestow the mutual tokens of immunity from death. Immortality is not a consequence implicit in the concept of "immateriality," it is a promise spoken to those existing in communion. Love, in being a revelation of the thou, is also a revelation of my self, and the trans-phenomenal character of my being. How do I affirm this? Only so far as I participate in communion. Love is "the active refusal to treat itself as subjective." It is charged with cognitive potentialities to the precise extent that it is love. Only a reflection which plunges into communion can make this affirmation, which is why communion is a source of knowledge.

Finally, for the same reason, in the opinion of both Marcel and Buber, the "I-thou" relation is cognitive in yet another way. The

Intersubjective Knowledge

abyss of existence is revealed to subjectivity and subjectivity is revealed to communion. As a member of a spiritual communion I move in a realm of an open presence. The finite thou is always to some extent also a thing, but the aura of the inexhaustible which surrounds communion is an intimation of an unfailing presence which sustains it. The light of the Absolute Thou is shed across human communion.[28] The transcendent is present to our experience as *intimation,* and this intimation is made to communion. The thou calls us beyond our isolated egos, and in calling summons us to a presence which founds a new being; but back of the discrete appeals which scattered selves fling out to us, there is the absolute appeal to found ourselves in a realm where love and fidelity make unassailable sense. For both Marcel and Buber, the I-thou relation is thus the avenue to the transcendent, and the proper name of God is Absolute Thou.

Once again we may ask whether all this should be called "knowledge," assuming that we grant value to the description of experience herein recounted. It is not knowledge that is accessible to "anyone at all"—but then this may be too narrow an idea of knowledge. It is knowledge which is available, if Marcel and Buber are right, to one who belongs to the I-thou relation and whose thought rejoins that relation. To the extent that they succeed in expressing this thought, they have raised the experience to a cognitive status; to the extent that this experience gives us a privileged access to an otherwise unavailable realm, it is a privileged sort of knowledge.

---

[28] Buber, *op. cit.,* p. 75; Marcel, *Du refus à l'invocation,* pp. 179, 218.

12 REMAINDERS

Certain of the problems in epistemology which are very much to the fore in contemporary speculation have not yet been touched on, nor could very much be done with them in a book of a fairly general character. Since they are so intrinsically interesting and important, however, and since they will call for so much continuing attention on the part of the philosophers of the future, it does not seem fitting to pass them by unnoticed. The following brief discussions are thereby appended, not in the belief that they do justice to their subjects, but only as indicators of territory still to be explored.

THE PHILOSOPHY OF SCIENCE

It is well known that most of the important problems in contemporary philosophy of science are epistemological in origin and character.

Since its inception in the mechanical approach to nature of Galileo, classical physics had tended to proceed on the relatively uncritical acceptance of the categories natural to that approach. Originally science had been set on this path by the growing exasperation with the futilities of Aristotleian physics, so forcefully expressed by Francis Bacon at the end of the 16th century. It was all very well for Aristotle's purely contemplative philosophical eye to stress a teleological appreciation of nature, but this viewpoint had not advanced the interests of humanity one iota. Really to "know" nature ought to confer on man the power to intervene effectively in nature and to wrest its processes to human advantage. In keeping with a now familiar outlook, men began to feel that to know nature and to control it were convergent ideals. What good to assert, in Aristotle's manner, that the natures of things acted for "ends" if this led either nowhere or up a blind alley?[1] It would be much better to seek out *how* events happen than to rest comfortable in the presumed knowledge of *why* they happen. The search for the how led to a search for efficient causes, the actual agencies involved in the step by step occurrence of physical processes.

This gave modern science a strong analytical turn, the ambition being to dissect a process into the serial activities which comprised it. Analysis once initiated must be pursued to the end, for science could not feel it was understanding the ultimate "how" of natural processes until it could discover the ultimate physical components efficiently causing activity. It led, therefore, to a reinstatement of the atomic theory at the center of scientific operations. The ultimate efficient causes at work in physical processes were these smallest elements of matter, influencing each other in the only way they could be plausibly conceived as influencing each other, *as* chunks of matter—in other words, through mechanical forces.[2] Since it is apparently impossible to conceive of mechanical forces acting otherwise than in a uniform and necessary manner, the outlook of classical physics inevitably became deterministic. When Laplace delivered his famous pronouncement in the 18th century, that for a hypothetical mind in possession of information as to the position and velocity of every ultimate particle in the universe, the whole future would be predictable, he was merely epitomizing a belief inherent in classical physics as such.

[1] The blind alley, for instance, of the explanation that fire "tends" upward because its "natural place" is "up," or the blind alley that the heavenly bodies travel in circular motion because the sphere is the perfect figure.

[2] The pre-eminence of mathematics is directly connected with both the analytical search for measurable constancies of interaction and with the only kind of unity possible in a mechanical system, the unity of *laws* which applied to integral sections of this system.

Objective reality came to be envisaged in the image of the new mechanics and this vision seemed to be justified by the unprecedented prosperity of theory and practice which it made possible for the burgeoning science. For classical physics, notions like mass, velocity, position, volume, pressure, force and the like were ultimate characteristics of an independently existing matter, and not simply abstract instruments by which man made his way in the world. On the contrary, "the" world was the world which corresponded to these categories, and whatever features could not be reduced to these were relegated to a subsidiary mental, and hence subjective, status.

This, we have seen, was the fate of the "secondary qualities," and it was also the fate of the notion of "quality" in general. The new science was a science of quantity; qualities could find a place within it only to the extent that they had measurable correlates: thus, red and green as experienced are qualitatively and therefore incommensurably different, but their correlated light-waves are measurable and therefore scientifically admissible. Once this approach is followed generally, it is a short step to the belief that these demoted qualities are not as "really real" as their assumed quantitative basis. The real world becomes, by scientific consensus, a system of geometrically conceived material particles in motion.

We have already seen some of the epistemological difficulties which arise out of this view, notably the difficulties inherent in the representationalist theory of perception. There is no need to go over these again. The present remarks will be chiefly concerned not with philosophy's problems with the views of science but with science's confusion about its own views. For, what has occurred in modern science is that the advances within science itself have forced a confused re-evaluation of many or all of the convictions of classical physics. The picture of the atomic universe as an indefinite number of sub-microscopic billiard balls soundlessly clicking together according to the rules of mechanics can no longer be held to be the portrait of the "real" world. Not only has the image of the atom as a solid chunk of matter been found inapplicable, but it is by no means clear that the newer notion of the atom as a miniature solar system with electrons in orbit around a nucleus, can be taken any more literally. In fact, there is such a wealth of problems now up for discussion in the philosophy of science that it would not even be possible to mention them all in any brief compass. Some attempt might be made to divide them into problems about the nature of scientific laws and principles on the one hand, and problems about the status of the *objects* with which science deals on the other. We will concentrate on the second sort of problem—(but these divisions surely overlap, due to the role of theory in identifying the "objects" of scientific inquiry)—and in doing so necessarily omit some problems of the first rank. Are scientific "laws" coercive edicts for the behavior of nature as classical physics tended to assume? Are they merely descriptive generalizations of the sequences of sense data, as Mach's positivism held in the last century? Are they tautologies, as some now hold? Is science's deterministic law of causality absolutely valid, as classical physics assumed and as some still hold—or is it a mere methodological rule as the Vienna Circle feels? Can the laws of statistics and probability which govern miscroscopic behavior really be incorporated into macroscopic order without philosophic anomaly? Should the Uncertainty Principle be construed as modifying the law of causality or is it simply a sign of a weakness in our powers of observation, as Einstein maintained? Such are some of the questions which we must pass over, but which would have to arise in any full discussion of the epistemology of science.

Even in selecting the second type of problem for concentration, the treatment must be sketchy. We will simply resort to the expedient of organizing several perplexities of contemporary philosophy of science around one central question: "What is the mode of reality which belongs to the objects about which science speaks?" Atoms, electrons, protons, nuclei, and the other sub-microscopic components are now practically household words, and that they are in some sense "real" is hardly open to question. But the precise manner in which their reality ought to be conceived is a matter of extreme perplexity. The natural thing to do would be to regard them as real in the same way that chairs, tables, rocks, and other familiar objects are real, only on a smaller scale. This was the older view, and the one which has now run into apparently insuperable difficulties. There has occurred in contemporary physics what might be called a "crisis of explanation." Physics has found itself called upon to speak of the entities with which it deals in a way that casts doubt both on their mode of reality and on its own mode of comprehending. Three sources for the confusion may be briefly cited:

1) Most familiarly, there is the Uncertainty Principle of Heisenberg,[3] according to which it is impossible to state at the same time the position and velocity of an electron. Experimentally, this impossibility derives from the fact that any quantity of light sufficient to detect its position would modify its velocity, and conversely, any quantity of light which would leave its velocity unaffected would not be sufficient to reveal its position. As far as the factual part of this situation goes, it is indisputable: our instruments of detection in this case thwart the discovery they seek to make possible. But so far forth, the impossibility might be regarded as a limitation on our instruments. One might continue to claim that the electron *has* a position and velocity, even though man is too clumsy to detect it. This is the view which Einstein defended, but the weight of contemporary physical authority is against him. According to the interpretation held by Heisenberg and the Copenhagen school, this impossibility is an impossibility in *principle*. It is in principle impossible to assert that the electron has a definite position and velocity at the same time. Briefly, their reasons are as follows: at the sub-microscopic level, we do not have a right to attribute *any* features to entities unless we can

[3] See Werner Heisenberg, *Physics and Philosophy* (New York: Harper Torchbooks), 1962, esp. chapters III and X. For a popular explanation, see J. W. N. Sullivan, *The Limitations of Science* (New York: Mentor Books), 1949, p. 69ss.

verify them experimentally (since these entities are not items for observation alone); but if we assume that the electron does have a definite velocity and position simultaneously, the results of an experiment conducted on this assumption will not tally with expectations; if, on the other hand, we introduce the concept of "probability" into position and velocity (as quantum physics does), our observations will tally with expectations. In other words, if it is right to assert that an electron has a simultaneous position and velocity, then the validity of quantum physics itself (which is firmly established) would have to be relinquished. Therefore it is not possible to speak of the electron having simultaneously definite position and velocity.

Now, to some ears such a statement may seem so outlandish as to invite instant dismissal—everything, we may insist, must be *somewhere* and moving at *some* speed at any given time. Yet to mitigate this kind of protest, we need only remind ourselves that this is so only if the electron is an object like familiar objects, and that is exactly the question. Thoughts and ideas, for instance, do not have to be confined to any definite point of place. When I have the idea of writing, my idea is effectively in my hand and in my head at the same time. Or more pertinently, we might ask ourselves at what position a "wave" is situated. The wave *as such* is not localizable at a definite position. These elementary considerations solve nothing, of course, but they bring us back to the issue. *If* we conceive an electron to be real as macroscopic objects are real, then the uncertainty principle, as well as other statements in quantum physics, becomes altogether opaque; but *should* we consider an electron in this way?

2) Secondly, there is the famous paradox in regard to the nature of light, which now assumes the same unresolved status in physics that the grace and free-will controversy assumed in theology. Until the contemporary era, it had been largely accepted that light was propagated in waves. Only if this was so could various properties, including the phenomenon of interference, be at all explicable. But there is now equally incontrovertible evidence in

another direction; the photoelectric effect, for instance, is only to be explained if light does not travel in waves but is emitted in discrete energy-packets called "quanta." There is, then, apparently conclusive evidence for the fact that light must be conceived as consisting *both* in waves *and* in quanta. Yet how can this be imagined? A wave is a continuous phenomenon, quanta are discrete. How can the same entity be the subject of such contradictory predicates? Certainly no image that we can form can ever succeed in representing such an entity—which is tantamount to saying that its reality cannot be comparable to that of perceptual objects.

3) Finally, we may cite the discovery which began the whole trouble, Max Planck's discovery of the fact that atoms existed only in discrete energy-states. An atom may exist at higher or lower energy levels, but these levels have discrete values, and the atom does not occupy levels intermediate between them.[4] To appreciate the anomaly of this, we may think by analogy of a pot of water being heated which, instead of passing continuously through a progression of temperature states, existed now at 30° C., now at 50° C., and now at 80° C. without ever being at the intervening stages. Not only is there discontinuity of energy, but many feel that there is title to talk of discontinuity of position; at least, there is no title to say that an electron successively observed at two different positions had to pass through intervening positions *between* the observations. Obviously, if such remarks are genuinely applicable to the atom and its components, an atom cannot be real in any way analogous to the reality of everyday objects and the question of its mode of reality is very much open.

One way of understanding the basis of such difficulties as the foregoing is to see them as manifestations of the breakdown of the "spectator" view of nature within science. Classical physics had regarded itself as a pure witness of natural events, to which its

[4] To explain this peculiarity consistently with the constellation picture of the atom, the notion of a "quantum jump" of an electron to a new orbit is well known.

witnessing made no difference, relying on a strict dichotomy between the subjective and the objective. This rested on a peculiar unacknowledged conception of the scientist as a sort of disembodied observer, but it raised no particular scientific difficulties as long as macroscopic objects were involved; after all, the influence of the light by which I viewed a falling body or a pulley and weight was negligible enough to be discounted altogether. But, as the Uncertainty Principle shows, this is no longer true at the microscopic level. The scientist is not only observer but *participant* in nature, and this participation may well set limits to the accuracy and even to the mode of the knowledge open to him.

Yet this physical interaction is only part of the story. It revives the philosophical view of the relational character of the whole perceptual field from which science sets out. And it has further led to a disposition to emphasize what might be called the "cognitional interaction" between theory and observation. That is why questions like the ones we have reviewed cannot be settled in terms of observation alone. The "objects" with which science deals are not items for observation alone: they are joint referents of theory and observation. The scientist cannot prescind entirely from theory in order to find a raw empirical given, for without theory he does not even know how to begin to look. The notion of a raw empirical datum now has the appearance of a limit-concept rather than something with which science begins.

The application for the notion of a "bare fact" becomes increasingly difficult to determine, for in science theory has a hand in deciding what the "facts" are. Often when we feel ourselves to be stating a brute fact about experience, it will turn out that we are expressing a consequence of our theory. A vivid example of this is given by Stephen Toulmin.[5] The familiar declaration that there is an absolute zero below which temperature cannot fall ($-273°$ C.) sounds like an expression of a rather peculiar empirical fact about nature—as if for some strange reason nature had decided

[5] Stephen Toulmin, *The Philosophy of Science* (New York: Harper Torchbooks), 1960, pp. 129–133.

that it would refuse to get colder than that. Actually, the existence of an absolute zero is a consequence of our decision to *measure* heat, and to measure it in a certain way. The very conception of an Ideal Gas scale logically entails that there will be a lower limit, for in such a scale temperature-units are defined with reference to the pressure of an ideal gas, and it is impossible that pressure fall *below* zero; hence any temperature defined with reference to decreasing pressure must have a lower limit. Thus, the statement about absolute zero is not a descriptive statement about a brute fact of nature, but is a consequence of our theory. Most scientists would probably agree with Ryle's opinion that scientific concepts are "theory-laden" rather than descriptive.[6] Even the "atom" is not an object of inspection which is divergently interpreted by classical and contemporary physics, but an object into whose conception theory enters essentially: the atom of classical physics and the atom of contemporary physics are two significantly different objects.

In one obvious respect the changed attitude of science is a healthy sign. For it bespeaks an end to the "imperialism of method" which had too long caused the scientist to dismiss as unreal those features of reality which were not available through his sort of cognition. There is much more disposition on the part of contemporary philosophers of science to recognize the abstract character of their own method and to refrain from hypostasizing the traits of reality with which this method is exclusively preoccupied. As Eddington has pointed out,[7] it would be a basic error for one who uses a fish net with two-inch holes to declare dogmatically that all fish in the ocean are larger than two inches. Just so, the scientist whose method is abstractly quantitative can only "catch" those features in the ocean of reality which can be caught by this method. Instruments have built-in limitations, and the theory which is the prime instrument of science allows it to

[6] *Dilemmas*, pp. 90–91.
[7] *The Philosophy of Physical Science* (Cambridge: Cambridge University Press), 1949, pp. 16, 62.

select out of the matrix of experience only certain aspects. The philosophically reflective scientist will not succumb to the tendency to project the abstract results of his quantitative method into independent reality, nor to derogate the cognitional value of other aspects of experience to which his method, by definition, prevents his access. It is one of the achievements of contemporary philosophy of science to have roused itself from a dogmatic rut and progressed towards this acknowledgment.

MORAL AND AESTHETIC EXPERIENCE

If a brief treatment of the problem of science is presumptuous, so is a mere glance at the cognitive status of moral and aesthetic experience. Yet not to glance at all in this direction would be to omit one of the important topics of current epistemological interest, and so we will once again be sketchy rather than default.

The issue may be put thus: in what sense do moral and aesthetic experience give us knowledge? Do these experiences merely tell us something about our individual selves *in* our individuality or do they allow us to stand in the presence of a facet of reality which is really there and otherwise inaccessible? Nobody is in the habit of claiming extra-individual value for his experiences of pain, or disappointment, or fatigue, or anger, and upon sophisticated reflection it might be felt that moral and aesthetic feelings are no more revelatory of reality than these. Yet we must beware of proceeding too quickly here. Just because certain "feelings" are non-cognitional does not mean that all are. We should not too hastily dichotomize knowledge and feeling, for there is the clear possibility that certain knowledge may only be obtainable *through* feeling.[8] Unfortunately even common sense has a tendency to do just this—to expand a concern to eliminate emotion, which may be desirable in certain areas, to a total rejection of the cognitive value of experiences in which emotion shares at all. But this is a

[8] Louis Reid, *Ways of Knowledge and Experience*, p. 81.

false "objectivity." It assumes that all facets of reality are accessible from the same mental vantage-point—and there is nothing self-evident about this assumption. It may be that if I want to get the scientific picture of the physical universe or to get the details of an auto accident, I must discount the prejudicial influence of my own emotions or of others' interests. But that does not prove that if I want to know whether justice or beauty is extra-individual, I must eschew all emotional involvement and assume the attitude of a neutral observer—for this may guarantee my inability to observe what is really there.

Our discussion will largely content itself with making that distinction clear, without attempting the extremely difficult task of deciding how I can determine whether a particular picture is beautiful, or more beautiful than another, or whether a specific course of conduct is right or wrong. Questions like this are of considerable everyday interest and even urgency, but they are better left to the philosophy of art or to ethics. Our question is more like asking whether the philosophy of art and ethics have anything to argue about—whether their disputes have cognitional status at all. It is a question of the *realm* of reality into which we are introduced by moral and aesthetic experience. Is there any conclusive objection to considering this as extra-individual? The logical positivist has a simple answer to this question, his "emotive theory" of value. Only statements which can be sensibly verified are meaningful and cognitional, according to him; other statements do not, in spite of their propositional form, make assertions about reality but are equivalent to exclamations.[9] "Promises ought to be kept" or "Beethoven's Fifth is beautiful" are, on this basis, no more revelatory of reality than is the exclamation "Ouch!" They are more refined expressions of approval or disapproval, but are revelations of subjective individual reactions only.

Now the obvious difficulty once this issue is raised is in deciding who settles it. Every answer to a disputed question must be given

---

[9] Ayer, *Language, Truth and Logic*, chapter VI.

by an answering consciousness and the problem is in deciding "who" responds. Certainly the neutral observer cannot really claim to settle the question, for the necessary data are not available to him: surely no moral hero and no poet would suppose that the exalted countenance which reality turns to him would be there if he looked as a "neutral observer" might look. Moral and aesthetic values are revealed only to one who experiences the exigence for them; if we deliberately set this exigence aside, there seems no way of authenticating their reality—any more than the poet's emotion could solve an equation or validate an historical document. But this in turn poses a problem. If reality in this realm is a function of an exigence, do we not again beg the question? If we feel this exigence, we will subscribe to the ontological uniqueness of the moral and aesthetic realm; if we do not feel it, we will not so subscribe. Between these positions there seems to be no effective mediation possible. One way or the other, we seem condemned to travel in a circle.

The difficulty probably stems from our spontaneous need to establish *universality* as the hallmark of true cognition. Failing some kind of standard of universality, we fear that we may be left at the mercy of subjectivism, everyone saying what he pleases and taking refuge in the contention that he sees what others do not see. If one is *really* seeing something, we tend to expect that others ought to be able to see it too. Genuine awareness ought to be at least universalizable in principle, we would think. Considerations like this were what precluded Kant's conceding the title "knowledge" to the moral and aesthetic realms, even though he was perhaps the foremost contributor to their philosophical exploration:[10] In the moral and aesthetic areas, the objective pole of experience is not characterized by being coercively imposed, subsumed under laws, and publicly available in the manner of scientific knowledge. With this in mind, too, certain modern Kantians have tried to enlarge his conception of consciousness, so as to

[10] The *Critique of Practical Reason* is devoted to moral experience, and *Critique of Judgment* in great part to aesthetics.

grant cognition scope beyond his confines: Ernst Cassirer sought to enlarge the Kantian notion of a synthesis, so that every symbolic unification of experience found a cognitive place, from science to myth.[11] T. M. Greene tries to show that the moral and aesthetic realms possess the Kantian characteristics of objectivity in their own way and deserve the title of cognition.[12] Yet Greene admits that the consciousness for which these characteristics are present is not the subject-in-general of phenomenal knowledge, but a special "cultivated" consciousness—and so again, we tend to become circular.

It is not evident that there is any way out of this circle. The universality which we desire to characterize knowledge seems to be an aspiration, an ideal to which the individual consciousness refers itself and from which it seeks to draw sustenance. If we were to confuse this aspiration to universality with either a real or potential unanimity on the part of a factual human community, it would be difficult to grant cognitive status to moral and aesthetic experience. Dietrich von Hildebrand follows the path of insisting that the reality of moral values in particular, but also of aesthetic values, must be viewed without reference to any consensus. For von Hildebrand, a value is an autonomous datum, as irreducibly given as any in terms of which anyone would seek to justify it: it justifies itself through its own luminous presence, and no one who really stands in the presence of a value would feel it necessary that others also acknowledge its presence.[13]

Martin Heidegger, too, instead of trying to break the circle, jumps into it. The poet, Heidegger holds, is the voice of the holy.[14] Poetic experience *is* the revelation of the trans-phenomenal depth

[11] See Ernst Cassirer, *An Essay on Man* (Garden City: Doubleday Anchor Books), 1956, pp. 15–41, 87–97.

[12] Theodore Meyer Greene, *Moral, Aesthetic, and Religious Insight* (New Brunswick: Rutgers University Press), 1957, esp. pp. 24–28, 59, 77.

[13] Dietrich von Hildebrand, *Christian Ethics* (New York: David McKay), 1953, pp. 34–63, 169–281.

[14] See the essay on "Hölderlin and the Essence of Poetry" in *Existence and Being*, trans. by Werner Brock (Chicago: Henry Regnery Co.), 1949.

of *Dasein,* but it is a revelation accessible only to the poet and to his genuine audience. He who has ears to hear, he hears—and that is the end of it. We might extend this, as Heidegger does not, to moral experience. Man's experience of himself as one who is called upon to actualize moral values *is* the experience of himself as a being transcendent in relation to phenomenal experience. But this call is present *as* call, as appeal, and his affirmation of this realm of being always has the character of a response. His assertion that he inhabits a unique moral realm is inseparable from his *decision* to inhabit that realm. Experience in this realm is cognitional, but it is cognitional as appeal. Perhaps I may affirm something about my existence from within the moral and aesthetic realm which I cannot affirm *without* that realm, and yet this affirmation is never "automatically imposed" on me. It shares with existential knowledge the character of being a "free certitude," and it gives us further reason to believe that man's freedom is never absent from the assertion of the transcendent dimension of his being.

13 REPRISE

Let us now briefly retrace the steps we have followed in this philosophical exploration.

The epistemological question, we found, arises from the fundamental ambivalence of the human situation: man both is and is not present to his own experience. This non-coincidence of man's existence with itself, the mark of his finitude and temporality, has as its cognitive counterpart the non-coincidence of his knowledge with itself: just as man is not what he is, so he does not know what he knows. This cognitional non-coincidence may be regarded as a fissure between thought and experience, and also as an estrangement of thought from itself. The philosophy of knowledge is an attempt to permit thought to come into explicit recognition of its own essence; it is thought's effort to express and exhibit to itself the grounds of steadfast certitude. Knowledge is tied to expression: to "know" is not only to experience but to express one's experience to oneself. The judgment is a pivotal form of expression, but the real preoccupation of epistemology is with the ground of judgment: the nature, range, and origin of *evidence*.

While human thought is characterized by the appearance/reality distinction, this distinction cannot render all thought null, since it cannot consume its own foundation: man's questioning existence. With this realization, subjectivism is overcome. The subject which raises the epistemological question is the subject which exists out of the primordial question and thus already surpasses the isolated Cartesian ego. There can be no irreducible problem of the existence of the non-self, for questioning consciousness is essentially bi-polar: it is the cognitional side of man's being-in-the-world. The real problem is not of the reality of the other, but of its status. The status of the non-self may vary, but the same situational existence which surmounts subjectivism conversely seems to preclude the "pure objectivity" of the rationalist. Knowledge is always *a-letheia,* always the revelation of being, but this un-veiling cannot be totally detached from the situational existence of the subject to which it is made.

In the same vein, knowledge must have an analogical character. The presence of being is not revealed in the same way, for example, in sense perception as it is to abstract thought, personal existence, or moral experience. In no case is consciousness purely "subjective," but the import of the reference to a non-self is clearer in some cases than in others. The precise assertion of "objectivity" which is underwritten by sense perception remains especially obscure, and while we reviewed the various opinions, we emphasized that in this area, the very meaning of "objectivity" stands in need of much greater clarification. The fact remains that sense experience is not intelligible in terms of "private experience": it even has a certain primacy as the most immediate and pervasive actualization of our being-in-the-world, the life-breath of human existence.

In the search for a more unconditional assertion, caution must be exercised. There is always a distance between the plenitude of meaning contained in the primordial question and the order of assertion. All assertion contracts the original question. Yet since the issue of truth is specifically raised in the order of assertion, what I at least know is that I can affirm unconditionally my right to affirm. Then there is a justice to the claim that the primitive assertion, "something is," and the first principles issuing from it are unconditionally known. Even this claim, however, is subject to the reservation that these principles are cognitional absolutes in a being which is not an existential absolute: that is, even this sort of knowledge is affected by the non-coincidence of thought with itself and the fissure between man's thought and his existence, and they should not be regarded as "automatically self-validating" in an abstract way. Kant's objection that these principles cannot have a transcendent use would only be valid if they were purely formal rules, empty of content. To recognize that they are more than this depends on recognizing that the idea of "being" really has *content*; this recognition, in turn, cannot be achieved except by the singular subject in all his singularity and contingence. Hence the *recognition* of the concretely absolute character of the first principles is a continual achievement of thought, a lived transmutation of existence into thought which is at the same time an appropriation of intelligibility by my existence.

It was not held that the primitive assertion provides the sole trans-temporal assurance possible for thought. As affirmer, I am a total openness to the real. The content of affirmation, however, arises from the side of my existence. I affirm the presence of reality. In this affirmation concepts play a key role. Nevertheless, concepts cannot be satisfactorily looked upon as merely registering what is already contained in experience considered pre-conceptually. Ideas are creative apprehensions of presences. They are an attempt to take up my total existence into the order of expression. Their universal character is also an expression of presence: a revelation of reality as specifically mind-ful, as answering to mind. In this light the controversy between rationalist and empiricist as to whether there is anything *more* in ideas than in experience is a vain one: it is based upon the error of thinking that the intelligibility of a concept must be either "dependent upon" or "independent of" experience. But if a concept is a creative apprehension, then, like the artist's creative idea, its meaning explicitly emerges in a perpetual dialectical interplay with experience. Like the artists's idea, it *both* transcends the temporality of processive experience *and* is only revealed in it. Here seems to reside the relevance of such views as pragmatism, sociologism and historicism. The meaning of our concepts explicitly emerges to view as we read them back out of the very experiences which they make possible: the conviction of the adequacy of this explicit meaning becomes firmer as the canvas of existence reveals it more plainly.

This dialectical relation by no means eliminates the possibility of trans-temporal insight or makes every judgment liable to future reversal. Just as the artist, while not able to give an exhaustive account of his creative idea, can recognize what is compatible with it, so though man cannot give an exhaustive account of his concepts (such as, "person," "liberty," "justice," etc.) he nevertheless can, when his consciousness is sufficiently developed, recognize what is compatible with them. Thus the perspectival character of thought, including its social and historical dimensions, does not eliminate the possibility of truth but rather is integral to it, just as the process of painting is integral to the recognition of the creative idea. A concept (at least one which is not purely formal) is not a brittle thought-checker with clearly marked outlines, but a plenitude of potential meaning. To know the meaning of a concept is not equivalent to being able to define it, and hence the dichotomy set up by logical positivism between merely tautologous necessary judgments and essentially corrigible empirical statements is a false one: if ideas are creative apprehensions, we may have genuine trans-temporal insights into experience.

Since the content of affirmation arises from the side of our existence, the character of knowledge must be analogical. There is a range of presence, since presence is a function of my mode of existing. Perceptual objects, scientific entities, persons, moral values, and the transcendent dimension of existence cannot be present in a univocal manner. If, for example, the I-thou experience is a unique way in which the self is open to the non-self, it has an irreducible and irreplaceable cognitional value. The meaning of evidence is manifold. Some evidence may be in function of my singular subjectivity. Hence the search for certitude cannot be construed as a search for relief from the weight of singular existence. Such a search is a quest not for assurance but for re-assurance, and would risk taking refuge either in formalism or in a social consensus.

Now there is some legitimate place even for this latter, since for man "seeing" is "seeing together." It is clear that man is most comfortable in dealing with "things," a thing being a triplex of concept, sense, and action. As such, a thing tends to be a correlate of a social convergence. It is no accident that man feels most at home in using the word "knowledge" in the re-assuring realm of science and every day practicality, where the applicability of "thing" is clear-cut. But transcendence is not a "thing": hence it is known only analogously. For instance, even though a man may contend that he "knows" that the soul is immortal, he still fears to die. This fear would be literally insane if "knowing" in the realm of the transcendent meant exactly the same thing as "knowing" in the phenomenal realm: one who was afraid to enter a room in which he *knew* a pleasant time awaited him would be psychotic. Even the notion of a "proof" undergoes a modification in the region of the transcendent, for every affirmation of the transcendent involves the response of my freedom. It is the most concrete of all affirmations, and supremely requires my creative participation in the truth which I pronounce. Perhaps as man fashions his human existence more and more in the image of his creative intuition of transcendence, this social convergence will bestow on knowledge of the transcendent something of the psychological security of our knowledge of "things"; if so, history has a very positive contribution to make to knowledge.

In conclusion, it should be emphasized that the view here enunciated does not lead to arbitrariness. Just because there are different types of things which are sayable, we cannot conclude that everyone has a right to say what he pleases. It is a correct instinct which leads us to associate knowledge with the attribute of universality. What is always contrasted to knowledge, throughout its range, is an assertion which has only intra-individual value. In effect what we have emphasized is that there is a universality proper to different realms of experience, and that they are not transferrable. For example, we cannot check a scientific pronouncement purely in terms of poetic experience, nor evaluate moral experience purely in terms of perceptual data. But that does not make *any* moral pronouncement or any scientific assertion equally acceptable. The moral fanatic and the victim of hallucination cannot take refuge in the claim that they see what others miss. For this claim is made in respect to realms which establish their own canons of truth. Error and confusion continue to be possible within each realm, but only the moral consciousness can recognize moral error, only the aesthetic consciousness aesthetic error, and so forth.

One who demanded an extrinsic criterion which would automatically guarantee him against going wrong would actually be guilty of arbitrariness; for he would be misconstruing what knowledge is. He treats it as something which I "have," something, as it were, into which I may come into "permanent possession." But knowledge is the reflective expression of what I am—or what my experience is. Both my experience and its expression admit of endless purification, but this does not eradicate their cognitional value. In this purification, an indispensable element is the *dialog* between minds. In the long run, it is "we" who think, and "we" who know. True, knowledge is a supremely personal act, yet it is an act by which I know myself to participate in an order of universal meaning. The existing universal which is human communion, in which my thought is born, is the medium through which I belong to the cognitional universal, to truth.

RELATED READING

The primary sources and many of the secondary sources germane to the subject matter of each chapter have been mentioned in the notes to the chapters; for the most part, the following bibliography does not duplicate books already mentioned, but adds further related material and is meant to be supplementary in a limited and selective way. Numbers refer to the chapters.

I. Henri Bergson, *An Introduction to Metaphysics*, trans. T. E. Hulme, New York and London, Putnam, 1912.
W. Macneile Dixon, *The Human Situation*, New York, Oxford University Press, 1958.
D. M. Harding, *The Hierarchy of Heaven and Earth*, New York, Harper, 1953.
José Ortega y Gasset, *What is Philosophy?*, trans. Mildred Adams, New York, W. W. Norton & Co., 1960.
L. M. Regis, O. P., *Epistemology*, trans. Imelda Choquette Byrne, New York, Macmillan, 1959.

II. James Collins, *A History of Modern European Philosophy*, Milwaukee, Bruce, 1954.
Etienne Gilson and Thomas Langan, *Modern Philosophy, Descartes to Kant*, New York, Random House, 1963.

III. William A. Luijpen, *Existential Phenomenology*, Pittsburgh, Duquesne University Press, 1960.
William J. Richardson, S. J., *From Phenomenology to Thought*, The Hague, Martinus Nijhoff, 1964. (on Heidegger)

IV. John V. Canfield and Franklin H. Donnell, Jr., *Readings in the Theory of Knowledge*, New York, Appleton-Century-Crofts, 1964.

Maxwell J. Charlesworth, *Philosophy and Linguistic Analysis*, Pittsburgh, Duquesne University Press, 1959.

Thomas E. Hill, *Contemporary Theories of Knowledge*, New York, Ronald Press, 1961.

John A. Passmore, *A Hundred Years of Philosophy*, London, Gerald Duckworth, 1957.

V. Peter Coffey, *Epistemology*, London and New York, Longmans, Green and Co., 1917, 2 vols., vol. II.

VI. Harry R. Klocker, S. J., *Thomism and Modern Thought*, New York, Appleton-Century-Crofts, 1962.

Jacques Maritain, *Distinguish to Unite*, or *The Degrees of Knowledge*, newly trans. under supervision of Gerald B. Phelan, New York, Scribner, 1959.

VII. Coffey, *op. cit.*, vol. I.

Etienne Gilson, *The Christian Philosophy of St. Thomas Aquinas*, trans. L. K. Shook, New York, Random House, 1956, pp. 187–248.

Yves Simon, *Introduction à l'Ontologie du Connaître*, Paris, Desclée de Brouwer, 1934.

St. Thomas Aquinas, *On Truth and Falsity and on Human Knowledge*, Chicago, Regnery, 1941. (*Summa Theologiae*, I, qu. 16, 17, 84–88, prepared for the Great Books Foundation.)

VIII. George Boas, *The Limits of Reason*, New York, Harper, 1961.

Irving L. Horowitz, *Philosophy, Science and the Sociology of Knowledge*, Springfield, Ill., Thomas, 1961.

William James, *Pragmatism* and four essays from *The Meaning of Truth*, New York, Meridian Books, 1955.

Raymond Klibansky and H. J. Paton, edit., *Philosophy and History*, New York, Harper Torchbook, 1963.

Jacques Maquet, *The Sociology of Knowledge*, trans. John F. Locke, Boston, Beacon Press, 1951 (a critical analysis of Karl Mannheim and Pitirim Sorokin).

Heinrich Rickert, *Science and History; a Critique of Positivist Epistemology*, trans., George Reisman, New York, Van Nostrand, 1962.

IX. Frederick Copleston, S. J., *Contemporary Philosophy, Studies in Logical Positivism and Existentialism*, Westminster, Md., Newman Press, 1956.

Robert O. Johann, S. J., "The Return to Experience," *The Review of Metaphysics*, XVII, 319–339 (March 1964).
X. James Collins, *The Existentialists*, Chicago, Regnery, 1952.
Jean Danielou, *God and the Ways of Knowing*, trans., Walter Roberts, New York, Meridian Books, 1957.
Karl Jaspers, *The Perennial Scope of Philosophy*, trans. Ralph Manheim, New York, Philosophical Library, 1949.
Kurt Reinhardt, *The Existentialist Revolt*, Milwaukee, Bruce, 1952.
XI. R. C. Kwant, *Encounter*, Pittsburgh, Duquesne Univ. Press, 1960.
Gabriel Marcel, *Royce's Metaphysics*, trans. Virginia and Gordon Ringer, Chicago, Regnery, 1956.
Roger Troisfontaines, S. J., De l'existence à l'être. 2 Vols., Paris, J. Vrin, 1953. Tome II, pp. 10–60 (on Marcel).
XII. a) Arthur S. Eddington, *The Nature of the Physical World*, New York, Macmillan, 1929.
Werner Heisenberg, *Physics and Philosophy*, New York, Harper Torchbooks, 1962.
Max Planck, *The New Science*, three complete works, trans. James Murphy and W. H. Johnston, New York, Meridian Books, 1959.
b) Ernst Cassirer, *The Problem of Knowledge*, trans. W. H. Woglom and Charles W. Hendel, New Haven, Yale University Press, 1950.
W. E. Kennick, *Art and Philosophy*, Readings in Aesthetics, New York, St. Martin's Press, 1964.
Joseph Margolis, *Philosophy Looks at the Arts* (readings), New York, Scribner, 1962.
Jacques Maritain, *Creative Intuition in Art and Poetry*, New York, Pantheon Books, 1953.
Yves Simon, *Critique de la Connaissance morale*, Paris, Labergerie, 1934.
Dietrich von Hildebrand, *Christian Ethics*, New York, David McKay Co., 1953, pp. 34–63, 169–281.

ADDENDA

General Works
Roderick Chisholm, *The Theory of Knowledge*, Englewood Cliffs, N. J., Prentice-Hall, 1966.
Arthur C. Danto, *Analytical Philosophy of Knowledge*, Cambridge, Cambridge University Press, 1968.
D. W. Hamlyn, *The Theory of Knowledge*, Garden City, N. Y., Doubleday Anchor Books, 1970.
A. D. Woozley, *The Theory of Knowledge: An Introduction*, London, Hutchinson University Library, 1949.

Rebuttals to Relativism
Edmund Husserl, *Logical Investigations*, 2 vols., trans. J. N. Findlay, New York, Humanities Press, 1970. (Vol. I, chapt. 3–7 contain the famous "refutation of psychologism.")
C. S. Lewis, *The Abolition of Man*, New York, Macmillan, 1965.
Roger Trigg, *Reason and Commitment*, Cambridge, Cambridge University Press, 1973.

Transcendental Thomism
Bernard J. F. Lonergan, *Insight*, New York, Harper & Row, 1970.
Joseph Marechal, *A Marechal Reader*, edit. and trans. Joseph Donceel, S. J., New York, Herder and Herder, 1970.
Otto Muck, S. J., *The Transcendental Method*, trans. William Seidensticker, New York, Herder and Herder, 1968.

Karl Rahner, *Spirit in the World,* trans. William Dych, S. J., New York, Herder & Herder, 1968.
(Also note that Van Riet's book, above, p. 22n23, has been translated: *Thomistic Epistemology,* trans Gabriel Franks, St. Louis, Herder, 1965.)

Repudiations of Epistemology
Richard Rorty, *Philosophy and the Mirror of Nature,* Princeton, Princeton University Press, 1979.
Ludwig Wittgenstein, *On Certainty,* trans. Denis Paul and G. E. M. Anscombe, Oxford, Basil Blackwell, 1974.

Philosophy of Science
Thomas Kuhn, *The Structure of Scientific Revolutions,* 2nd edit., Chicago, University of Chicago Press, 1970.
Michael Polanyi, *The Tacit Dimension,* Garden City, N. Y., Doubleday Anchor Books, 1967.
Karl Popper, *Objective Knowledge: An Evolutionary Approach,* London, Oxford University Press, 1972.

Special Topics
Franz Brentano, *The True and the Evident,* edit. Oskar Kraus, trans. R. Chisholm, I. Politzer, and K. Fischer, New York, Humanities Press, 1966.
H. D. Lewis, edit., *Clarity Is Not Enough,* New York, Humanities Press, 1963 (an anthology of essays on linguistic philosophy and logical empiricism).
Don Locke, *Memory,* Garden City, N. Y., Doubleday Anchor Books, 1971.
Arthur Pap, *Semantics and Necessary Truth,* New Haven, Yale University Press, 1958.
George Pitcher, edit., *Truth,* Englewood Cliffs, N. J., Prentice-Hall, 1964.

Wilfrid Sellars, "Empiricism and the Philosophy of Mind," in *Science, Perception and Reality,* London, Routledge & Kegan Paul, 1963 (contains his critique of the "myth of the given").

Hilary Staniland, *Universals,* Garden City, N. Y., Doubleday Anchor Books, 1972.

Robert Swartz, edit., *Perceiving, Sensing, and Knowing,* Berkeley, University of California Press, 1976 (a book of readings from twentieth-century sources).

Alan R. White, *Truth,* Garden City, N. Y., Doubleday Anchor Books, 1970.

INDEX

Absolute, knowledge as open to, 62, 128–131, 140, 146, 194
Abstraction, theory of, 167–168
Action, and knowledge, 151, 187–191
Analogy
  of being, 17
  of knowledge, 15–19
Analytical propositions, 219
A priori, 116, 143–144, 199
Aristotle, 3, 156, 161, 276–277
St. Augustine, 5, 32, 231, 246
Ayer, A. J., 91–95, 213–218, 286

Bacon, Sir Francis, 276
Being
  as absolute idea, 129, 146
  not an objectified notion, 238, 244–245
Bergson, Henri, 178, 217, 226
Berkeley, George Bishop, 76–83
Broad, C. D., 90–91, 97–98
Brunner, Auguste, 57–58
Buber, Martin, 267–275
Burtt, E. A., 120

Cassirer, Ernst, 288

Causality
  philosophical principle of, 135–136
  and science, 140–141
Certitude, 9, 27
  absolute, 129–130
  "free," 246–250
  types of, 147–151
Childe, Vere, 16, 193
Circle, epistemological, 59–61
Cogito, 27–33, 163
Common sense. 7–9, 68–69
Concepts
  as creative apprehensions, 171–178
  distinguished from sense, 152–157
  and experience, 177–178, 190
Conceptualism, 160–163
Connaturality, knowledge by, 20
Consciousness
  bi-polarity of, 47–51
  diverse realms of, 125–126, 287
  intentionality of, 49
  judgmental and perceptual, 119–121
  not a container, 44–47
  not a thing, 67

Consciousness *(Cont.)*
  of self, 49–50
  structure of, 44 ss.
Contradiction, principle of, 131–132
Creative character of knowledge, 171–178, 183, 204–205, 249–250
Criterion of truth, 24, 246–247

Descartes, René, 7, 63, 148, and all of Chapter 2
Determinism, 140–141
Dewey, John, 69, 187–197
Dialog, 57–58, 65–66, 295
Doubt, 152
  critical, 25ss.
  dream-doubt, 29–30, 40–43
Dualism, Cartesian, 40

Eddington, Sir Arthur S., 84, 95–97, 284
Einstein, Albert, 280
Empiricism, sense, 71, 158–159, 222
Epistemology
  def., 12
  method, 19–23
Error
  not in senses, 104–105
  paradox of, 24–26
  sources of, 27, 105–106
Essence
  and existence, 130–131
  knowledge of, 171–178, 179–187
  ontological and gnoseological, 183
Evidence, 20, 147–148, 226–231

Existential aspects of knowing, 12–15
Existentialism, 226–250

de Finance, Joseph, 224, 245
Finitude, 13
Forms, Plato's theory of, 42, 160, 163
Foundations of knowledge, 61–62

Gilson, Etienne, 9–10, 11
"Given," 221
God
  knowledge of, 242–246, 275
  ontological argument for, 38
Gorgias, 11
Greene, T. M., 288

Hartmann, Nicolai, 186
Hegel, G. W. F., 51, 132, 197, 232, 267
Heidegger, Martin, 5, 18, 53–55, 65, 288–289
Heisenberg, Werner, 118, 141, 280–281
von Hildebrand, Dietrich, 218–225, 288
Hirst, R. J., 93–94
Historicity, 197–206
Hoenen, Peter, 138–139
Hume, David, 141–147, 209–213
Husserl, Edmund, 49, 66, 123, 228–231

Idealism, epistemological, 35
Ideas
  as objects of knowing, 72–75
  Descartes' clear and distinct, 37–38
Identity, principle of, 131–132

Index

Illusion, 8, 89–90
Images, and distortion of thought, 44–47, 172–173, 226–228
Induction, 207–218
Insight, 201, 219–222
Intentionality, 49, 167
Interpersonal experience, 266–275
Intuition
  Descartes on, 38
  in von Hildebrand, 218–221

James, William, 18
Judgment, 19, 119, 168–170
  primary, 130

Kant, Immanuel, 52, 116–117, 142–147, 203–204, 287–288
Kierkegaard, Sören, 14, 231–236
Knowledge
  and action, 187–191
  analogy of, 15–19
  by connaturality, 20
  creative character of, 171–178
  of essences, 171–187
  and existence, 12–15, 62
  and expression, 19–20, 271
  as identification, 46
  indefinable, 15
  and love, 21, 271–274
  Plato's theory of, 42
  proper object of human, 223–225
  question as fundamental form of, 61–67
  of self, 50
  of the singular, 170
  situational character of, 51ss.
  social and historical dimensions of, 197–206
  through concepts, 153–157
  as trans-temporal, 201–202, 219–221
  variety in meaning of, 5

Language
  and distortion of thought, 47
  essentially social, 58
  "ordinary language," 100–102
  "two-language" theory, 91–92, 96, 99
Laplace, Pierre, 141, 277
"Laws of nature," 210, 279
Lean, Martin, 97–99
Lewis, C. I., 193, 201, 203
Locke, John, 70–75
Logical positivism, 246. See also Ayer.
Love, 21, 270–275

Mannheim, Karl, 199–200
Marcel, Gabriel, 21, 51–53, 236–241, 243, 245, 247, 248, 249, 267–275
Maréchal, Joseph, 130, 176
Maritain, Jacques, 7–8, 12, 20, 183
Material objects, notion of, 91–95, 98
Matter, 80
Mead, George H., 267
Mechanism, 277
Merleau-Ponty, Maurice, 56–57, 123
Mill, John Stuart, 93, 253–255
Miller, Barry, 17
Moore, G. E., 88–89

Moral experience, 285–289
Mystery vs. problem, 236–241

"Natural view," 66
Newman, John Henry Cardinal, 150
Nominalism, 157–160
Noumena, Kant on, 116–117

Objectivity,
 ambiguity in meaning of, 119–127
 and relativity of knowledge, 197–203
Objects, of science, 118–119, 279–285
Ortega y Gasset, José, 18, 55–56, 64
Ostensive signification, 97–100
Other minds, 251–260
 argument by analogy for, 253–255

Paradigm argument, 95–97
Pascal, Blaise, 231, 246
Perception, Chapters 5 and 6
 objectivity of, 113–115
 and science, 83–87, 112, 118–119
Phantasm, 174
Phenomena, Kant on, 116–117, 143–144
Phenomenalism, 91–95, 107
Phenomenology, 228–231. See also Husserl, Heidegger, Merleau-Ponty, Marcel, von Hildebrand.
Pieper, Josef, 181
Planck, Max, 282

Plato, 3, 4, 6, 42, 158, 160, 161, 163, 164, 246
Polanyi, Michael, 205
Pragmatism, 187–197
Principles, first, 131–140
Protagoras, 11
Proust, Marcel, 125
Psychology, distinct from epistemology, 22, 167–168
Pyrrho, 11

Qualities, sense, 69–70
 primary and secondary, 73–75, 108–110, 123, 125, 195, 278
 tertiary, 85–86, 195
Question, as fundamental cognition, 63ss.

Realism, 9–10, 35
 immediate, 110
 moderate, 163
 naive, 68–70, 103
 virtual, 108–119
Regis, L. M., 17, 22
Reid, Louis Arnauld, 285
Relativism, 11, 200
Relativity of knowledge, 197–203. See also Sensations, Concepts.
Representationalism, 75, 86–87
van Riet, Georges, 22, 183
Rousselot, Pierre, 171, 177, 183, 231
Royce, Josiah, 266–267
Russell, Bertrand, 16, 22, 36, 88–89
Ryle, Gilbert, 40, 101–102, 284

Sartre, Jean-Paul, 14, 263–265
Scepticism, 9–12

Index

Scheler, Max, 69, 201, 254, 261–263
Science
  and perception, 83–87
  philosophy of, 276–285
  world view of, 8, 74–75, 276–277
Scientism, 83–87
Self
  consciousness of, 49–50
  social character of, 260, 266–267
Sensations
  conditions for, 105
  objectivity of, 86–87, 113
  relational character of, 108, 123
Sense-datum theory, 87–95
Sensibles, proper and common, 106, 111–112
Sextus Empiricus, 11
Shame, 264–265
Situation, being-in-a-, 51–58
Smith, Norman Kemp, 37
Sociology of knowledge, 197–206
Socrates, 3, 156, 233–234
Solipsism, 35–36
Soul, immortality of, 233–234, 274
Spencer, W. Wylie, 258
Stark, Werner, 199, 200, 201
Stebbing, L. Susan, 95–97, 99–100
van Steenberghen, Fernand, 22, 111–112, 114–115
Subjectivism, 33–36
Subjectivity, 231–236, 241, 244, 248–250
Sufficient reason, principle of, 132–135

Sympathy, 262–263

Tautology, necessary truth as, 213–215
Teilhard de Chardin, Pierre, 205
Testimony, 150–151
Theory, and fact, 283–284
"Thing," notion of, 144, 203–204, 294
St. Thomas Aquinas, 22, 48–49, 167, 171–172, 174, 181, 222
Time, 13–14
Toulmin, Stephen, 283–284
Transcendence, 242–246, 275
Transcendental ego, 229–231
Truth
  def., 19
  criterion of, 24, 246
  pragmatism and, 191–193
  of the trans-phenomenal, 243–248
  trans-temporal character of, 201–202, 219–221

Universality
  as criterion for truth, 287–288, 294–295
  not equivalent to impersonal validity, 244–245
Universals, 152–157, 164–166

Verifiability, principle of, 215

Whitehead, Alfred North, 75
Wilhelmsen, Frederick, 22
Wisdom, John, 256–257
Wittgenstein, Ludwig, 100–102
Wonder, 3–7
World, being-in-a-, 51–58